THE AMERICAN GOVERNMENT

Before publication the several chapters of this book were read and approved by the following authorities:

I.—The President.
  WILLIAM H. TAFT, *President of the United States.*

II.—The Department of State.
  PHILANDER C. KNOX, *Secretary of State.*

III.—The Treasury Department.
  FRANKLIN MACVEAGH, *Secretary of the Treasury.*

IV.—The Army.
  Maj. Gen. LEONARD WOOD, *Chief of Staff.*

V.—The Navy.
  Rear Admiral RICHARD WAINWRIGHT, *Aid for Operations.*

VI.—The Postal Service.
  FRANK H. HITCHCOCK, *Postmaster General.*

VII.—The Interior Department.
  CARMI A. THOMPSON, *Acting Secretary of the Interior.*

VIII.—The Patent Office.
  EDWARD B. MOORE, *Commissioner of Patents.*

IX.—The Geological Survey.
  HENRY C. RIZER, *Acting Director.*

X.—The Department of Agriculture.
  JAMES WILSON, *Secretary of Agriculture.*

XI.—The Weather Bureau.
  WILLIS L. MOORE, *Chief of the Weather Bureau.*

XII.—The Department of Commerce and Labor.
  CHARLES NAGEL, *Secretary of Commerce and Labor.*

XIII.—The Census Bureau.
  E. DANA DURAND, *Director of the Census.*

XIV.—The Bureau of Standards.
  S. W. STRATTON, *Director.*

XV.—The Public Health.
  Dr. HARVEY W. WILEY, *Chief of the Bureau of Chemistry.*

  Dr. WALTER WYMAN, *Surgeon General of the Public Health and Marine-Hospital Service.*

XVI.—The Smithsonian Institution.
  RICHARD RATHBUN, *Acting Secretary.*

XVII.—The Panama Canal.
  Col. GEORGE W. GOETHALS, *Chairman and Chief Engineer.*

XVIII.—The Interstate Commerce Commission.
  JUDSON C. CLEMENTS, *Chairman.*

XIX.—Our Insular Possessions.
  Brig. Gen. CLARENCE R. EDWARDS, *Chief of the Bureau of Insular Affairs.*

XX.—How Congress Legislates.
  Senator THOMAS S. MARTIN, *Chairman of the Democratic Conference.*

XXI.—The House of Representatives.
  CHAMP CLARK, *Speaker.*

XXII.—The Senate.
  JAMES S. SHERMAN, *Vice President of the United States.*

XXIII.—The Library of Congress.
  HERBERT PUTNAM, *Librarian.*

XXIV.—The Government Printing Office.
  SAMUEL B. DONNELLY, *Public Printer.*

XXV.—The Civil Service.
  JOHN C. BLACK, *President Civil Service Commission.*

XXVI.—The Supreme Court.
  JAMES H. MCKENNEY, *Clerk of the Supreme Court of the United States.*

XXVII.—Other Federal Courts.
  WILBUR S. HINMAN, *Deputy Clerk of the United States Commerce Court.*

XXVIII.—The Department of Justice.
  GEORGE W. WICKERSHAM, *Attorney General.*

XXIX.—The Pan American Union.
  JOHN BARRETT, *Director General.*

XXX.—The National Capital.
  CUNO H. RUDOLPH, *President of the Board of Commissioners of the District of Columbia.*

THE AMERICAN GOVERNMENT

BY
FREDERIC J. HASKIN

ILLUSTRATIONS FROM PHOTOGRAPHS
TAKEN ESPECIALLY FOR THIS EDITION BY
BARNEY M. CLINEDINST

NEW YORK
PRINTED FOR THE AUTHOR
BY
J. J. LITTLE & IVES CO.
1911

353
H273a

Copyright, 1911, by
FREDERIC J. HASKIN

Entered at Stationers' Hall
London, October, 1911

75th Thousand.

Feb. 5, 1998
Gift

CONTENTS

CHAPTER	PAGE
Introduction	xi
I.—The President	1
II.—The State Department	14
III.—The Treasury Department	27
IV.—The Army	40
V.—The Navy	53
VI.—The Postal Service	65
VII.—The Interior Department	78
VIII.—The Patent Office	91
IX.—The Geological Survey	103
X.—The Department of Agriculture	117
XI.—The Weather Bureau	130
XII.—Department of Commerce and Labor	143
XIII.—The Census Bureau	157
XIV.—The Bureau of Standards	170
XV.—The Public Health	183
XVI.—The Smithsonian Institution	196
XVII.—The Panama Canal	209
XVIII.—The Interstate Commerce Commission	221
XIX.—Our Insular Possessions	235
XX.—How Congress Legislates	248
XXI.—The House of Representatives	261
XXII.—The Senate	274

CHAPTER	PAGE
XXIII.—THE LIBRARY OF CONGRESS . . .	287
XXIV.—THE GOVERNMENT PRINTING OFFICE	299
XXV.—THE CIVIL SERVICE	312
XXVI.—THE SUPREME COURT	325
XXVII.—OTHER FEDERAL COURTS . . .	337
XXVIII.—THE DEPARTMENT OF JUSTICE. .	349
XXIX.—THE PAN AMERICAN UNION . . .	362
XXX.—THE NATIONAL CAPITAL	374

LIST OF ILLUSTRATIONS

	PAGE
Entrance to White House	4
Tourists waiting to ascend Washington Monument	12
Declaration of Independence	20
Printing Dollar Bills	28
Troopers at Fort Myer	44
Clock that regulates time for the United States	52
The Naval Observatory	60
Destroying Old Paper Money	76
Searching the files in the Patent Office	92
Observation Tower at Weather Bureau	132
Machine that tests Standard Weights	172
Dr. Wiley at Work	180
Preparing Tuberculin for Shipment	188
Government Taxidermist	196
Roosevelt Lions in National Museum	204
Testing Steel for the Panama Canal	220
A View in Washington	252
Bearing the Mace	268
Grand Stairway in Library of Congress	284
Court in Pan American Building	364

PREFACE.

WHILE this book is a generally comprehensive review of the actual work of the Federal Government of the United States, it does not pretend to relate the complete history of the several departments nor to present a full account of all of the details of their present activities. To do so would require many, many volumes of this size. However, the reader who would be informed on the actual operations of his Government will find this presentation a dependable source of information on the more important phases of the subject.

INTRODUCTION.

This book is to tell about the work of the Federal Government of the United States of America, the most active and powerful Nation in the world, what is required of the servants of its people from the President down, and how these officers perform that service.

It is not designed as a treatise on the science of government, nor as an exposition of the peculiar political structure of the United States. It is, rather, an effort to tell in the ordinary language of everyday life what the Government does and how it does it.

The United States is the largest Nation in the world, in population, area, and wealth, whose people speak one language and enjoy the privilege of self-government. The American people govern themselves by means of a complicated machinery unlike that of any other Nation. Things that are local in their nature, or that were local at the time the Constitution was adopted, are under the control of the semi-independent governments of the several States. These States, in turn, acknowledge certain rights of local government to more restricted areas, such as cities and towns, counties and school districts.

The Federal Government, with which this book is solely concerned, derives its powers from the States and the people, and is strictly limited in its activities to affairs concerning the whole Nation, or more than one State, as defined in the Constitution of 1787 and its amendments of subsequent dates.

Measured in terms of receipts and expenditures of public money, the Federal Government represents but little more than a third of the business of government in this country. Yet in spite of this limitation, the national governmental machine is in many respects the most powerful and most active in the world.

The work of the Government in this advanced and advancing age is not confined to the things usually denoted by the word "government." No longer a mere collector of taxes and a wager of war, the modern government must needs aid its people in the creation of wealth and the progress of culture.

Our Government is a builder. It undertakes to construct almost anything, from a gun that will hurl two-thirds of a ton of steel a distance of 15 miles to a pair of scales so delicate that the balance will turn sharply under the weight of a millionth part of a grain. Our Government is an operator. It takes observations of temperature with a thermometer so sensitive that it will measure the heat of a candle 5 miles away, and it operates a gigantic testing machine that will register a strain of 10,000,000 pounds.

It performs functions ranging from the conduct of international diplomatic affairs to the driving of mules; from making maps to feeding hogs; from coining money to making ice cream; from digging canals to flying kites.

The service of a half million men and women and the expenditure of more than a billion dollars a year are required to keep this huge machine going.

This is the same machine that was set going a century and a quarter ago by the impoverished people of the Atlantic seaboard, numbering altogether not 3,000,000. They established the Government more in hope than in confidence, and not the wisest seer nor the most optimistic dreamer among them would have dared to predict the things that this book sets forth.

That baby Government was so poor that it was forced to borrow money upon the personal credit of its officers, or to beg the little better credit of one of its constituent States. When the Capitol was built at Washington (the central part of the same building in which the laws are now made), the United States was forced to borrow the money to pay the laborers from the wealthier governments of Maryland and Virginia. Now the credit of the United States is greater than that of any other Nation, and it borrows money upon more advantageous terms than can any of the great Nations of Europe that so lately smiled indulgently upon what they called "the American experiment."

It is a great country as well as a great Government. Having only one-sixteenth of the world's population, the United States has a fourth of its wealth, owns a third of its railways, distributes a third of its mail, wields a third of its banking power, and prints more than half of its newspapers and magazines.

Having only one-twentieth of the landed area of the civilized world, the United States produces one-fifth of its wheat, one-third of its coal, one-fourth of its gold, one-third of its manufactured wares, nearly one-half of its steel, more than half of its petroleum, nearly two-thirds of its cotton, and four-fifths of its corn. It is the land of plenty, for it is the only country on earth, excepting some of the British colonies, where an ordinary laboring man may eat meat every day if he wants it.

Unlike all Governments that had preceded it in the history of politics, the United States Government is established upon a principle of divided authority and responsibility. Not only are restrictions placed upon the powers of the Federal Government by the reservation to the States and the people of all powers not enumerated in the Constitution, but there is also the separation of the executive, the legislative, and the judicial functions of government into three branches of equal majesty and importance. In a constitutional monarchy like Great Britain, or a parliamentary Republic like France, the legislative branch of the Government is supreme. In a Federal Empire like Germany, or an autocratic Empire like Russia, the executive branch of the Government is supreme. In our country, in theory, the three branches are coordinate and equal, although sometimes one asserts its power over the other two in a particular matter.

For instance, the Supreme Court may nullify a law passed by Congress on the theory that it is unconstitutional; the President may refuse to execute a decree of the Supreme Court; and Congress may refuse to vote money for the supply of the executive departments. But these are exceptional things.

The executive, or law-enforcing function of the Government is vested in the President. He appoints the Cabinet officers who superintend the departments, and is, finally, responsible for all of the varied activities of the executive branch of the Government—a responsibility that includes by far the greater part of the work of the Government and is greater than that laid upon the shoulders of any other mortal man.

The legislative, or law-making function of the Government is vested in Congress. Representatives, elected by the people, compose the House of Representatives, or lower chamber, and in this body must originate all bills having to do with taxing the people. Senators chosen by the States, two from each State, compose the Senate, or upper chamber. The concurrence of the Senate is required in all legislative acts and also in certain Executive deeds, including the appointment of officers and the ratification of treaties with foreign powers. The President has a part in the legislative function, also, since he may veto a bill passed by Congress and unless it is passed a second time by a two-thirds vote in both Houses it can not become a law.

The judicial or law-interpreting function of the Government is vested in the Supreme Court of the United States, and other Federal courts created by Congress. The Supreme Court is the final arbiter of all disputes arising under the laws of the Federal Government, and as the interpreter of the Constitution it can set aside the acts of Congress or of the President on the ground that the power delegated by the States and the people in the Constitution has been exceeded.

Upon this triangular framework has been erected the marvelous machine that we call the American Government. Its political complications are such that no man may describe them without provoking controversy, and with them this book has nothing to do.

Leaving on one side the considerations of the statesman who is concerned with theories, and on the other those of the politician who is concerned with expedients, this book represents an effort to tell of the work and the workers of the Federal Government.

It is a plain account of how the President, the Congress, the Supreme Court, and all of the other half million servants of the American people do the work of the people for the people.

It is the story of the actual doings of the men who, as officers of the Government, protect this Nation against foreign foes, administer its laws to preserve peace at home, safeguard the public health and prosperity, conserve the use of its national resources, encourage its inventive genius, and do all in their power to advance its moral and material interests.

It is a story to make every American breast swell with pride, a story whose hard facts loom so large in the record of the world's accomplishments that the knowledge of them can not but increase the love and honor all of us have for the Land of the Free and the Home of the Brave.

THE AMERICAN GOVERNMENT

CHAPTER I.

THE PRESIDENT.

The President of the United States is the foremost ruler of the world. He is not a ruler by accident of birth, but by virtue of the will of 90,000,000 people, who fight the world's greatest political battle every four years for his selection, and then willingly and fully acquiesce in the verdict of the ballot box.

Election to the presidency carries with it a vast responsibility. The successful candidate faces four years of administering the laws of the greatest Nation on earth, acting as the master mind of a huge machine manned by nearly half a million men and women, a machine which can patch a mail bag, study a plant louse, maneuver an army, or dig a Panama Canal.

Congress makes the Nation's laws, the courts interpret them, and the President executes them. Congress may appropriate a billion dollars a year, but the President must execute the laws by which this vast sum is raised, as well as those under which it is spent. When he assumes the presidency, he undertakes to carry out laws which, during his term, call for the expenditure of nearly $4,000,000,000. Not only is it incumbent upon the President to execute the laws, but he must take an important part in framing them. He must, from time to time, send messages to Congress, advising that body of the condition of the country and as to what legislation is needed for the improvement of those conditions. Through the Secretary of the Treasury he must also inform Congress just how much money will be needed to keep the Government going during the next year, and when Congress appropriates these funds that action is not completed until the President has scrutinized and signed the appropriation measures.

While the President has a Cabinet to assist him in his supervision of the execution of the laws of the Nation, under the Constitution he is solely responsible for any official action any member of the body may take. As a collective organization, the Cabinet has no constitutional standing, its decisions being in nowise binding upon the President. This is illustrated by a story of Mr. Lincoln. He brought before his Cabinet a proposition which he favored and the Cabinet voted against it. He declared the votes to be 7 noes and 1 aye. "Therefore," said he, "the ayes have it." The President, with his attention demanded upon every kind of matter, from the appointment of a postmaster at Podunk to the determination of the proper course to pursue in a great international situation, is a very busy man. But he has so systematized his work that he has almost as much time for recreation as the average man of affairs.

For instance, although his mail is the largest received by the head of any Government on earth, it is so handled that the task of going through it is not a very burdensome one. The daily number of letters ranges from 500 to 2,000, but less than a hundred of these require the personal attention of the President. There is one clerk in the Executive Offices whose sole duty is to classify this correspondence as it comes in. A card-index system of all correspondence is maintained with a complete filing system in connection. Probably a hundred letters of a day's mail may be answered by a single form letter, without even engaging the attention of the Secretary to the President. Several hundred of the remainder will be distributed to the various departments and perhaps less than half will reach the Secretary to the President. Of those which do, the secretary makes a digest and when the President has a moment of leisure his secretary gives him their substance and receives instructions as to the replies to be made. Letters are often addressed to the President and his wife marked "personal" and "private," but these marks are necessarily disregarded. Only letters initialed by intimate personal and political friends reach the President unopened.

Probably no other official in the world receives more begging letters than the President of the United States. It is estimated that in many instances the letters of this nature received in the course of a single day ask for as much as $20,000 in the aggregate. Often the letter-writing proclivities of the beggars are stimulated by jokes which the Washington correspondents sometimes perpetrate upon the President. When Mr. Roosevelt first enunciated his celebrated antirace suicide doctrine, some humorous newspaper writer sent out a story to the effect that the President had received 28 baby carriages. It was published broadcast, and hundreds of poor families wrote asking him for these carriages.

Writing to the President has become much more general in recent years than formerly. It is said that during the Grant administration the Executive force used to play croquet during the dull hours of the day and only upon the arrival of the mail would be summoned to the Executive Offices.

The constant stream of callers and the vast amount of routine business make the heaviest demands upon the time of the President. During the first three or four weeks of his administration, he may have to shake hands with from 50,000 to 75,000 people. Unless he learns to grip

ENTRANCE TO WHITE HOUSE.

the hand of his visitor before the visitor grips his, he is sure to have a badly swollen arm. The President may transact the business of his office at any place he may elect, and there is nothing to prevent his spending the major portion of his time elsewhere than in Washington. Congress once asked President Grant to advise it as to what part of his duties were performed outside of the District of Columbia. He replied in a polite, but none the less pointed, note that it was none of Congress' business. Never since then has this right been questioned. There is nothing in the Constitution which prohibits the President from going beyond the borders of the United States, but Mr. Cleveland was the first President to do so. On a fishing trip he went beyond the 3-mile limit in the Atlantic Ocean.

Aside from the great power accruing to the President through his right to appoint all of the administrative officers of the Government, and to supervise the expenditure of the billions of dollars appropriated by Congress, and beyond the prestige which his office gives him, he possesses the power which, prior to the admission of Arizona and New Mexico, amounted to the legislative influence of 14 Senators and 65 Representatives, this many votes being required in addition to a majority to override his veto. The only method by which the President can be thwarted in his purpose by Congress, so long as he keeps within his constitutional powers, is by its refusal to appropriate the money he needs for carrying out his plans. As Commander-in-Chief of the Army he has the right to handle it as he sees fit. But Congress controls the appropriations for the support of the Army, and it provides that this money shall be available only when the Army is handled in a specific way. This same check upon the President is used in other instances.

The person of the President is inviolable during his term of office. Theoretically he can not be arrested or restrained by any official, even should he commit murder. The only remedy against him while President is the cumbersome proceedings of impeachment. Even in these proceedings he can not be compelled to answer, to attend, or to do any other thing which in the slightest degree might interfere with his personal liberty. This is upon the theory that such restraint would restrict either the negative or the positive powers of his office, and enable other individuals to circumvent the supreme authority of the Constitution. In practice, however, the President may be arrested and otherwise restrained. General Grant was once arrested by a negro policeman for fast driving. He commended the officer for doing his duty, put up $20 collateral and forfeited it in the police court next day.

As far as the courts are concerned, the President may also do as he pleases. Interested parties have sought to restrain him from doing certain things by injunction proceedings, or to compel him to do other things by mandamus, but the courts have uniformly refused to take any action hampering the discretionary power of the President. Congress and the President often clash, but the judiciary and the President seldom do. In one instance Chief Justice Marshall handed down an opinion with reference to an Indian tribe, which did not suit President Jackson, who declared: "John Marshall has made his decision, now let him enforce it."

While many people complain that the President is a poorly paid and poorly housed Chief Executive, considering the size and importance of the American Nation, nevertheless he manages to live in a style which would be pleasing to the average American citizen. The annual appropriation for the upkeep of the White House amounts approximately to $86,000. A fine conservatory is maintained for his benefit, and it is estimated that the 5,000 or more plants used to decorate the White House at a single reception would cost at least $2,500, if bought in the open market. A single set of china used at the big state dinners may cost as much as $6,000. When the supplies for one of these big dinners are bought, only the best things in the market get into the White House market basket, and only the choicest morsels of these are served. A large roast of lamb is provided for each five people at the dinner so that only the most select bits reach the table.

The salary of the President now amounts to $75,000 a year, or $6,250 a month. He is the only official of the Government who is not required to sign the pay roll. In the time of President Cleveland the salary of the President was $4,166.66⅔ a month. So accurate is the Treasury system of bookkeeping that the salary check of the President was drawn for $4,166.66 one month and $4,166.67 for the next two months. At the end of his term it was found that there was still due President Cleveland the amount of 1 cent, so a check for that amount was drawn in his favor. It has never been cashed, but is one of the souvenirs of the Cleveland home in Princeton, N. J. The President of the United States is one of the most photographed persons in the world. It is said that one Washington photographer has taken more than a thousand pictures of President Taft.

The quadrennial election at which the American people choose their President for the ensuing four years is the greatest political battle of the world. Investigation discloses the fact that the names of more than 700,000 candidates are on the ballots which are cast the day of a presidential election. Every telegraph and telephone company in the country lends itself to the public that night for the transmission of the returns. No one has attempted to estimate the amount of business they carry over their wires election night, but if paid for at the usual rate it would cost hundreds of thousands of dollars. Even the wireless companies make special efforts to keep ships at sea informed as to the progress of the count.

The President is inaugurated about four months after his election. While a presidential candidate always receives notification of his nomination, the President-elect receives no such advice, but gets his information from the newspapers, and presents himself in Washington a few days before his inauguration. A presidential inauguration is one of the finest governmental spectacles in the world. Its impressiveness lies in its simplicity rather than in its display. Each inauguration is on a larger and more brilliant scale than its predecessor. Over 30,000 men march in a present day inaugural parade. Nearly 200,000 people come to Washington from all parts of the country to witness it. Daniel Webster said of the crowd which attended the first inauguration of Andrew Jackson that it was "a multitude, too many to be fed without a miracle, and that it seemed that the whole Nation rushed to the Capital." The "great multitude" was computed to be about 8,000 people. The first real inaugural ball occurred when James Madison came into office. The crowd which attended was estimated at 400. Provision was made for 15,000 at the Taft inaugural ball.

George Washington had to borrow $3,000 to defray his expenses to New York, where his inauguration took place. When he arrived at the Federal Hall it was found that there was no Bible in the building, and an attendant saved the day by getting one from a Masonic lodge room nearby. John Adams wrote after his inauguration that there was more weeping when he took the oath of office than he had ever witnessed at a tragedy, but whether it was from the loss of a beloved President or the accession of an unpopular one, he could not say. When he was succeeded by Jefferson he moved out the night before and refused to ride to the Capitol with his successor or even to welcome him to the White House. President Johnson refused to meet General Grant, it having come to his ears that General Grant had said he would not ride to the Capitol with Johnson. James Monroe was the originator of the custom of holding the inaugural ceremony on the East Portico of the Capitol.

After a President is inaugurated, unless the state of public affairs demands the convening of an extra session of Congress, he has but little work to do other than to name the higher officials of the Government, until the ensuing fall, when he sends his first annual message to Congress. In it the President outlines in full his policies, and tries to win the approval of the Nation by its contents. In order that it may be as widely circulated as possible, he has copies of it sent into every newspaper office in the country before it is officially published, and linotype operators from Maine to Mexico read the message before it reaches Congress. The moment its reading is begun in the halls of Congress every newspaper is informed that the message is "released," whereupon the paper goes upon the street within a few minutes, containing the whole thing.

Great care is taken to prevent a premature publication of a presidential message. There has never been a leak through a newspaper betraying the confidence reposed in it, but there have been leaks otherwise. During the Harrison administration an employee of the Government Printing Office sold a copy of it to the Washington correspondent of a New York newspaper. During the Roosevelt administration the President himself sent advance copies to the magazines, and some of these took the message into Wall Street before it was officially released.

President Roosevelt was the champion message writer of American history. He wrote more than twice as many messages as were written by President Cleveland, and it is said that if the vocabularies of all the other Presidents were boiled down into one composite whole, it would be found that he used a greater range of words in expressing his views than all of the others together.

The literary merit of McKinley's messages improved after John Hay became his ranking adviser, and the literary folk say that even Washington's Farewell Address shows a good deal of Alexander Hamilton in it. On the other hand, J. Pierpont Morgan has the original letter written by George Washington to James Madison asking him to prepare the Farewell Address and outlining completely the proposed paper. James Madison also wrote the famous nullification proclamation issued by Andrew Jackson. What is perhaps the finest message in the history of the presidency is credited to Andrew Johnson, who had fewer educational advantages than any other man who has ever been President of the United States. However, it was written by George Bancroft, the historian. The original draft is now in the Manuscript Division of the Library of Congress, in Bancroft's handwriting, with only a few unimportant additions and references added in the hand of President Johnson.

Sometimes a presidential message declares a principle which comes to be universally accepted as fundamental, and thus becomes as much a part of the organic law as if it had been incorporated in the Constitution itself. An instance of this is the Monroe doctrine. When in one of his messages President Monroe declared that the United States would not tolerate further extension of European dominions in the Western World, he laid down a principle ever since accepted as a cardinal precept of American diplomacy.

President Taft, in six years of speechmaking, before and after becoming President, has uttered nearly 2,000,000 words in his public addresses. A stenographer always goes with him to take down his speeches exactly as they are delivered. This stenographer afterwards transcribes his notes

TOURISTS WAITING TO ASCEND WASHINGTON MONUMENT.

and files the typewritten copies away. When enough have accumulated to make a 400-page volume, they are sent to the Government Printing Office to be bound. Already President Taft has more than 20 volumes of bound speeches. Each of these volumes contains nearly twice as much as this book.

CHAPTER II.

THE DEPARTMENT OF STATE.

The Department of State employs the smallest force of any department of the Federal Government, but it is first in rank among them, and its official head is regarded as the premier of the Cabinet. As a rule, when the President makes up his official family, he selects the ablest man he can get for the State portfolio. If there should ever come a time when both the President and the Vice President should die or in any other way become unable to serve as Chief Executive, the Secretary of State would become President, provided he were constitutionally eligible to that office. Should he not be eligible, the position of President would pass to the next lower Cabinet officer, and so on down the list, until one was found who did possess the necessary constitutional qualifications to become President. The presidential succession act was passed before the Department of Agriculture and the Department of Commerce and Labor were established, hence there is no provision by which the heads of these two departments could succeed to the Presidency by reason of the disability of any Cabinet officer above them.

The Secretary of State takes official precedence in the Cabinet, and usually holds first position in influence as well. There have been a few instances, however, where he has yielded first place in influence to the head of another department.

The Department of State has its official headquarters in Washington, but the larger portion of its activities are conducted in other countries. The Diplomatic and Consular services represent the most important work of the department, and while the plans are mapped out in Washington they are largely executed abroad. It was found advisable from the earliest history of the American Colonies to have representatives in Europe, whose mission it was to look after the interests of the Colonies abroad. Benjamin Franklin was a diplomatic agent of some of the American Colonies before the Revolution.

In order that they may be in a position to do their most effective work in the transaction of difficult diplomatic business, the diplomatic representatives of the United States in foreign countries are supposed to keep in close touch with the officials of the country to which they are accredited, and to be on terms of friendship with the foreign officials with whom they have to deal.

A few of the leading countries send ambassadors to Washington, and the United States sends officials of like rank to their capitals in turn. An ambassador is the personal representative of the ruler of the country from which he comes, and is supposed to have the same standing with the Government to which he is accredited that the ruler who appoints him would have. As the personal representative of the President of the United States, an American ambassador is supposed to have access at all times to the person of the ruler of the Government to which he is accredited.

If he is to make the most of his position he must be well fitted for taking a leading part in the social affairs of the official set of the capital at which he is stationed, and this calls for expenditures far in excess of his salary as ambassador. It is said that Ambassador Reid, in maintaining the American Embassy at the Court of St. James, spends $250,000 a year—more than ten times his salary. This means, of course, that only men of wealth can fill these important positions.

It is the hope of those who wish to see American citizens eligible to these positions without reference to their wealth, that the United States ultimately will supply embassy and legation buildings, and also funds for representation, including necessary official entertaining, etc.

The diplomatic representatives next in rank are the ministers, officially designated as envoys extraordinary and ministers plenipotentiary. These are stationed in countries which send ministers rather than ambassadors to Washington. Their official residences are known as legations. Usually a minister spends fully as much as his

THE DEPARTMENT OF STATE

salary in the endless round of entertaining which is regarded as an essential, although not an official, part of a minister's duties.

The Consular Service deals with problems of commerce arising in foreign countries as distinguished from problems of statecraft handled by the Diplomatic Service. There are about 700 consular officers of the United States scattered throughout the countries of the world. They are America's lookouts on the watchtowers of international trade. Few nations enjoy such extensive business abroad as the United States, our foreign trade now aggregating more than $3,000,000,000 a year. The men in the Consular Service are continually spying out new promised lands of commercial opportunity, and seeking for every kind of data which will enable the American export business to continue its growth.

Not long ago a New England manufacturer of knives asked the Consular Service for a list of retail dealers in cutlery in England. He got the list and is now carrying coals to Newcastle by shipping American knives to Sheffield. In another case the Department of State sent a new office safe to a certain consular office abroad. Since then more than 50 duplicates of this safe have been ordered from the American manufacturer by foreign business men who saw the one in the consular office. The Department of State points with pride to the success of the American foreign service in securing a single order amounting to $23,000,000 for battleships and armament from Argentina.

The office of consul is not a bed of roses. If a consul expects to get ahead, he must keep his eyes open. He has keen competition from the consular officers of other Governments, and often his salary is small in comparison to the services rendered. There are American consulates in all trade centers and some in very remote places. Probably the most inaccessible of the American consulates is that at Chung King, far back in the interior of China, almost on the frontier of Thibet. To reach it requires six weeks' travel from Shanghai by river. Much of the distance is traversed in a small river boat, pulled by a hundred Chinese coolies, who are paid a cent a day each. So deep are some of the gorges in this water route that at times the towing ropes seem to stand straight up in the air.

Foreign Governments consider the American Consular Service the best in the world. They are constantly using it as an example of efficiency which they would have their own consular representatives emulate. During recent years there has been a determined effort to promote the efficiency of the service. President Cleveland first took active steps toward applying the merit system in the appointment of consular representatives. Prior to that time, consular positions were regarded as a part of the spoils of political warfare and were filled more for the purpose of paying off political obligations than with a view of securing the highest possible type of men to fill them. President McKinley added strength to the policy begun by his predecessor, and President Roosevelt in 1906 and 1907 effected sweeping reforms, reorganizing the Consular Service, and providing for comprehensive competitive examinations. His aim was to have merit applied, both with respect to appointment and promotion in the service. President Taft has extended the same system of appointment and promotion to the Diplomatic Service, up to the grade of ministers.

In former years it was customary for consular representatives to charge fees for their service. Under that system many positions were worth a great deal to the incumbents. The consul generalship at London usually paid from $25,000 to $30,000 a year. The Paris consulate general was a splendid berth, and in exposition years was worth about $100,000 to the man fortunate enough to hold it. To-day all fees are turned into the United States Treasury, and the consular officers are paid specific salaries. The only exception to this general statement is that consular agents, who are simply men who perform consular services in communities where it would not be profitable to maintain a regular consulate, are allowed half the fees they collect up to the sum of $1,000, in payment for the services they render. The collections in consular agencies seldom exceed $200 a year. The consular agent is usually some established business man in his community who carries the agency as a side line. The result is that the Stars and Stripes sometimes float over strange places. It has not been many years since the consular agent of our great Republic stationed in a South American city had his office in a laundry.

Although the Consular Service has given a fine account of itself in the past, it has done so largely in spite of the indifference of American exporters to the necessity of meeting foreign conditions where they desire to build up an export trade. The average American manufacturer seems totally indifferent in the packing of goods, and as a result much of that which he does export reaches its destination in a damaged condition. On the Pacific Coast of Latin America it seems that the words, "handle with care," mean to the Indians an equivalent of "throw it down hard." The result is that many a costly piece of machinery is broken in transit, and long delays are the result. One may stand by the rail on a Pacific Coast steamer unloading into lighters and recognize every piece of American goods by the character of its packing. The Consular Service is constantly urging the American exporters to meet the essential conditions of foreign trade, but largely without success. Although the annual exports now aggregate more than $2,000,000,000, they are small when compared upon a per capita basis with the exports of other countries. If we

DECLARATION OF INDEPENDENCE.

THE DEPARTMENT OF STATE

exported as much per capita as the people of the Netherlands, we would ship $12,000,000,000 worth of goods to other countries each year. If we sold as much per capita as the people of Belgium, we would have more than five times as large an export trade as we have to-day. If we exported as much per capita as Argentina, our export trade would total more than $5,000,000,000 a year.

In its efforts to make the Diplomatic and Consular Services thoroughly efficient, a sort of foreign-service school has been established at the Department of State, and those receiving appointments attend this school for at least 30 days. Here they are given a course of lectures and instructions by experienced and competent men upon the duties of foreign representatives. They learn how to certify invoices; how to watch out for would-be smugglers in their prospective fields of work; how to prepare quarantine papers, which will entitle ships sailing from their ports to land their passengers in American ports; how to settle the estates of Americans dying abroad; what are a consul's duties with respect to the merchant marine, and what relief the law requires a consul to afford to stranded sailors in foreign ports.

The activities of a consulate cover a wide range. Consuls usually keep a complete list of all American citizens residing either temporarily or permanently in their jurisdiction; their offices serve as post offices for traveling Americans;

and they do everything within their power to assist their fellow citizens abroad. They make extensive reports to the Government at Washington concerning all sorts of commercial opportunities, and this information is placed on file or published, as conditions may warrant, and is put at the disposal of every interested American.

There are a great many matters in which the Department of State comes into direct contact with individual citizens. When Americans are deprived of their treaty rights abroad, or those of aliens are infringed upon in the United States, the department conducts the resulting international correspondence. If a zealous constable should happen to arrest a foreign diplomat for an infraction of the speed law of some small American village, the matter would be taken up and satisfactorily adjusted by the Department of State. If an American residing in some foreign country finds himself being deprived of his property or his liberty unlawfully, he appeals to the department to protect his rights. When Congress wishes information about any sort of conditions in foreign countries, the department acts as its agent in gathering it. Likewise, when any foreign Government wishes to know anything about American railroad or banking systems, American marriage and divorce laws, or other matters, it appeals to the Department of State for the data it desires. When cases are tried in the courts of one country and testimony is de-

THE DEPARTMENT OF STATE

sired from another country, it issues the letters rogatory through which it is secured.

The department, under the direction of the President, negotiates all treaties, attends to all matters of extradition, and has charge of all foreign and international tariff relations. When an American or a foreigner commits murder abroad and flees to the United States, the department issues the papers which enable him to be taken back for trial. Likewise when a murderer in America flees to a foreign country the Department of State acts as the agent of the American courts in bringing him back.

All matters pertaining to the American end of international conferences and congresses are arranged through the Department of State. Various institutions, such as missionary societies, have their protection assured through its labors, as in the case of the establishment of schools, hospitals, and the like. The department maintains a record of the marriage of all American citizens abroad, when performed in the presence of American consuls, and also of all American children born abroad. Many Americans use the agencies of the Department of State to ascertain the whereabouts or fate of friends and relatives who have dropped out of sight. For instance, an electrical engineer goes to South America and his friends lose track of him. When they appeal to the department it uses its entire machinery in the effort to locate the missing man.

The Department of State has charge of the publication and distribution of the laws of Congress, so as to make them accessible to all men and to forestall any excuse for the plea of ignorance of the law. When an amendment to the Federal Constitution is adopted, it becomes the duty of the Department of State to promulgate it, and its Secretary proclaims the admission of new States into the Union. He is also a medium of correspondence between the President and the governors of the several States. He has custody of the Great Seal of the United States, which he affixes to all Executive proclamations, to various commissions, and to warrants for the extradition of fugitives from justice. The original copies of all laws in force in the United States are filed with him for permanent keeping.

The card index of the Department of State covers diplomatic matters and all matters in which the Consular Service has a hand as well. Through this index the State Department officials have at their finger-tips a million things which, without it, would be needles in haystacks of voluminous records. The smallest and seemingly the most insignificant matter of to-day may affect the diplomacy of the world a decade hence. It is important that information concerning these things be filed away, and equally important that it be made readily accessible when needed. That the volume of this information is large is demonstrated by the fact that it has required nearly half a million cards to index the matter accumulated in four years. That it covers a wide range is shown by the fact that it may relate to an international situation affecting all of the Governments of the earth, or to the registration of the marriage of John Smith and Susie Brown in Paris or Singapore.

This index also serves as a sort of diplomatic "who's who" of the world. For instance, when any other nation appoints one of its citizens on a board or court of arbitration, it is very desirable for the United States to know the antecedents of that person, and to be sure that he is fitted for such a position. The Department of State needs only to look at its card index to determine this matter. Again, when another country sends an ambassador or a minister to Washington, it is essential that the United States should know whether or not he will be persona grata. Here again the great card index answers all questions.

The Department of State possesses the only fund in the administration of which no accounting to the people of the country is required. This is known as the contingent fund, and amounts to about $100,000 a year. It is used for the purpose of enabling the Secretary of State to keep a close watch on affairs in other nations, in order that the United States may at all times be apprised of any foreign developments which might affect its interests. If the Secretary were required to present an itemized statement of the expenditures of this fund to Congress and to the people of the country, there would be no means of keeping this work secret, and that fact alone might result in foreign complications. Another charge against this fund is the expense of entertaining the guests of the Nation. When a foreign dignitary like Admiral Togo visits this country, he is made the guest of the Nation, and representatives of the President and the Department of State are among those who welcome him. It is intended to have a suite of apartments in the new State Department Building where these honored guests may be quartered during their stay in the Nation's Capital.

CHAPTER III.

THE TREASURY.

The Treasury Department of the United States Government handles more money than any other one institution on earth. As the national tax collector, as the supervisor of the national-banking system, as the conservor of the national credit, and as the guardian of the financial resources of the country, the Treasury Department occupies a position of unique importance.

The Treasury Department collects all taxes levied by Congress for the support of the Federal Government, and expends the money thus collected upon the order of Congress. The Secretary of the Treasury, as the head of the department, at the beginning of each regular annual session of Congress advises that body what amount of money will be needed for the operation of the governmental machine for the next fiscal year, giving his estimates in detail.

The department not only acts as the fiscal agent of the Government, but it has direct control of the currency of the Nation, mints its coins, prints its paper money and its postage and revenue stamps, and protects the people from counterfeiters.

Other activities of the department include the maintenance of a fleet of armed vessels for the suppression of smuggling and the enforcement of the quarantine laws, the Life-Saving Service, the Public Health and Marine-Hospital Service, the construction and maintenance of all public buildings, and the audit and control of the accounts of the other executive departments of the Government.

The most interesting part of the work of this department is that of making money. For the making of its paper money it maintains an establishment known as the Bureau of Engraving and Printing, in which an average of fully a million dollars a day is printed. The paper used is of the toughest linen, made by a secret process. The flax from which it comes may once have been the garments of babes, the confirmation robes of children, or the graduation gowns of girls. After it reaches the rag bag it goes to the paper makers. Perhaps it comes back as money and dowers the bride who wore it as a baby.

The plates from which money is printed are made with the most exacting care. The public is not permitted to see the engravers at work, nor does any one engraver prepare a whole plate. It usually takes about a year of continuous work to complete one of the original plates. The money

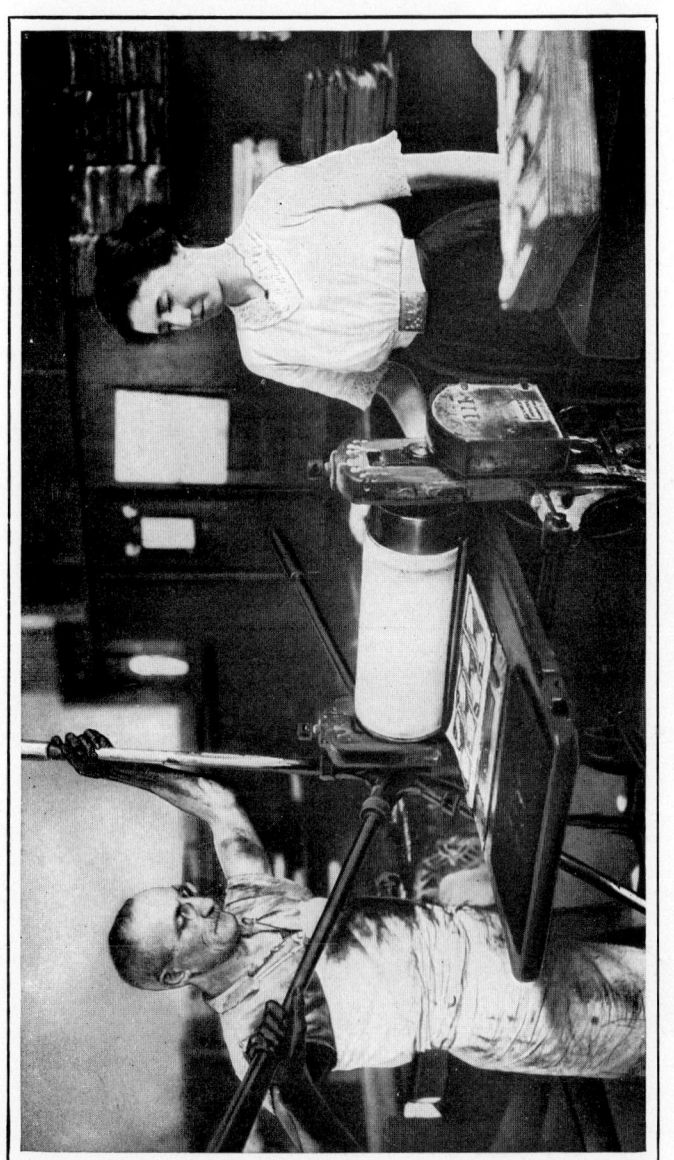

PRINTING DOLLAR BILLS.

is never printed from these originals, but by duplicates made from them by a mechanical process. If this were not so it would be practically impossible to detect counterfeiting. The fine lines on the paper money were made upon the original plates by a geometric machine which has as many combinations as the best safe lock, each combination producing a different design. Until the appearance of the counterfeit Monroe head hundred-dollar bill in 1897, it was thought that these lines could not be imitated. The portrait on a bill is regarded as the best guarantee against counterfeiting.

One of the most thorough systems of accounting in the world has been installed to insure the Government against loss during the process of printing. Out of the million or more dollars of paper currency printed every working day in the year, only one piece of paper went astray in 15 years. The officials of the bureau were morally certain that this was lost, but the workmen in the room where it disappeared had to pay its printed value. Each bill contains many symbols which tell the initiated what plate it was printed from, who engraved the plate, who printed the bill, and the like. It requires about 30 days to complete the intricate processes of getting a piece of paper money ready for circulation, during which time it is counted more than 50 times. It costs the Government about 1½ cents to issue and redeem each note, and less than one-fifth of

1 per cent to maintain the paper circulation of the country.

One-half of 1 per cent of the money going out never gets back. Uncle Sam is the gainer every time a piece of paper money is lost, for he will never be under the necessity of redeeming it with good hard gold. He maintains a force in the redemption bureau where torn, burned, or otherwise damaged currency may be redeemed. If three-fifths of a damaged note is sent in, the bill may be redeemed at face value; if less than three-fifths and more than two-fifths be sent, half value will be given. Any part less than three-fifths is not redeemable unless proof be brought in showing that the rest was destroyed. From the San Francisco fire came many charred notes, a majority of which were redeemed, while bits of cloth taken from a cow's stomach, and tiny shreds of green and yellow paper from a thrashing machine have proved to be redeemable currency when brought under the keen eyes of Government experts.

The average life of paper money in the United States is less than three years. The low denomination silver certificates get into the macerator, the machine with which worn-out money is destroyed, and which chews up a million dollars at a mouthful, in one and one-half years after they start their rounds of the pocketbooks of the country. Treasury notes reach their allotted term of life in two years, while the average yellow-back gold certificate is able to continue its travels for three years. The largest piece of paper money printed is the ten-thousand-dollar note. Four thousand of these were issued, of which only 641 have ever come back for redemption. Notes of the thousand-dollar denomination are highly prized by the big banks, as they occupy very little space in the vaults and are easily counted. Twelve pounds of ten-thousand-dollar notes would take the place of 2,000 tons of silver in a bank vault.

The seal which appears on the paper money of the United States is a relic of days antedating the Constitution. The words abbreviated are "Thesauri Americana Septentriomalis Sigillum." In English these words mean "seal of the Treasury of North America." To the well informed in history this tells of a time in American events when it was hoped that Canada would become a part of the United States. The die from which the present seals are made was prepared in 1849.

The processes of coining metallic money are no less interesting than those of making paper money. Anyone may take gold to the United States Mint and have it coined. After the metal has been assayed to ascertain its degree of purity, it is next put through a process which removes all foreign material from it. As pure gold would be too soft for money, an alloy is then added to give it the proper degree of hardness. It is next put through what is known as an annealing process, in which it is run between rollers, heated and worked over again, and put through rollers once more, until it becomes a thin bar of gold. This in turn is put through a giant stamping machine, which acts like a huge cake cutter, cutting hundreds of little golden cookies out of the bars of gold. These little golden cakes are next put into a huge squeezing machine, with engraved dies above and below them, and are squeezed with a pressure of 275 pounds. When they come out they are money. The same process is used in the making of silver, nickel, and copper coin.

The Government makes a profit on all coins except those of gold. The difference between the actual value of the metal in a coin and the face value of the coin is known as seigniorage. The metal in a 1-cent piece is worth only a small fraction of its face value. The remainder represents a clear profit to the Government. Every time a coin is lost Uncle Sam makes the difference between its actual value and its face value. How many of these get lost is shown by the fact that although the little half-cent pieces that were issued many years ago are very seldom seen nowadays, over 8,000,000 have never been returned to the Treasury. It is estimated that 6,000,000 of these have been lost forever. The 2- and 3-cent pieces are also unusually scarce, and yet more than a million dollars' worth of them have never come back to the Treasury.

One of the most interesting bureaus under the Treasury Department is that known as the Secret

Service. Its main work is to guard the currency of the country against counterfeiting. It is said that the best guardians of the currency are the tellers in the banks, and that more than nine-tenths of all the counterfeit money discovered in circulation is detected by them. The counterfeiter of to-day takes advantage of every modern process in his work, and by using photomechanical methods is able to produce results that can be detected only by the skilled handler of money. How comparatively little counterfeit money there is in circulation is shown by the fact that out of some $3,000,000,000 which passed through the hands of Treasury officials, less than $12,000 worth of bad money was found. After the spurious money is detected, it becomes the duty of the Secret Service to run down its makers. This often requires a vast amount of patience and keen detective work on the part of the Secret Service officials.

There are cases on record where counterfeit coins are worth more than those which they imitate. In former times platinum, which has about the same weight as gold, was worth only one-third as much as the yellow metal. The counterfeiter sawed the real coin into three sections, substituting for the middle section of gold a layer of platinum. A milling machine and a little soldering did the rest. Since those days platinum has increased tremendously in value, and a counterfeit coin of this kind now is worth more than the genuine. A band of counterfeiters in Mexico coined a lot of silver dollars. When these were discovered it was found that they contained $1.09 worth of metal each. There was a streak of gold in the silver, and they did not know it.

The United States Government recognizes the fact that the moving-picture show may prove an incentive to crime, and prohibits the display of films showing the processes of counterfeiting. Not long ago such a film was exhibited, and the Secret Service insisted that it be destroyed. Men have sometimes been arrested for passing real money. Not long ago a traveler offered a hundred-dollar note with a red back in payment of a hotel bill. He was arrested for attempting to pass spurious money. The bill turned out to have been a gold certificate of 1866. There is another note in circulation printed only on one side, which not one man in a thousand would cash for a stranger. It is the compound-interest note of 1864, and is worth much more than its face value.

The major portion of the revenues of the Federal Government is collected by the customs and internal revenue bureaus of the Treasury Department. Since the foundation of the Government, approximately $10,000,000,000 have come into the Treasury through the customhouses of the country. Two-thirds of all the customs business of the United States is transacted at the port of New York, where it costs 2 cents to collect each dollar of customs duties. There are a number of other customhouses, usually located at important cities along the coast and along the frontiers, while others are found at smaller towns. At Beaufort, N. C., it costs $1,500 to collect $1.55, and at a Maryland port it costs $1,000 to collect 61 cents.

Elaborate precautions are taken to prevent the smuggling into the United States of goods properly subject to tariff duties. Men conceal diamonds in secret holes in the heels of their shoes, women convert their bodies into huge spools for rare laces and silks, or sew Chicago or New York tags on Paris gowns in order to escape the payment of duties; while vessel owners sometimes attempt to land dutiable goods at places where there are no customhouses. The Secret Service keeps a card index of every known smuggler in the world, and closely follows his movements. Reports of all big purchases of jewels or other valuables abroad are made to the Treasury Department by its foreign agents, and its officers keep watch for these goods on every ship that comes into port.

The tariff laws of the country afford many anomalies. For instance, pearls come into the United States as precious stones, dutiable at 10 per cent, when unstrung. When strung, they are passed as jewelry, dutiable at 60 per cent. Some years ago there was a steady importation of pearls and the customs authorities concluded they were to be used as a single strand. The authorities held that the mere presence or absence of a string did not determine whether they were strung or unstrung pearls, but that the determining factor was whether or not they had been selected and matched for the purpose of making them into a string of pearls. Upon this theory they levied on them a duty of $110,000. The importer carried the case to the Supreme Court, which decided that he should pay only $18,000. Thus the absence of a string saved the importer $92,000. Another anomaly is the fact that a piece of goods at the customhouse may be linen to-day and cotton to-morrow. The law provides that textiles shall be rated according to the ingredient of principal value in them. In the fluctuations of the market the linen in a piece of mixed goods may be worth more than the cotton in it to-day, while to-morrow the cotton may be worth more than the linen. So to-day it will come into the United States as a piece of linen and to-morrow as a piece of cotton.

The Internal Revenue Bureau is the second best tax collector the United States has. Its receipts amount to several hundred million dollars a year. This bureau was organized in the early history of the Government, and in 1791 a tax of from 7 to 18 cents a gallon was levied on whisky. This tax led to the first threatened civil war in America. The distillers of western Pennsylvania did not fancy paying it, and began what is known as "the Whisky Rebellion." The present tax is $1.10 a gallon, and this tends to make moonshining a profitable business. There are no braver men in the Government service than the revenue agents whose duty it is to seek out and bring moonshiners to justice. The revenue agent who is seeking an illicit still must look for it in all guises and forms. Some years ago there was evidence of illicit whisky in a certain community, and the only clew to the place of manufacture was in the fact that in a certain piece of woodland the soot was thicker on the leaves of the north side of the tree than it was on those on the south side. After a prolonged search the revenue agents discovered traces of smoke issuing from a knot-hole in a hollow tree. It developed that this tree stood over a cave, and was used as a chimney for the still.

The national-banking system of the United States, comprising nearly 8,000 banks, is under the control of the Treasury Department. The capital of these banks aggregates nearly a billion dollars, and their surplus nearly seven hundred million. They have outstanding loans and discounts amounting to more than $5,000,000,000, and their total deposits aggregate as much more. Much of the money in circulation in the United States consists of national-bank notes. These are printed by the Treasury Department and sent to the national banks, where the president and the cashier sign them and they become full-fledged pieces of paper money. The bank is required to deposit with the Treasury Department Government bonds equal to the amount of the notes issued to guarantee the redemption of these notes.

Although the national banks of the country play such a large part in its fiscal affairs, only one-third of the money on deposit in the banks of the United States is carried in the national banks. In other words, the people of the United States have $15,000,000,000 to their credit in the banks of the country. There is a total of only slightly more than $3,000,000,000 of money in circulation upon any given date. A large percentage of this is in the pockets of the people. It will be seen that, upon an average, every dollar of the three billion is deposited to the credit of five different people.

The Supervising Architect of the Treasury Department has charge of the erection and maintenance of the public buildings authorized by Congress. He selects the sites, secures the necessary cession of jurisdiction by the States affected, prepares estimates and drawings, and has general oversight of the preliminaries in the construction of these buildings.

One of the most powerful officials in the Government service is the Comptroller of the Treasury. He is charged with the duty of revising all accounts upon appeal from settlements made by the auditors for the various departments. Whenever any question with reference to appropriations is raised, it is referred to the comptroller, and his verdict as to what the appropriation laws mean can not be reversed. It was the comptroller who decided the famous question of whether a tip is legal or not. He has expressed his opinion that a tip of 25 cents to a Pullman porter for a day's ride is warranted by law as a part of traveling expenses.

Thus the Treasury Department includes in the range of its activity every financial function of the United States, from coining money to tipping Pullman porters.

CHAPTER IV.

THE ARMY.

ALTHOUGH more than two-thirds of the revenues of the United States Government is expended in preparing for future wars and on account of wars of the past, this large expenditure is not reflected by the size of the United States Army. In the Regular Army at the present time there are 4,939 officers and 82,685 enlisted men, which includes the 180 officers and 5,732 enlisted men composing the Philippine Scouts. The authorized strength of the Regular Army is not to exceed 100,000 men. Both the Regular and the Militia Regiments are maintained on a peace footing at a little over half war strength. As the Organized Militia embraces about 120,000 officers and men, it will be seen that it would require a reserve of about 200,000 men to bring all of the regiments of the Regular Army and Organized Militia up to their war strength. Only about one man to each four hundred and fifty people in the United States is numbered in the organized forces of the American Military Establishment. The unorganized militia consists of more than 16,000,000 men, which embraces every able-bodied man in the United States between the ages of 18 and 44.

Although it does not take as long to recruit and equip a strong army as it does to build a naval fleet and put it into commission manned by an efficient personnel, it does take a considerable period of time to bring such an army up to a standard which makes it an efficient fighting force. The country is commencing to realize the importance of establishing in time of peace an organization from which an efficient army can be quickly made in time of war, and with this end in view a provisional field army has been established in the New England States and New York. The National Guard and regular troops have been grouped into what is known as the First Provisional Field Army. The Commanding General, Department of the East, is its commander. The Organized Militia and Regular Army, while furnishing a very considerable portion of the troops needed for this army, are not adequate to furnish certain technical troops, nor is the quota of field artillery or cavalry sufficient. A serious effort is being made to organize additional field artillery and cavalry organizations in the militia, and to organize and train certain technical troops, such as sanitary troops, engineer troops, signal troops, etc., and to provide reserve supplies of clothing, transportation, guns, ammunition, etc. The policy will probably be carried out throughout the United States and a certain number of provisional field armies organized and reserve supplies gradually accumulated. The great shortage in the

Army to-day is in field artillery guns and ammunition.

The task of provisioning the Regular Army is no small one. The commissary department issues 30,000,000 rations a year. Each of these costs approximately 21 cents. For an army of 100,000 men, there is required (for each day's rations) 50 tons of meat, 50 tons of bread, 50 tons of potatoes, and 40 tons of other food. Experience has taught that the feeding of an army is one of the first essentials to its efficiency in the field, and the War Department is using every possible facility for insuring good food for the soldiers in the service.

The recruiting service of the Army is a busy one, even in times of peace, and if Uncle Sam does not get good soldiers it is not because he has lack of applications for service in the Army. In a recent year 134,000 such applications for enlistment were received. Of these 125,000 were attracted by advertising. The Adjutant General keeps a card index in which is recorded full data about the Army service and the men who constitute it. This index now contains nearly 60,000,000 individual cards, 8,000,000 of them being medical cards, giving the history of all cases of sickness in the Army.

When a soldier enlists in Uncle Sam's Army he is assured that he will receive the best possible medical attention, which is provided free of charge. The medical department of the Army consists of hundreds of graduate physicians who are appointed after competitive examinations. If a soldier is only slightly indisposed, he is treated by the post-medical officers and is furnished with medicine at the regular dispensaries free of charge. If his ailment is more serious, he is sent to a hospital, and the army hospital has the reputation of being one of the most sanitary and best conducted in the world.

Humanity owes a vast debt to the Army medical officer. Many of the most valuable lessons learned by medical science during the past 20 years have been taught by him. For instance, the mosquito theory of the transmission of yellow fever was proved by a board of American medical officers consisting of Drs. Reed, Carroll, and Lazear. The support given them by Gen. Leonard Wood resulted in the sanitary triumph of the American occupation in Cuba. Later this work bore fruit in the even greater achievement of making possible the digging of the Panama Canal. The use of vaccination for the prevention of typhoid fever was borrowed from the British Army surgeon, but it has been pushed further by the American Army surgeon than by the British. In the last mobilization of the American Army there were only two cases of typhoid fever among 24,000 men, one a teamster who avoided the prophylactic, and the other a man who had developed typhoid before he had been vaccinated. This is a record without parallel in the medical history of any army. So thoroughly has the theory of sanitation been mastered that there are now less than one-thirteenth as many admissions to the Navy and Army hospitals on account of malaria as there were 13 years ago.

Although some other Governments spend large sums in the encouragement of rifle practice, the American people have the satisfaction of knowing that in both team and individual marksmanship their soldiers and sailors stand at the head of every list. Almost every international trophy to be competed for is now in their keeping.

A new device has been invented for teaching schoolboys marksmanship without danger to themselves. It is known as the subtarget machine. No ammunition is used with it; the boy simply aims the gun and pulls the trigger, and a needle-like rod registers on a minute target the point where the bullet would have struck on a regulation target had the gun been loaded. This machine is not a toy, but has been adopted by many militia companies, and several thousand are in use in the French Army. After the schoolboys are taught to take accurate aim in this way, they are put to work with 22-caliber rifles having the same weight and sight as the regulation Army rifle. After indoor practice with these has made the schoolboys proficient in the handling of guns, they are then taken to the rifle ranges and started in regular practice. It has been calculated by Army statisticians that for every man hit in

TROOPERS AT FORT MYER.

THE ARMY

battle by small arms, there are from 3,000 to 5,000 shots fired.

The Ordnance Bureau of the War Department has charge of the work of providing the Army with all its munitions of war, from the big 14-inch coast-defense gun down to the cartridges for an Army rifle. The heaviest guns weigh as much as a railroad engine and shoot a projectile weighing as much as ten ordinary men. The machine guns can fire eight rifle bullets in a second. No battleship can resist the concentrated fire of modern coast-defense guns. It has become only a question of marksmanship, and the American coast defenders have solved that problem by becoming the best marksmen in the world. They are now provided with 60-foot moving targets, and the troops at Fort Hancock, N. J., some months ago scored four shots in less than a minute with a battery of two guns. All four shots struck in a rectangle of 24 by 53 feet. The target was 4 miles away, and was traveling 5½ miles an hour. With such firing as this, it would be impossible for any foreign fleet to pass through the Narrows below New York.

The big guns are mounted on disappearing carriages. The gun is loaded and is then aimed according to directions given by the fire-control station, in the making of which a minute knowledge of physics and geometry is required, and the gun is raised into position. When it is fired, the recoil throws it back and down into the pit again.

There it is loaded once more, driven up into position again and fired. Two of these guns are placed in a single pit, and together they can keep a shot in the air nearly all the time, their combined capacity being a shot every 15 seconds.

In addition to the long coast-defense guns, there is a liberal supply of mortars, which shoot 16-inch projectiles. They have scored as high as 70 hits out of a hundred. These mortars are at all times out of sight of the enemy, and are not fired directly at the object they seek to destroy, but their tremendous balls are hurled high into the air and allowed to drop on the deck of an enemy's warship. The mortars are fired only after the most careful calculations involving the force of the winds, temperature, and many other conditions. Their projectiles carry in them charges of as much as 60 pounds of high explosives and do great damage when they hit. If one wishes to get an idea of the exactness of the aim of these mortars, let him lay a piece of money on the ground a hundred yards away and toss a baseball up in the air so that it will fall directly upon the coin.

The biggest gun ever built is the great 16-inch monster now at a New York fort. It carries a projectile weighing a full ton and can reach an enemy 21 miles away. At 17 miles it can toss its 2,400-pound ball as accurately as a baseball player throws a ball to a team-mate 17 yards away. This gun has been fired only a few times, and is regarded as satisfactory. The newest coast-defense guns fire a 14-inch projectile and could probably sink a battleship at a distance of 10 miles.

The War Department has provided for the United States, it is believed, the best system of coast defense possessed by any country. It is believed that all our principal harbors are adequately defended, and the fortifications in our insular possessions are being rapidly pushed forward to completion. Work is also being commenced on the fortifications at Panama. Additional works at the entrance of Chesapeake Bay are about to be commenced. All the principal Atlantic and Pacific coast cities are well defended.

In addition to the coast-defense guns, many harbors in American waters possess a complete layout for the planting of mines. In the case of threatened hostilities, these harbors would be literally underlaid with death-dealing mines, some of them to be exploded by contact, and others by touching a button on a switchboard on the shore. It is said that Uncle Sam has worked out the most complete system of harbor mining that exists in the world. Furthermore, every harbor from Portland, Me., to Portland, Oreg., could be completely mined at a cost much less than that required to build a single battleship. The moral effect of these mines in time of war can not be overestimated, since no nation would care to risk a fleet in a thoroughly mined harbor. A mine costing a few hundred dollars may destroy a battleship costing millions. Military and naval experts say that it was the knowledge that its harbors were amply protected that allowed Japan to fear nothing from the Russian Navy and enabled the Japanese fleet to assume the offensive. With a complete system of high-power guns, mortars, searchlights, fire control, and everything else that tends to give a land fort the advantage over a battleship, it seems that the American coast-defense system is a perpetual guarantee of the safety of American cities from bombardment by a foreign fleet.

No nation on earth is so liberal to its soldiers after they have retired from the service as the United States. Four billion dollars is too large a sum for the human mind to grasp. It is enough to build 300 or more modern battleships, or to run the postal service of the United States for forty years without the collection of a cent from the people. It is this sum that a grateful nation has given freely, voluntarily, and without a single regret to the men who have served it in its wars. And it is probable that a like amount will be given before the last pensioner now on the list shall have cashed his last voucher.

The pension payments of the American Government are greater than those of all the other nations of the earth combined. At one time and another more than 2,000,000 pension claims have been allowed, and nearly a million and a half of other claims have been rejected. Perhaps nine-tenths of these pension claims have grown out of the Civil War.

The Corps of Engineers of the United States Army, in addition to its duties relating to the construction and repair of all fortifications and other works of defense, also has charge of the work of improving the rivers and harbors of the United States. If the American people would spend as much per capita on their inland waterways as Canada already has spent, every inland waterway project in the United States could be perfected. Projects which will require the expenditure of half a billion dollars have already been approved by the Board of Engineers, and others involving the expenditure of another half a billion dollars have been carried out. Those already constructed carry more freight than the 80,000 miles of perfected canals of continental Europe, which cost ten times as much. The improvement of the Harlem River, under the very shadow of Wall Street, was undertaken in 1878, the total cost to be less than $3,000,000. The project is now about half completed. In 1875 it was decided to give the Ohio River a slack-water navigable depth of 6 feet. In all the intervening years since then the work has gone on, and it has been decided to increase the depth to 9 feet. At the rate the Army Engineers are carrying it forward, 50 years must elapse and $63,000,000 must be spent before this work is done. The trouble, however, does not lie with the Corps of Engineers, but with

Congress. That body has so many demands upon it for appropriations that it is not able to have the work completed more expeditiously.

The War Department has charge of the United States Military Academy at West Point. This academy is one of the foremost military schools in the world, and employs 111 officers and instructors. Over 500 young men compose the cadet body. They are appointed by competitive examinations, upon the recommendations of the Senators and Representatives from the several States. In recent years there has been something of a lack of interest in military education, as is shown by the fact that more than 200 of the vacancies in the Cadet Corps are not filled each year, and that the corps is nearly one-third smaller than the maximum capacity of the school, which is placed at 730. It is a remarkable fact that during a ten-year period the Military Academy has not been able to furnish a single graduate to fill a vacancy made by increases in the Army, but that the graduating classes have averaged more than 50 short of the number necessary to replace ordinary casualties, such as deaths, resignations, and retirements.

The War Department also has charge of the military parks and cemeteries of the country. The park at Gettysburg is regarded as the finest military park in the world. Steps are being taken for marking the position of the Confederate troops on that battlefield, and when this work is

THE ARMY

completed, it will represent the most comprehensive effort ever made to mark the position of troops on a battlefield. There are military parks also on the Civil War battlefields of Chickamauga, Shiloh, and Vicksburg.

A law was passed in 1903 creating the office of Chief of Staff and the General Staff Corps of the Army. The Chief of Staff is the military advisor of the Secretary of War, and keeps him informed on all military matters. He receives from the Secretary of War directions and orders given in behalf of the President, or by the President directly. All orders of the Secretary of War affecting the Regular Army and Organized Militia when called into the service of the United States are issued by him through The Adjutant General; and through the Chief of the Division of Militia Affairs in matters affecting the Organized Militia not in the service of the United States. He supervises all staff departments and corps, all troops of the line and staff, and all other matters pertaining to the Military Establishment within the scope of the War Department. Under authority of the Secretary of War he can call for information, make investigations, and exercise all other functions necessary to secure proper harmony and efficiency. His supervisory powers cover duties pertaining to the command, training, and discipline of the Army, its recruitment, and military operations, distribution of troops, inspections, armaments, fortifications, military education and instruction, and kindred matters. In short, his office constitutes a supervising military bureau of the War Department, which is expected to handle all of the military matters in behalf of the Secretary of War.

CLOCK THAT REGULATES TIME FOR THE UNITED STATES.

CHAPTER V.

THE NAVY.

WITH the exception of Great Britain, the United States has what is perhaps the most powerful Navy in the world. It costs approximately $130,-000,000 a year for the maintenance and expansion of our fighting force on the seas, of which approximately $100,000,000 goes toward its upkeep. The authorized enlisted force of the Navy embraces 47,500 men of the seamen branch and 9,521 marines. If Congress follows the recommendations of the naval authorities, in 10 years the United States will have about 40 first-class battleships, 40 scout cruisers, and 120 torpedo-boat destroyers. The cost of building such a number of scout cruisers and torpedo-boat destroyers would be more than $100,000,000. With 40 battleships on the list, only 21 would be kept in active commission, as at present, the remaining ones being kept in reserve. Likewise, only four or five of the scout cruisers would be kept in active commission continuously, and no more destroyers would be kept in full commission than at present.

Although the active battle fleet has been increased from 16 to 21 ships, and the torpedo fleet has been added to in an even greater proportion, the cost of maintaining the entire Navy has decreased, and should Congress authorize all of the new construction desired by the Navy Department in the way of battleships, cruisers, destroyers, repair ships, etc., the aggregate expense would not be materially increased, since it is expected that the economy resulting from improved administrative methods will offset the cost of maintenance of an increased number of ships in reserve.

Although the United States now leads the world in naval construction, with its projected 30,000-ton battleships, only 28 years ago this Nation did not have a single armored seagoing warship. Although the size of battleships has risen from 16,000 tons displacement to 30,000 tons in 10 years, the cost has not risen in proportion. It cost but little more to build the 26,000-ton *Arkansas* than it cost to construct the 20,000-ton *Delaware*. The *Vermont,* whose keel was laid in 1904, and which has a displacement of 16,000 tons, cost a quarter of a million dollars more than the *Utah,* of 22,000 tons displacement. Battleships have grown greater, not only in size and in the strength of their armament, but also in their efficiency. The *Delaware,* of 20,000 tons displacement, burns less coal than the *Connecticut,* of 16,000 tons displacement.

One of the most interesting factories in the world is the Naval Gun Factory at Washington, which is the largest gun-making establishment on earth. Here 60-ton guns are picked up and carried around with as little apparent exertion as a boy makes in lifting an air-rifle to his shoulder, and the largest guns built are the 14-inch monsters which will be placed on the new battleships. With a 365-pound charge of smokeless powder, they hurl a 1,400-pound shell through the air with an initial speed of nearly half a mile a second. So great is the force with which this shell is propelled that it has a possible range of 25,000 yards. One of these shells would pierce at least 5 feet of wrought iron. The charge of powder by which it is hurled on its death-dealing mission generates a force which would lift the great Masonic Temple of Chicago, 2 feet in the air in a single second. At 7 miles one of these shells would pierce the heaviest armor. At every broadside of the twenty 14-inch guns of two of the latest battleships, more than 12 tons of metal would be hurled against the opposing fleet. This is much more than the entire gun power of Dewey's whole fleet at Manila. This metal will be propelled by more than 3 tons of smokeless powder and the aggregate cost of each broadside will represent much more than the annual salary of the Admiral of the Navy.

It is believed that the naval battles of the future will be fought at long range, and that the issue will be determined largely by the effectiveness of guns at a distance of 7 miles or more. In this particular the American naval gunner has the advantage of those of any other country. In the battle of Santiago, Admiral Evans estimates only 5 per cent of the shots were effective. In recent naval practice the American gunner has registered hits in from 60 to 90 per cent of the shots fired, and Admiral Evans thinks that 40 per cent of the hits would be registered in actual war. The guns of the *Connecticut* shoot five times as fast as did those of the *Oregon* at Santiago, and "Fighting Bob" figures that in five minutes the *Connecticut* would hurl 35,000 pounds of steel against a hostile fleet, whereas the *Oregon* landed only 790 pounds.

Among the most interesting sights one sees at the Naval Gun Factory is the shop where jackets are fitted to the big barkers. So great is the explosive force of a charge of modern powder that the breech section of a great gun has to be strongly reenforced. Anyone who has ever seen a rural blacksmith "cut a tire" on Farmer Brown's road wagon will understand the principle of togging out a big gun in a new jacket. The jacket is heated for a long period in an electric furnace at a temperature of from 400° to 500°. After it has sufficiently expanded, the big gun is lifted up and the small end put down through the jacket. When the breech end comes in contact with the jacket, it is in position, and the steel is gradually cooled and tempered by the application of jets of water. One hears much about the muzzle speed of the cannon ball, and wonders how it can be accurately told. Two targets are connected with a chronograph by an electric current. As the projectile passes through the first target it releases a weight from an electromagnet, which, in falling, records the exact instant the projectile passes through the target. Another weight is likewise released when the projectile passes through the second target and the difference in the time registered shows how long it required for the projectile to cover the distance between the two targets.

To measure the pressure in gun fire, two methods are used. In the one method a piece of brass is placed in a steel case. A piston is connected with this piece of brass and the pressure produced by the explosion, acting on the piston, compresses the brass in proportion to the amount of pressure exerted. This gives the basis for the calculation as to the amount of pressure.

One of the most interesting of all the munitions of war is the modern Whitehead torpedo. Its motive power is furnished by compressed air, stored in a tank within the torpedo, at a pressure of about 1,100 pounds to the square inch. In a chamber back of the compressed-air tank is a mechanism for regulating the depth at which the torpedo shall glide along in the water. A piston is held in a balanced position by the pressure of springs on one side and of water on the other. When the torpedo goes too low in the water, the pressure drives the piston out of its former position, and this in turn forces the submergence rudders upward and drives the torpedo toward the surface. When the torpedo gets too near the surface, the springs force the piston the other way and the torpedo is guided downward. This would keep it gliding first upward and then downward unless an additional mechanism were provided to regulate the action of the piston. To meet the difficulty, a pendulum has been introduced, which keeps the torpedo submerged at a previously determined depth during its entire flight. In addition to a mechanism for keeping the torpedo at its proper depth, there is also a mechanism which prevents it from turning to the right or to the left. This is controlled by a little gyroscope. If the torpedo attempts to turn either to the left or to the right, the gyroscope, true to its laws of motion, adheres to its own straight line, and in so doing opens a little valve in a small steering engine which moves the guiding rudders in such a manner as to bring the torpedo back to its course. The gyroscope acts in the same way as a person handling the reins in driving a horse and is the driver which guides the steed of death on its errand of destruction. The torpedo has a war head on it when put in service, which explodes the charge when it hits its mark. There is a sea-valve in the torpedo, which automatically scuttles it and sends it to the bottom of the sea if it misses its mark.

The Navy uses smokeless powder for all its big guns. This is perfectly harmless, unless ignited when it is confined. In the open air a stick of it can be held in the hand and lighted and it will burn slowly, without an explosion. At the Indian Head Naval Proving Ground near Washington, where smokeless powder is made by the Government and stored in large quantities, for a long time there was a workman who daily smoked a pipe with a stem made of smokeless powder. A former chief of the Bureau of Ordnance of the Navy Department used to carry a cane made of a stick of smokeless powder. Occasionally he would set the end on fire to light his cigar. Gun-cotton, which is the principal ingredient of the smokeless powder used by the Navy, produces a gas having a volume 750 times greater than the original substance.

The task of provisioning a battleship fleet is a great one. It required 133,000 tons of coal to take the world-girdling fleet from Hampton Roads to San Francisco and across the Pacific. The cost of transporting this coal alone amounted to $755,000. The fleet was provided with 9,000 pounds of dried eggs, which is equivalent to 36,000 dozen fresh eggs, and 26,000 pounds of dehydrated vegetables.

Realizing that an error of a minute of two in time might lead the commander of a fleet to miscalculate his position, and that such an error of position might decide the fortunes of a naval battle and of a war, the Navy Department established the Naval Observatory for the primary purpose of providing the exact time for its ships.

It keeps a great master clock in a hermetically sealed case in an isolated vault, the temperature of the vault never being allowed to vary more than the hundredth part of one degree. This clock is so accurate that it never varies more than three-tenths of a second, and at times it has run for three weeks without varying the hundredth part of a second. The temperature of the vault is maintained at an even degree by a thermostat and a small electric light. The change of the hundredth part of a degree of temperature would affect the delicate thermostat as much as a change of 40° affects a human being. When the temperature in the vault becomes the two-hundredth part of a degree hotter than normal, the thermostat automatically turns off its little electric stove. When the temperature falls below normal, the thermostat starts the stove to work again. It often switches the little electric bulb off and on as much as a dozen or more times a minute.

Yet with all the wonderful accuracy of the big master clock, a careful check is kept upon its performance. This is done with a transit instrument, which looks like a cross between a telescope and a cannon, and which is mounted on two great pillars of granite, on the exact meridian of Washington. It is adjusted with a delicacy almost unbelievable. It can not rest but a small percentage of its weight on its pivots, being supported by a sling arrangement which allows only enough

THE NAVAL OBSERVATORY.

of the weight on the real bearings to give it steadiness. At its side there are two delicately adjusted wheels which may be turned the smallest conceivable fraction of an inch, and while they are about 2 feet in diameter, it is necessary to use four microscopes to see the lines in the silver on the rims which constitute the gauge by which the instrument is set. In spite of the greatest exactitude that is obtainable in the mounting and operation of a transit instrument there is always a remaining margin of error; but it happens that this margin of error may be determined when the observations are made and are compensated for in the resulting computation. These errors are caused by such conditions as the variations of temperature, changes in barometric pressure, and the personal equation of the observer. When the observer wishes to fix the time, he takes the transit of about five of the fixed stars. He knows the exact instant at which one of these stars ought to be at an exact position in the heavens. He aims his telescope at the star and watches the stars cross each of the 10 minute spider threads. Each time the star crosses one of these lines the observer presses the key of a chronograph, and the fact is registered electrically, showing the exact time of crossing. From these observations he gets the data by which he is able to determine to the hundredth part of a second how accurate his clocks are.

One of the rooms at the observatory is used

for the purpose of testing the chronometers, clocks by which time is kept on shipboard in the Navy. Before being sent out these clocks are kept under observation for six months and are regulated so that they measure time with remarkable precision. In this room it is aimed to keep the temperature and moisture conditions as near to an approximation of sea conditions as may be. Wet clothes are hung up around the room in order to obtain the proper degree of humidity. Every vessel in the Navy must carry at least three chronometers. If only one were carried there would be no means of knowing when it went wrong. If two were carried it would be impossible to tell which one was right and which one was wrong, in case of variation. So they carry three and when two of them agree it is reasonably certain that it is the third one that is wrong.

The Naval Observatory has made some remarkable experiments in the past. One of the most interesting of these was the determination of the velocity of light by former Prof. Michaelson, and the late Simon Newcomb. Light travels so fast that it might girdle the globe more than seven times in a single second, yet these scientists were able to measure the time it required light to travel from the Washington Monument to Fort Myer, 2¼ miles distant, and return. In the grounds at Fort Myer they stationed a revolving mirror with a speed of 250 revolutions to the second, and by revolving this mirror they were able to note how long it took for a ray of light to flash across the intervening space and back again. They found that it could cover the distance in the forty-thousandth part of a second, and thus were able to settle the question of the velocity of light, proving former theories to be correct.

The work done by the Naval Observatory with reference to the measurement of time finds a counterpart in the careful surveys of harbors into which American warships may have occasion to go made by the Hydrographic Office. Lack of knowledge of obstructions in the usual channels of the ocean and in the harbors of the world might not only imperil commercial navigation, but it might prevent the proper maneuvering of a fleet in a naval battle. In conjunction with the Coast and Geodetic Survey, the Hydrographic Office prepares charts showing the condition of every harbor and waterway in the world. The charts are printed from copper plates, of which more than a million dollars' worth have been made.

The Navy Department is the world's greatest user of the wireless telegraph, already possessing equipment worth more than half a million dollars. This will be more than doubled in a short time. The instruments of the Navy are so tuned up that outside instruments can not read its messages unless they come within 3 per cent of having the same number of vibrations per second. It is the intention of the department ultimately to have four big wireless towers, each with a range of 3,000 miles around it. One of these will be located at Washington, another at Panama, another at Honolulu, and the fourth on the western coast of the United States. It is also intended to equip two or three of the large cruisers with similar outfits, so that the department will be able to keep in touch with its vessels in all parts of the world at all times.

CHAPTER VI.

THE POST OFFICE DEPARTMENT.

The Post Office Department of the United States Government is by far the largest postal institution in the world. Its 300,000 employees handle more than 15,000,000,000 pieces of mail each year, which is one-third of the aggregate postal business of all the civilized nations. The American post office handles more than 800,000 letters every hour of the 24, every day in the year; it issues and redeems daily more than 250,000 money orders; it registers daily more than 115,000 letters and parcels, and it handles thousands of tons of second and third and fourth class matter every hour.

For many years there has been a deficit of from $10,000,000 to $18,000,000 in the operation of the postal service, and it remained for Postmaster General Frank H. Hitchcock, of President Taft's Cabinet, entirely to eliminate this deficit and to make the postal service not only a self-supporting but a paying institution. In doing so his main effort was to stop up the little leaks without adversely affecting the service in any way. He continued the application of the new divisor in the readjustment of pay to the railroads on the weights of mails carried until the effect had been felt throughout the entire service. He recommended to Congress a change with respect to the rates payable for service on land-grant roads, which Congress enacted into law. The withdrawal of empty equipment from the mails and its transportation by freight was extended throughout the weighing sections.

In the money-order business, until recently, the handling of the domestic advice slips, which were in every instance required to be mailed by the issuing to the paying office, cost the Government about $600,000 a year. A new form of order has been introduced in which the advice slip forms a part of the order itself, and is presented at the paying office by the holder of the money order. This radical change has resulted in the entire elimination of the six-hundred-thousand-dollar expense incident to the handling of the advice slips under the former method. It formerly was the custom to furnish a return receipt card showing delivery for every domestic registered letter or parcel handled in the mails. This required the handling of more than 30,000,000 such cards a year. By the authority of Congress these cards are now furnished only when requested, and this resulted in the saving of approximately $77,000 a year. Economies in the purchase of supplies also cut down the total expenditure of the postal service. The annual supply bill amounts to about $4,000,000. The twine used by the service in

THE POST OFFICE DEPARTMENT

tying packages of letters costs $200,000 a year, nearly a billion yards of it being used. This amount of twine would go around the earth 20 times. The Post Office Department long sought a substitute for twine, but has given up the quest.

In addition to the four Assistant Postmasters General, who are the aids of the Postmaster General in commanding the postal army, the Post Office Department has its own legal staff, and its own force of traveling representatives or inspectors. The Assistant Attorney General for the Post Office Department has charge of the enforcement of the law against lottery schemes, swindlers, and greengoods men who use the mails. More than 3,000 persons and firms have been denied the use of the mails on "fraud orders."

The growth of the mail business of the United States has been one of the marvels of American progress. In 1837 the average citizen spent 32 cents a year for postage. Now he spends $2.29. The receipts of the Chicago post office to-day are larger than those of the entire country at the beginning of the Civil War. The receipts of the post offices vary from $5 a year at the smallest office, in Alabama, to more than $23,000,000 a year at the largest, New York City.

The Railway Postal Service, with its 17,000 employees, constitutes the backbone of the American postal system. The transportation of the mails on railways costs $50,000,000 a year and the pay of the clerks $20,000,000 more. Each clerk must be familiar with the location of from 5,000 to 20,000 post offices, and is required to be able to tell instantly on what railroad each post office is located, through what junction points a letter dispatched by him to that office may pass, and a multitude of other details which can be mastered only by very retentive minds. A letter addressed to the little village of Mount Crawford, Va., mailed in Washington before a certain hour, will reach its destination in the shortest time by one railroad, but if mailed after that hour, it will arrive sooner by another. Every change of schedule on a railroad affects the method of dispatching mail so that it will reach its destination at the earliest possible moment, yet the railway-postal clerk is expected to be familiar with these things at all times. The accuracy to which they can attain is illustrated by the experience of one clerk who made a record by handling 17,000 cards addressed to as many post offices at the rate of 60 a minute without putting a single card in the wrong pigeonhole in the mailing case.

The Rural Free Delivery Service costs nearly $43,000,000 a year, and does not bring in more than a fourth as much in return. Yet the Fourth Assistant Postmaster General insists that it is one of the most valuable features of the entire postal service.

Uncle Sam is the champion letter writer of the world, but the Post Office Department receives no direct revenue in postage therefrom. A few

THE POST OFFICE DEPARTMENT

years ago Congress decided to ascertain how much mail the Post Office Department was carrying free for the Government. The weighing and counting was done during the last six months of the year 1907. The latter part of the period was considered dull commercially, but this would not necessarily affect the business of the Government. During this half year 24,000,000 pounds of Government mail was handled, which was at the rate of 24,000 tons a year. The report showed that 2,277,000 pounds of congressional mail matter and 21,663,000 pounds of departmental mail matter was dispatched. Congressional mail is larger, however, in proportion, than these figures indicate, since Congress was in session only a portion of the time the weighing was made, and the vast amount of free seeds and free Government documents usually sent in the spring were, therefore, not included. During the count of seven days the postal service handled 633,000 pieces of departmental mail for each of the seven days. Nearly 50 per cent of all the mail dispatched by the Federal Government is handled in the post office in Washington City.

Although Government mail travels free and private mail has to pay its own way, Government mail travels farthest. Paid mail travels an average of 622 miles; congressional mail, 750; and departmental mail, 782 miles. The last count of mail received by Senators and Representatives showed that nearly 20,000 letters a day are received at the Capitol. The Post Office Department is the greatest producer of Government mail, with the Department of Agriculture second, and the Treasury Department third. The Treasury Department receives an average of about 4,000 letters a day. One word saved in every letter mailed by the Federal Government would enable it to lay off enough stenographers to do the work of a business corporation transacting an annual million-dollar business.

Counting the stamps on stamped envelopes, postal cards, and newspaper wrappers, over 11,000,000,000 postage stamps, or more than a thousand for every man, woman, and child in the country, are issued every year. These range in value from 1 cent to $5. The average stamp user has never seen a 5-dollar stamp, yet more than 3,000 of them are sold each year, while over ninety thousand 1-dollar stamps pass through the stamp windows of the country. In years gone by the Government issued a stamp worth $100. It was a newspaper stamp, and was never seen by the public. It was placed on the book in the office of the dispatching postmaster and canceled there. All newspaper stamps have been discontinued.

The story of the origin of the postage stamp has in it a pleasing little romance. Some 65 years ago Rowland Hill was staying at an English inn when the daughter of the landlord received a letter by mail. Looking it over from

THE POST OFFICE DEPARTMENT 71

one end to the other she inquired of the postman what the charges were. He replied that it was a shilling. She did not have the money to pay the charges and Hill paid them for her. Afterwards she told him she was sorry he had done so, that she and her lover had evolved a little code of their own by which they put their messages on the outside of the letters and thus could send them through the mails without paying, allowing the postal authorities to destroy the letters after they had looked them over and refused to pay the charges. This put Hill to thinking, and the pay-in-advance stamp was the result.

The Post Office Department has long striven to do everything in its power for the convenience of the big users of the mail. Large business houses long felt the loss from the petty grafting of stamps by office boys and others higher up. To provide means of identification so as to protect the buyers of large quantities of stamps, it was arranged that the stamps may be perforated with numbers or letters not over half an inch square. This has resulted in a large decline in the petty pilfering of postage stamps.

Another order which has resulted in a great saving of time and expense to the postal service, and also to the big users of the mails, is the privilege of sending unstamped third and fourth class matter through the mail. To a firm which sends out a million circulars, the work of stamping them is very tedious, and the actual cost of the stamps to the Government is not insignificant. So it is provided that where a business house sends out 2,000 or more identical pieces of mail, it may be granted the privilege of printing on the wrappers or envelopes a statement showing the amount of postage paid, the office at which paid, and the number of the permit under which this form of postage paying was substituted for stamps.

Another convenience is the privilege of precanceling stamps. A big firm, for instance, mails 50,000 calendars. Each of these is in a roll. If the firm placed a stamp on each one of these calendars and took it to the post office in the ordinary way, the office would be swamped, since no other method than the old hand stamp has been found for canceling the postage on package mail. By permitting the precancellation of stamps both the patron and the post office are saved a vast deal of trouble and expense.

It costs the United States a half million dollars a year for the upkeep of old and purchase of new mail bags. Over 900,000 locks are used in the ordinary transportation of the mails, each of them opening to every key in the postal establishment used in connection with the ordinary mail pouch. To protect them the greatest possible care must be observed to prevent a single one of these keys from going astray. There are 56,000 rotary registry locks in use. These locks are used on pouches which contain registered mail

THE POST OFFICE DEPARTMENT 73

only, the mail being checked in the pouches by two clerks who keep a duplicate record of the number of pieces placed in the pouches and who send the original record in the pouches to the receiving offices. The locks are opened by a special key, and have a registering equipment like that of a bicycle cyclometer, which moves up one number every time the lock is opened. When a registry pouch arrives at its destination two clerks open it and check its contents with the bill inclosed. When the numbers on the lock correspond with those in the record, it shows that the lock and pouch have come through unopened. When the lock numbers do not correspond it indicates that the lock has been opened by some unauthorized person.

There are many curious things in the postal service. The strangest post office from which the American postal service receives mail is one on the Galapagos Island, off the coast of Ecuador. It is nothing but a barrel in which letters are dispatched semioccasionally. All mariners in those waters know of this post office, and when in that vicinity go to look in the barrel for letters. Recently some of these showed up in Washington much the worse for wear.

Mail usually gets to its destination in the shortest possible time, but occasionally a letter or a package of letters will not show up for years. Recently a letter came to the post office in Paterson, N. J., that had been mailed three years before at Midvale, 5 miles away. In another instance a letter arrived in an eastern city bearing congratulations to a proud father upon the birth of a son. When it arrived, that son three times had been congratulated upon the birth of children of his own.

The Post Office Department is a maker of maps as well as a carrier of mails. Using all Government surveys, it makes post-route maps of the States, showing post offices and all mail connections, and also rural-delivery maps of the principal counties on an enlarged scale, showing all the roads and residences, the dimensions of the latter maps averaging 30 by 36 inches. The sheets of the post-route maps are sold at 80 cents each, and those of the county maps at 50 cents each.

There has been much controversy over the question of a parcels-post system for the United States. The country merchant thinks such a system would be ruinous to him. On the other hand, the advocates of the parcels post point out that the Rural Free Delivery Service will never reach its greatest usefulness until such a system is established, and that the express companies will continue to swell their dividends by reason of its absence. While the controversy is being waged the American citizen enjoys the somewhat novel privilege of being able to send a parcel through the mails to England at a smaller cost than he can send it to his next door neighbor. Also, he

THE POST OFFICE DEPARTMENT 75

can send a 11-pound package to England, but can not dispatch a package weighing more than 4 pounds to his friend in the next town.

The Dead Letter Office of the Post Office Department is one of its most interesting institutions. It receives about 12,000,000 "dead" letters and parcels a year and some 8,000,000 post cards and postals. Ten million letters and parcels are opened, and of these about 6,000,000 are either forwarded to the addressees or returned to the writers. One can scarcely imagine the great number of queer things which show up at the Dead Letter Office. A museum is maintained where many of these strange relics of the mail are put on exhibition. One of these exhibits is an old white hat bearing lines and rhymes telling of the romances of school days. Another is a rattlesnake's hide. There are doll-baby legs, a grinning skull, an old-fashioned wooden stirrup, and the hind legs of a wolf. More than 85,000 photographs come to the dead letter office each year.

Often live animals and insects are found in the mails. Once a clerk opened a package and released a whole swarm of Kansas chinch bugs. Another clerk opened a small pasteboard box and out of it came a deadly tarantula. In another box there appeared a large rattlesnake, accompanied by a card on which was written, "I hope this puts an end to you." A careful record is kept of all valuable inclosures received in dead letter mail, including money, commercial papers, wills, deeds, etc. Of some $60,000 of actual money received in a year only about $40,000 could be returned. The remainder was turned into the United States Treasury.

One of the most unique events in the year's work of the postal service is the annual dead letter sale. This sale is held just before Christmas, and the proceeds approximate $10,000 a year. Formerly it was one of the greatest lotteries imaginable. A young woman made the highest bid on a package containing a set of false teeth. A woman-hating man was the successful bidder on a package containing a lot of false hair, and a colored woman got a package containing six boxes of white face powder.

Each year thousands of letters come to the post offices of the country addressed to Santa Claus. Formerly these were all destroyed, as the department was never able satisfactorily to find the permanent address of good old Kris Kringle. Later President Roosevelt granted Miss Elizabeth Phillips the right to take these letters and, as far as lay in her power, to grant the requests contained in them. Within a year Miss Phillips became widely known as "The Santa Claus Lady." Her untimely death caused much sorrow among the poor children of the country.

One of the innovations of the present administration is the establishment of a postal-savings

DESTROYING OLD PAPER MONEY.

THE POST OFFICE DEPARTMENT

system. The Postmaster General has taken a personal interest in the system from the beginning and as a result it has been extended with great rapidity. In fact, none of the many countries of the world, operating postal savings, ever tried to operate so many depositories in so short a time after its installation. The receipt of deposits was started first on January 3, 1911, in 48 post offices in as many States and Territories. Since that time the system has been extended as rapidly as practicable. There are approximately 60,000 post offices in the country, and it is the purpose of the present administration to have a savings department in the 50,000 money-order offices.

One of the most widely desired improvements in the postal service that is indicated for the early future is the adoption of 1-cent letter postage. It has been asserted by congressional leaders that as soon as the Post Office Department could make itself a self-supporting institution, Congress would grant penny postage to the people of the United States. If this reduction is made, it is predicted that the postal business in the United States will soon increase to a point equal to that of all other nations combined.

CHAPTER VII.

THE DEPARTMENT OF THE INTERIOR.

The Department of the Interior is little more than a collection of unrelated governmental bureaus. There is no relation whatever between the work of the Pension Bureau and that of the Geological Survey, nor is there any reason why such widely divergent activities as those of the Patent Office and the Office of Indian Affairs should be placed under the control of the same department. When the Department of the Interior was established it was intended that it should have charge of all matters relating to the internal affairs of the country.

Its establishment grew out of the large accession of territory following the Mexican War, and the consequent increase in population, wealth, and business. The act under which the Department of the Interior was established was entitled "An act to establish the Home Department." Since the establishment of the Department of Agriculture and the Department of Commerce and Labor, there have been many instances of duplication of departmental activities and divided jurisdiction over the same subject matters. This is illustrated by the fact that the Departments of

Agriculture and of the Interior have joint supervision of the lands in the National Forests, but the powers and duties of each are clearly defined.

Former Secretary Richard A. Ballinger declared in one of his official reports that the Department of the Interior ought to be consolidated with the Department of Agriculture. He thought that the supervision of the Capitol Building and Grounds should be transferred to the Supervising Architect of the Treasury, that the Patent Office should go to the Department of Commerce and Labor, and the Pension Office to the War and Navy Departments.

The activities of the Secretary of the Interior are now taken up by the supervision of the affairs of the unrelated bureaus which make up the department. Holding first rank among these bureaus is the General Land Office. Uncle Sam has been one of the most bountiful distributers of land in the history of the world. From the time the Government was founded down to the present, 1,835,000,000 acres of land have come into his control. He has disposed of all of this to the people of the United States except 700,-000,000 acres. As a buyer of real estate Uncle Sam has been a notable success. The entire amount of land received by him cost him less than 5 cents an acre. The great "Louisiana Purchase," embracing some of the finest land in the entire country and now representing an aggregate value of many billions of dollars, cost considerably less than a nickel an acre. A large proportion of the public lands has been given away as free homesteads to those who would settle and improve them. The free homesteads consist of 160 acres. A law has recently been enacted by Congress providing that a homesteader can secure a surface patent for his land where it is underlaid with coal. This will permit the farmers to go upon coal lands and raise crops there while the Government reserves the coal deposits which may be found in the ground beneath. This law will result in millions of acres of public lands being utilized for farming purposes which might otherwise lie completely idle pending the utilization of the coal beneath it.

The General Land Office also has charge of national monuments, forest-reserve work, and power-site reserves. Among the national monuments under its control is the Rainbow Bridge, a natural arch, resembling a rainbow, 309 feet high, and 278 feet in span, which lies in the southern part of Utah. Another is the Sitka National Monument in Alaska, upon the site of the decisive battle grounds of the Russian conquest of Alaska in 1804. It has numerous totem poles, which contain the genealogical history of several clans of Eskimos.

The Pension Office is an important bureau of the Interior Department. The number of survivors of the Civil War now on the pension roll exceeds half a million, but their names are being erased by death at the rate of more than 30,000 a year. The total number of pensioners on the roll now approximates 900,000. The annual payments on account of pensions at the beginning of the fiscal year 1911 was $158,000,000. The average value of each pension per year was $171.90. The total amount paid out for pensions at the beginning of the fiscal year 1911 was more than $4,000,000,000. Of this $3,837,000,000 was paid out for Civil War pensions. In other words, more than fourteen-fifteenths of all the pensions paid by the National Government have been on account of the Civil War. The admitted pension claims in the files of the Pension Office are so numerous that they fill 27 rooms and weigh more than a thousand tons. More than three-and-a-quarter-million claims have been filed since the establishment of the American pension system. A million and a quarter of these have been rejected.

Mrs. Phoebe M. Palmeter, of Brookfield, N. Y., aged 89 years, pensioned by a special act of Congress as the daughter of Jonathan Wooley, who served under George Washington, in a New Hampshire company, was the only pensioner on account of the Revolutionary War remaining on the roll in 1911. The last widow pensioner of that war was Esther S. Damon, of Plymouth Union, Vt., who died in 1906, at the age of 92. The last survivor of the Revolutionary Army was

Daniel F. Bakeman, who died at Freedom, Cattaraugus County, N. Y., in 1869, aged 109 years, 6 months, and 8 days. The last survivor of the War of 1812 was Hiram Cronk, of Ava, N. Y., who died in 1905, aged 105 years. More than 350 widows of the War of 1812 were still carried on the pension rolls in 1911.

The Bureau of Education is a part of the Department of the Interior and aims to serve as a sort of national clearing house for educational information. It seeks to gather such data with reference to the educational activities of every progressive community of the world as will enable the more backward communities to take advantage of the lessons of progress, and to bring themselves to the forefront of educational work. If one community happens to make a marked success of a system of transporting pupils to rural schools, the Bureau of Education sends experts to study all the details of its operation, and then prints the results of this investigation in pamphlet form so that interested educators and legislators the country over may have the benefit of the experience. The School Administration Division of the bureau aims to secure the establishment of better systems of school accounting and school statistics throughout the country. A specialist in higher education is engaged in gathering information relating to standards of collegiate and professional education, the statistics and accounting systems of colleges and universi-

DEPARTMENT OF THE INTERIOR 83

ties, cooperation in graduate studies, the opportunities afforded in this country for students from foreign countries, and many related matters. The bureau also has charge of educational work among the Eskimos in Alaska, and is giving them instruction in agriculture, cooking, sewing, bench work, washing clothes, cleaning houses, sanitation, and hygiene. It also helps the destitute natives in their hours of need, requiring all able-bodied natives who receive such help, to perform, in exchange for supplies received, an equivalent amount of labor in furnishing fire wood for use in the schools, in cleaning the premises, or in the removal of refuse from the vicinity of the native houses. The bureau also has charge of the reindeer herds of Alaska. There are 22,000 reindeer in the 34 herds in the Territory. The income from the sale of reindeer products more than quadruples in a single year, and the natives are finding the reindeer industry one of the most important features in their economic life.

The Commissioner of Indian Affairs has charge of Indian tribes of the United States exclusive of those in Alaska, their lands, moneys, schools, the purchase of their supplies, and their general welfare. There are now approximately 300,000 Indians on the reservations of the United States. Formerly it was the policy of the Government to deal with the Indians as tribes instead of as individuals. All of this has been changed, and the efforts of the Interior Department are toward the progressive assimilation of the Indian into the body politic, with the greatest degree of protection to the Indian and with a minimum of injury to the community to which he may belong. It has come to be recognized that the only way to accomplish this is to deal with each of them as an individual. Therefore, as rapidly as an Indian demonstrates his ability to perform the duties of a citizen and to be subject to the same social, political, moral, and legal obligations, he is given his freedom from the tutelage of the Federal Government and made to hoe his own row as any other American citizen. To change the characteristics of a race, compelling it to surrender its traditions, its customs, and its impulses, is a matter of generations rather than years. The full-blooded Indian of to-day still asserts a stubborn resistance to the efforts of the Government to transform him into a farmer, with fixed habitation, or to interest him in the trades or common vocations of life. In the Government's policy of individualizing the Indian for civic usefulness, one of the most potent influences is the distribution of tribal properties among the individuals who constitute the tribe. This distribution has resulted in the saving of millions of dollars to the Indian by obviating the litigation of trumped-up claims for fees by alleged representatives and speculating attorneys. The Indian is usually ready to sign away his birthright for a mess of pottage, and in some instances the fees of attorneys in a single cause amounted to hundreds of thousands of dollars. Under the new policy such claims will not be recognized by the Government. As the Indians become free and their property becomes subject to taxation by the States, the educational system now supported by the Federal Government will become a part of the State educational systems.

Perhaps the most trying and difficult work the Bureau of Indian Affairs has to do is to prevent the sale of liquor to the Indians outside of Alaska. They are proverbially fond of the white man's fire water, and despite the utmost vigilance upon the part of the Government officials in the prosecution of offenses of this nature, a vast amount of mischief is still done. Sixty thousand dollars a year is appropriated to keep liquor out of the hands of the Indians. As a rule, the Indian gives little encouragement to the Government's efforts in this direction, but now and then Indians themselves have circulated petitions addressed to their home city or town councils asking that saloon licenses be revoked and the barrooms closed.

In the process of making free the property of the Indians now being carried on by the Interior Department the thumbprint is figuring largely. Heretofore it has been the custom to let the Indian who could not write simply make his mark. In after years he was inclined to forget that he had made such a mark, and could usually make a showing toward proving an alibi. An Indian inspector suggested the thumbprint in addition to the mark and all new Indian deeds bear this imprint. The result is that Lo is given to understand that no amount of false swearing will serve to disprove his signature as witnessed by the unerring thumbprint, and it is said to have shown already a very excellent effect on the commercial morality of the illiterate Indian. The supervision of liquor traffic among Indians and natives of Alaska is under the direction of the governor of Alaska.

Perhaps the richest people on earth, per capita, are the Osage Indians, whose property is now being turned over to them as individuals. This tribe consisted of 2,230 persons, and they were the joint owners of nearly 2,000,000 acres of excellent farming lands. In addition to that their ready-money funds amounted to nearly $9,000,000. Under the law each Indian has been permitted to take 480 acres of land and has been given nearly $4,000 in cash. As soon as each individual Indian becomes capable of managing his own affairs he will be given certain privileges and at the end of 25 years will come into fee simple ownership of all his property.

It is said that when Columbus discovered America, there were at least 48 different stocks of Indians inhabiting the territory north of the Gulf of Mexico. It is estimated that there were not more than a million Indians here at that time. The aggregate Indian population is growing to-day, but the number of full-blooded Indians is gradually decreasing. There are now 26,000 pure-blooded Indians within the continental United States who still adhere to their blankets and their primitive mode of life.

The work of the Reclamation Service, another bureau of the Interior Department, is largely that of irrigating the desert places of the Western States and Territories. This work promises to produce a great expansion of the national wealth in years to come. An act of Congress passed in 1902 set apart as a fund for the reclamation of arid lands all moneys received from the sale of public lands in certain Western States and Territories, except 5 per cent of the proceeds of such sales, which was set aside for educational and other purposes. This has resulted in making available for reclamation work nearly $68,-000,000. With this money, the Government goes into a section of arid country and constructs the necessary irrigation works. Congress has since appropriated additional funds and as a certain project is completed it is made available for settlement, and each settler may take 40 acres of ground for a homestead. The settlers go together and constitute a water-users' association, paying the expenses of operating the plant and establishing a sinking fund to reimburse the Government for the cost of constructing the work.

As this money comes back to the Government new works are undertaken elsewhere.

More than 11,000,000 acres of land have been irrigated by the Government and private interests. It is estimated that there is enough additional water available to irrigate 30,000,000 acres more. At the rate of one inhabitant to every 2 acres this would give a population of more than 20,000,000 on land that once was arid. The Government will permit men without much ready money to work out the cost of the water rights for the land they buy by assisting in the construction of canals, ditches, dams, and other works. It is estimated that the irrigated area of the earth amounts to 75,000,000 acres, of which more than one-seventh lies within the boundaries of the United States. More than 3,000,000 Americans are now living upon crops grown on lands made fertile by irrigation.

That irrigation is a profitable enterprise is illustrated by the experience of the State of Colorado. During a recent year the value of its wheat crop was $18.65 per acre as compared with $12.19 in Wisconsin, $11.22 in Illinois, $9.00 in Minnesota, and $8.45 in Kansas. Its yield per acre of oats was double in value that of its nearest rival, Wisconsin. Its barley yield was valued at $19.12 an acre as compared with $13.65 per acre for Wisconsin. Its yield of hay was valued at $19.47 per acre as compared with $13.14 per acre in its closest rival, Wisconsin. Many an acre of irrigated land has been made to yield profits of from $200 to $500 a year.

Deeds of daring and resourcefulness almost without parallel in history have been performed in the perfecting of this great scheme of desert redemption, and engineering feats have been accomplished which have astonished the entire world. Of these deeds the Uncompahgre project in Colorado is an example. In the valley of the Uncompahgre River lies land of exceptional value, but until the United States took a hand there was no way to water it. Flowing parallel to this river is the Gunnison, whose route lies through a canyon, whose volume of water is large, and which has no contiguous land needing it.

These two streams flow 10 miles apart, separated by a mountain 2,000 feet high. It was decided to take the superfluous water from the Gunnison River, divert it into the Uncompahgre, and so make fertile the hundreds of thousands of acres in that valley. Then came the men of daring who were to survey the route. Swinging by ropes over precipices, clinging to crevices of rocks, floating down unexplored rivers on rubber rafts, and otherwise encountering many dangers, they completed the survey of the tunnel to be cut under the mountain. This tunnel is 6 miles long and is the greatest underground waterway in the world. In the work of the Reclamation Service covering eight years an amount of material one-third as large as that to be removed from the Panama Canal has been excavated.

The Department of the Interior also has oversight of the work of the Geological Survey and the Patent Office. In addition to this it looks after the eleemosynary institutions of the Federal Government, the national parks, the administration of affairs in the Territories, and work connected with the United States Capitol Building.

CHAPTER VIII.

THE PATENT OFFICE.

ALTHOUGH the patent-right system of the world had its inception in England and now finds the most effective application in Germany, it probably has rendered its greatest service in the United States. The civilized nations of the earth have issued 3,000,000 patents, and of these more than a million have been issued by the American Patent Office.

The genius of invention came with the empire builders to Jamestown and Cape Cod, and in 1641 the colony of Massachusetts granted Samuel Winslow a patent for a new method of making salt. In 1646 a patent was granted to Joseph Jenks for an "engine for the more speedy cutting of grass." This "engine" was nothing more than an old-fashioned mowing scythe, but it was the first of a long line of American agricultural machines which have revolutionized the farm life of the world.

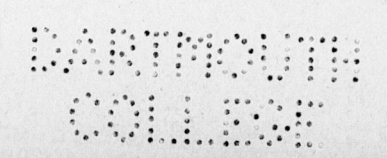

The patent system was provided for in the Federal Constitution, and the First Congress passed a law creating a patent commission made up of the Secretary of State, the Secretary of War, and the Attorney General. They waited for three months before the first applicant for a patent appeared. Samuel Hopkins had invented a new process of making pot and pearl ashes, and was granted a patent thereon on July 31, 1790. Three years later another act was passed and the Secretary of State became the head of the system. Since that day the American inventor has led the world. He is bringing out new ideas at the rate of more than 30,000 a year. During the recent fiscal year 36,000 patents were granted out of 64,000 applications filed.

These patents covered the entire range of human ingenuity. Each decade brings some epoch-making basic invention, which in turn brings in its train thousands of other inventions. When the automobile was first patented there had been no need for the thousand-and-one attachments that have followed. No such thing as a siren horn or an antijoy-riding device was dreamed of before the automobile came into popular use. As soon as the flying machine becomes commercially feasible, the Patent Office will do a tremendous business in patents on appurtenances for the improvement of aerial navigation.

Indirectly the development of American inventive genius has been due to the fostering care of the Patent Office. It is estimated by statisticians that two-thirds of all the national wealth is the product of inventions. Great industries have been called into existence through the patent system, and have given employment to hundreds of

SEARCHING THE FILES IN THE PATENT OFFICE.

thousands of people with wages and salaries aggregating hundreds of millions of dollars. In less than 40 years the activities of the inventor in the field of electrical application have resulted in the filing of patents which have built up an industry with a total investment of $7,000,000,000.

There are 43 general divisions in the Patent Office under which applications for patents are made, embracing all the known arts. These general classes in turn are each divided into subclasses, and there are many thousands of subjects upon which patents are issued. Every applicant for a patent pays a stated fee ($35) for his patent. This, with the other receipts of the Patent Office, has created a net surplus of over $7,000,000. In other words, in spite of the vast benefit conferred upon the Nation by inventors, they have been taxed $7,000,000 more than it cost to maintain the American patent system.

A great celebration was held in the city of Washington in 1891 in honor of the first centennial of American patent history. Four hundred and fifty thousand patents had been issued up to that time. Statesmen, inventors, and publicists were enthusiastic in boasting of the achievements of the century. Since that time only 20 years have passed, yet in those 20 short years more patents have been granted than in the full century that went before. In that year Congress made an investigation of the wage problem which showed that the average mechanic was then getting twice as much wages as his predecessor in 1840. The average mechanic of 1911 gets twice as much as his predecessor of 1891. It will be seen, therefore, that wages for labor have practically quadrupled since the dawn of the age of labor-saving machinery in America. Yet at the beginning laboring men were violently opposed to the adoption of such machinery.

More patents have been issued for inventions relating to transportation than upon any other line of human activity. These inventions have resulted in a great saving to the people and have made possible a civilization which could never have come into existence but for them. In the early history of the country it was no unusual thing to pay from 20 to 30 cents a ton per mile for the transportation of freight. To-day the average ton of freight in the United States is hauled a full mile for less than 1 cent.

In no other realm have the labors of the American inventor and the fostering care of the Patent Office served a better purpose than in the development of the apparatus with which the farmer produces the things that men eat and the raw material out of which they make their clothing. Without the farm machinery which the United States has given to the world, mankind necessarily would be still a race of small farmers. There could be no big cities; a thousand arts and sciences could flourish only in an indifferent way if at all.

The development of agricultural machinery has so enhanced the productive power of the individual farmer that fully three-fourths of those who formerly obtained their living by tilling the soil may now find profitable occupation in other vocations. According to authentic statistics it cost an average of $4.95 an acre to cut wheat with the old-time sickle. The invention of the grain cradle reduced this cost to $2.60 an acre. The big steam harvester threshers have lowered it to 50 cents an acre. When the Chicago World's Fair was held a delegation of foreign agriculturists were taken to a big Dakota ranch and shown how American wheat may be harvested at a smaller cost per bushel than the mere cost of food of slave labor under old-time conditions.

It is estimated that if the world's crop of wheat were harvested without the aid of modern machinery of American invention, the annual additional expense would be half a billion dollars. More than 50,000 patents have been issued upon inventions relating to agriculture by the American Patent Office, and the present day value of the farm machinery and tools in the United States aggregates a billion dollars. With these the farmer has been able to make his property holdings worth some $40,000,000,000 and his annual gross income greater than the capital value of all the trusts of the United States.

Yet the maker of agricultural implements declares that the application of machinery to farm work is only in its infancy. It has been demonstrated that denatured alcohol can be utilized as motive power for all sorts of farm operations, and that the farmer may make this motive power from potatoes grown on his own farm, and that with it he can conduct his farming operations more economically than with the horse. The arrival of the horseless age on the farm would result in the saving of nearly a hundred million tons of hay and grass, with grain in proportion.

Another illustration of the future which the Patent Office hopes some day to make possible is the wonder-working results that would be accomplished by the discovery of an economical process of gathering nitrogen from the air. This element, when applied to the soil in proper quantities, possesses the almost magical power of making four blades of grass grow where one grew before. It is one of the most plentiful things in the world, existing in incalculable quantities in the free air, but coming down to serve as plant food only upon the wings of the lightning and the bosom of the rain drop. The inventor who will find a cheap method of extracting it will make the United States able to support a population of 300,000,000 people more easily than it now supports 90,000,000.

It is only 60 years since manufacturing became one of the national activities of the United States, largely under the stimulating influence of the American patent system. Since that time the value of our manufactures has increased more than fifteenfold; the wages of the factory employees of the country have been multiplied by 10; and the number of men and women finding employment in factory work has been quintupled. Statisticians figure that under former conditions it would require at least a hundred million employees to turn out the products now made in the factories of the United States by the 5,000,000 men and women engaged in factory work.

The inventor of machinery for the factory has rendered a signal service to humanity. He has proved himself wonderfully versatile. He has devised a huge hydraulic forge able to exert a pressure of 14,000 tons; he has made a machine which will cut a screw thread with 260 turns to the inch. One of his machines will produce a giant cable many inches in diameter and another a wire one-tenth the diameter of a woman's hair. One machine will weave an iron netting so heavy that it will serve as the front of a tiger's cage, and another a steel gauze so fine that it has 40,000 meshes to the square inch. One inventor will produce a cutting machine which will make slices so thin that thousands may be piled up in a layer an inch high, and another a steel saw so strong that it will cut a groove through the hardest metal with as much ease as a knife cuts a slice of bread.

The manufacturer is able to take a piece of

iron and transform it into a giant boiler, into hairsprings for watches worth 13 times their weight in gold, or into watch screws so small that a hundred thousand may be put into a thimble. One of the most striking cases of labor saving through the patent system is that of mechanical shoemaking. By the old-fashioned cobblers' methods, it took the shoemaker two days to produce a pair of shoes. To-day that pair of shoes may be made in 20 minutes, 60 operatives and 45 machines being utilized in the process.

It requires billions of boxes to carry the fruit and berries of the country to the urban consumer. The same ingenuity that has made it possible for the American inventor to produce a bit that will bore a square hole has enabled him to evolve a machine which takes in raw strips of lumber and turns out completed boxes. One girl and a box-making machine will turn out 12,000 berry baskets or 4,000 grape baskets in a day.

The genius of the inventor brings hundreds of comforts to the poor which could not be enjoyed by the rich before the rise of the American patent system. A century ago it took the earnings of 32 days of common labor to buy a single linen bed sheet. Now even the poorest may have them. A century ago it required the labor of days to buy a gridiron. To-day the workman in the street makes enough in an hour to buy a good one. A little more than a century ago the activities of one-half of the civilized world were entirely absorbed in providing clothes for the people.

Although many marvelous inventions are included in the files of the Patent Office, it is quite generally believed by patent authorities that the years to come will far surpass those that are gone. One of the problems engaging the attention of inventors to-day is that of economically using the fuel which has been stored in the earth in the form of coal. It is said that the coal mined in the United States in a single year represents almost as much work as the entire human race could do in a full generation. The energy in a pound of anthracite coal is equivalent to that expended by a hod carrier in 10 hours' work. Yet the proportion of this energy utilized under present-day methods is less than the hod carrier would spend in 50 minutes. A piece of coal weighing less than 2 pounds has in it as much power as is exerted by a horse pulling a plow from sun to sun. If all the energy of coal were utilized it would require only 300 tons to drive a *Lusitania* across the Atlantic. Gradually the patents that are being issued are increasing the percentage of energy which may be extracted from coal, and there is even hope that the laboratory processes of making electricity directly from coal may become commercially feasible.

But suppose none of them work out, and the present wasteful methods of coal mining and use finally exhaust the coal supply? Will we then be deprived of the necessarily abundant supply of motive power? The inventor has already answered this question by bringing out a solar engine. It needs only cloudless skies and hot climates for its successful operation. Along the water fronts of the desert regions of the world may be found strips of land a mile wide with an aggregate length of more than 8,000 miles. With solar engines to develop the wasted sunshine of these regions, 2,000,000,000 horsepower could be utilized through 9 hours a day—enough to turn every wheel in the world. There men could cool their houses with refrigerating machinery driven by the heat of the sun. They could drive their factories, turn the desert into a land perennially flowing with the milk and honey of plenty by irrigation, and could eliminate a majority of the wasteful processes of modern civilization, all by the direct application of the heat of the sun as motive power. The electricity for their railroads, their automobiles, and their lights could be generated by it. They could lead lives all but independent of mundane weather conditions, and might look back upon the civilization of the twentieth century as we now look back upon that of centuries ago.

If the records of the Patent Office could reveal all of the comedy and tragedy they contain they would furnish a fascinating chapter in the story of the activities of the American Government. Thousands of men and women have pursued that will-o'-the-wisp of invention—perpetual motion. Many of them, at last realizing that their long quest has been in vain, have committed suicide; other hundreds have wrestled with the problem until their minds have broken down under the strain. The Patent Office tells every applicant that the one essential thing to be produced is a working model. Of course, no such model is possible, and the would-be inventor goes away disappointed and certain that the Government has maltreated him by demanding it. The ingenuity of those who have tried to devise perpetual motion machines is worthy of a better cause. One of them used a water wheel for pumping water into a basin above the wheel. This water, in turn, was expected to pump more water into the basin by turning the wheel as it descended. Another wrestler with the problem used a wheel and a large number of metal balls. Arms were so arranged on the wheel that as it turned around the balls would roll out to the extremity of the arm until they reached the lowest point, and then would roll back to the hub of the wheel as they ascended on the other side. The inventor believed that the power applied by the balls going downward would exceed that required to raise the ones traveling upward, and that thus a perpetual motion would be established.

The officials of the Patent Office often have very amusing experiences. Some years ago a minister from a southern city came to the Patent

Office and asked the chief of the Drafting Division to have made for him a drawing of an apparatus he had for finding keyholes in doors after dark. The number of peculiar patents that have been issued is surprising. One of these is a device to enable a man buried alive to signal to the people outside his desire to be released from the grave. Another covers a device in the shape of a collision-proof railroad train. It carried trucks fore-and-aft with rails running over the roof of the train so that one train overtaking or passing another would run over the top of the other train instead of colliding with it. Another invention for the prevention of collisions consists of a large truck several hundred feet long built on the lazy-tong principle.

It required 120 years for the Patent Office to issue its first million patents, the millionth one having been issued August 8, 1911. At the rate patents are being issued to-day the next million will be issued in less than 30 years.

It is probable that in the early future the Government will undertake the erection of a new patent office building. The patent records, representing the ingenuity of a century, and worth millions of dollars to the Government, are now housed in such a way that a fire breaking out in the building would probably end in almost total loss of these records. Many years ago there was such a fire, and at that time thousands of models of vast historic interest were destroyed.

CHAPTER IX.

THE GEOLOGICAL SURVEY.

WHAT the Department of Agriculture is to the farmer, the Geological Survey is to the miner, the manufacturer, the builder, the railroader, the irrigationist, the drainer of swamp lands, the digger of deep waterways; in short, to everybody who has occasion to know anything about topography, geology, mineral and water resources, structural materials, and waste utilization. It is a sort of John the Baptist in the wilderness of undeveloped resources, preparing the way for those who would most effectively utilize these vast resources, and laying the foundations for future engineering, construction, and conservation work. It is a sort of watchdog over the natural wealth of the Nation. In this capacity it stands guardian over millions of dollars of natural wealth, where the watchdog of the Treasury stands guardian over thousands of dollars of actual gold and silver.

One of the most interesting activities of the Survey is the making of a great geologic map of the United States. This map is so exhaustive and requires such close investigation that work has been carried forward on it for some 30 years, and yet it covers only a comparatively small portion of the United States. It is a map which in large part is being made on the scales of 1 and 2 miles to the inch. Such a map on a scale of 1 mile to the inch would require a sheet of paper about 240 by 180 feet, practically half a city block in area. Of course, it will be impossible to make such a map on one plate, so it is being made piece by piece, and the individual sheets are bound together with descriptive text accompanying them.

The first essential in the making of this map is a topographic survey and map of the land to be geologically platted. This topographic map, which is also in sections to correspond with the geologic map, is made by another branch of the Geological Survey. The topographic map sheets are in themselves peerless results of geographic surveying. They show every physical characteristic of the surface of the area surveyed. Every mountain, hill, valley, slope, stream, swamp, and all the works of man are exactly portrayed; indeed, a clever model maker may take one in hand and by it construct a miniature model of the area shown on the map. Over one-third of the United States has been thus mapped. Aside from its use as a base for geologic work, the topographic map has come to have a high intrinsic value as a base map for all engineering work.

In order to map the geology of a region, the geologist must determine the character and distribution of the individual rough masses and their relation to one another. He must travel over the whole area and plat all outcrops and ledges of rock. The dips of the rocks must be measured in order to determine the amount of deformation they have undergone and other most particular studies must be made.

A knowledge of fossil remains of plants, birds, animals, and fishes is often of great assistance to the geologist in locating various mineral deposits. For instance, there is a particular fossil mollusk which is of the same geologic age as certain coal deposits. When the geologist discovers one of these he knows that coal may be not far distant. These fossils are utilized as keys to translate the secrets below the surface of the ground.

When this great geologic map is completed it will constitute a most remarkable exposition of the mineral resources of the United States. Each section of the map reveals minutely the mineral resources, the geologic formation, the character of the soil, the underground water, and a hundred other things which are of immeasurable value to the people of the United States. The topographic map upon which the one dealing with the geologic formations of the country is based is being projected on a scale of a mile to the inch in the more thickly settled regions of the United States; approximately 2 miles to the inch in other sections and, in most cases, 4 miles to the inch in Alaska. A surveying party is able to cover a maximum of 500 square miles in a season in making this map, and the cost of the work varies from $12 to $30 a square mile, according to the nature of the country.

In addition to being a mapmaker, engraver, and printer, the Geological Survey is perhaps the world's greatest prospector. By the expenditure of less than 10 cents an acre in examination to ascertain the presence and quantity of coal deposits, the Survey has increased the value of thousands of acres of land from $20 to $400 an acre. Some 70,000,000 acres of coal lands still remain in the possession of the United States Government. Under the construction of the coal law, all such lands within 15 miles of a railroad were to be sold at not less than $20 an acre; all over 15 miles from a railroad should be sold at not less than $10 an acre, the minimum price. In practice $10 and $20 was made the uniform selling price.

A new order of things now prevails. The Survey geologist goes upon these coal lands, locates an out-cropping bed of coal, measures its thickness at many points, studies its altitude, determines its faults, and passes on its quality. A board of geologists then calculates the amount of coal on each tract of 40 acres, plats it on the official maps, and computes the value of the tract on the basis of the coal in the ground. The price then fixed is a nice adjustment which shall encourage development, but prevent the acquisition

THE GEOLOGICAL SURVEY

of the coal lands for speculative purposes. According to quality of coal and ease of mining, the prices range from one-half cent to 3 cents a ton.

But even at this remarkably low figure, the Government is able to dispose of the coal lands at a largely enhanced value. The maximum value of a single township in Wyoming under the old regulations was $2,088,600. Under the new regulations its value is $15,777,660. Probably not more than a third of the coal lands owned by the United States have been surveyed in detail, but when the work is completed Uncle Sam will find himself vastly richer than if he had continued to dispose of his properties on the old basis of sale. From April, 1909, to August, 1911, the Survey classified and valued 16,873,370 acres of coal land with a total new system valuation of $711,992,537, as against $266,652,431 under the old system. The latest estimates show that there are over three trillion short tons of coal still unmined in the United States and nearly five billion tons of easily available coal, perhaps half of which is to be found in the lands still under Government ownership and control. Over 40 per cent of the landed area of the United States is still owned by the Federal Government, and of this practically half a billion acres remain unsurveyed.

One of the prospecting activities of the Geological Survey is that of determining the location and extent of the phosphate beds of the country. Phosphorus is absolutely essential to the growth of the plant life which constitutes the prime source of the American food supply. As food, raiment, and water are the three essentials of human welfare, so nitrogen, potash, and phosphoric acid are the absolute essentials of plant growth.

Potash exists in the rocks in unlimited quantities, awaiting only the perfection of a cheap method of extraction to supply every need. The great German deposits of potash salts also afford an enormous supply. The leguminous plants, with their little chemical laboratories at their roots, can take enough nitrogen from the air to supply this necessary element as can also a recently discovered electrochemical process. But when the phosphate beds are gone no one yet has solved the problem of where the world's future supply of phosphoric acid will come from. There are thousands of acres of phosphate beds in the western part of the United States, and it is the aim of the Geological Survey so to protect them that they will continue for many generations to come to supply the needs of the crop-growers of the United States. The Geological Survey is also prosecuting a potash search in the West, and is drilling into the depths of the earth for deposits of potash salts, which will make the United States independent of Germany for this necessary fertilizer.

The oil wells of the public domain are also the subject of much study on the part of the officials of the Survey. The petroleum supply has a different status from the other mineral supplies of the country. The oil deposits are entered under the old placer gold mining law. A man must discover some mineral before he has a right to the public land on which it is located. If a man thought he had found oil and had begun to bore for it, some other fellow could run in and bore close to him and the one who got oil first would get the right to the property by discovery. Consequently, it was not a profitable thing to gamble on finding oil under such circumstances. The result was that subterfuges were resorted to. Gypsum deposits that are commercially worthless are to be found in the oil territory in California. An oil prospector finds gypsum on a tract of land, and claims it by right of discovery, on the ground that gypsum is a mineral within the meaning of the law. The law requires that $500 shall be spent in the development of these tracts, and one may travel through the oil country and see magnificent gypsum stairways standing in the open. They lead nowhere but to a perfect title for oil lands, and are standing proof of the technical fulfillment of the law and the absolute violation of its spirit. The Government now holds several million acres of oil lands withdrawn from public entry until Congress shall make a new law which will protect the oil resources from being gobbled up by speculators.

Not only has the Geological Survey been a prospector and gatherer of important information with reference to the public domain and concerning the mineral industries of the country, but it has been an experimenter of the first rank in solving problems of conservation. A notable instance of this is its work of fostering industries for the utilization of the coal dust and slack coal from the mouths of the coal mines of the country. This material was always a menace around the mouth of the mine, consisting of coal dust and coal too poor for shipping or for burning in any ordinary grate. No one knows when a big pile of this material will catch fire and do untold damage. The Survey experts saw these piles of unusable coal and lent their efforts to their utilization. In Europe such waste material is pressed into blocks called "briquettes." The Survey installed experimental briquette machines, and to-day the briquetting industry has reached the commercial stage. Small sizes of coal, heretofore wasted, are now being burned in specially constructed grates. The Survey also installed a huge German briquetting machine for making briquettes out of the unsold millions of tons of lignite coal by simple pressure and without the use of a "binder," the most expensive factor in briquette making.

Another line of experimentation which promises much for the future was carried on for a number of years by the Survey. Its investigations demonstrated that by using producer-gas engines, the power derived from a ton of coal

THE GEOLOGICAL SURVEY

may be trebled as compared with the power derived from the same ton of coal through a steam engine. Furthermore, the very lowest grades of coal may be used in making producer-gas, a ton of such coal going as far as a ton of the best Pocahontas coal used with steam power. Largely through the educational work being done by the officials of the Geological Survey, it is believed, the number of producer-gas engines in use was quintupled in a single year. The general adoption of producer-gas power would result in the saving of hundreds of millions of dollars annually, and, by making the cheapest grades of coal available, would extend industrial enterprises into sections of the country heretofore considered to be without fuel and would further extend the date of the exhaustion of the coal supply to a period far beyond the interest of the living generation.

The wonderful expansion in the use of concrete and structural steel and other fire-resistant building materials, which has come about in recent years, has been due in a large degree to the exhaustive experimental and educative work of the Geological Survey. These investigations were made primarily for the purpose of ascertaining for the Supervising Architect of the Treasury, the Engineering Board of the War Department, the Isthmian Canal Commission, and the Navy, the behavior of concrete, reenforced concrete, clay products, stone, and miscellaneous building materials, under the action of fire, water, acids, alkali, stress, and other destructive agencies. The result of these investigations, however, has been published widely. The investigations embrace studies of relative cost, durability, and strength, and give every sort of information with reference to structural materials needed in the erection of any sort of structure, from a bungalow to a 40-story skyscraper. Since 1910 this work has been continued by the Bureau of Standards. The work of investigating mine accidents and testing fuels has been transferred from the Survey to the new Bureau of Mines, whose field of operation covers the technical work of mining.

Records of the daily flow of streams have been collected at more than 1,500 points throughout the United States by the Geological Survey, and at present 500 stations for stream measurements are being maintained. Studies have been made of their mean flow, their flood stages, their low-water marks, and all other essential data which will serve the developers of power, the irrigationists, the swamp drainers, and the deep waterway diggers. The Survey is often put to a severe test in its efforts to measure correctly the flow of a river, and many unusual contrivances have been devised to measure the depth and velocity of water at a given point in a river bed. One may wonder of what practical use such studies are, but a hundred activities depend upon them. The Government is spending over $60,000,000 on irrigation projects, and is expecting to get three

THE GEOLOGICAL SURVEY

times as much back in national wealth, and the basic water resources investigations made by the Survey are absolutely essential to the success of this work. It is as important that the irrigationist know the water flow on which he bases his project, as it is that the architect shall know the character of the foundation upon which he rears his skyscraper. The same may be said of water-power development. No river and harbor improvement program can be carried out successfully without details as to silt deposits, stream flow, and low-water marks. The Survey has been making these investigations for more than 15 years, and it is largely upon the data thus gathered that Congress provides for the deepening of rivers throughout the United States.

The activities of the Geological Survey show results in many unexpected places. One would hardly look for effects of this work in the monetary affairs of the Government, but it has recently developed into an important factor in maintaining a stable money market. The work of the Survey in the single little arm of Alaska, known as Seward Peninsula, may have had some bearing on the development of a gold supply which yields a steady stream of from five to seven million dollars' worth of gold every year. This is enough to pay the entire purchase price of Alaska. The Survey has but little more than begun its investigations in this giant young Territory, but it has already ascertained enough to show that it is the biggest land-buying bargain a nation ever drove, if we except the great Louisiana Purchase.

The work which is now being done by the Bureau of Mines formerly was part of the activities of the Geological Survey. How important is the matter of protecting the mining industry of the United States is indicated by the fact that 65 per cent of the traffic of the railroads of the country originates in the mines, and that about 2,000,000 wage-earners are constantly engaged in mining operations. Without the products of the mine the factories could not have been built; the railways never could have been constructed. But the miner has been wasteful in his methods, and in some cases has taken out as low as only 40 per cent of the coal in the mine. The difference between the greater cost of clean mining, as compared with the lesser cost of wasteful mining, often means the difference between profitable and unprofitable operation. One of the tasks assigned to the Bureau of Mines is to attempt to discover methods of operation whereby it will be profitable to take practically all of the coal out of a mine. The coal production of the country now aggregates a half billion tons every year, and it is calculated that the annual waste of coal amounts almost to half as much.

In addition to investigating economical methods of mining, the Bureau of Mines is assigned the task of trying to determine the conditions which lead up to mine explosions and the methods of preventing them. It seeks to determine what explosives can be used with least risk in mines where gas or inflammable dust may be found; what conditions permit the safe operation of electric equipment in coal mines; what types of mine lamps are safest, most efficient, and least liable to produce explosions; and what sort of artificial breathing apparatus is best suited for use in the rescue of victims of mine disasters.

In the prosecution of investigations looking to the ascertainment of what explosives are least dangerous in coal mining, large explosion-proof closed tubes are used, with only such openings as will permit the engineers to watch an explosion. All conditions found in mines are simulated and the explosives on the market are carefully tested under every imaginable kind of working conditions. The results of these tests are used in making up a list of such explosives as are regarded as safe in mining operations. The list of "permissible explosives" numbers about 50.

The investigations and educational work in connection with the use of artificial breathing apparatus and other types of mine rescue equipment have been useful in developing better methods for using such equipment. Thirteen branch mine rescue experiment stations have been established. These stations guard the lives of miners and the property of the mines in the same way that a fire department guards the property of a city. There are emergency cars fitted up with all sorts of rescue equipment. Not only do the bureau experts rush to every mine explosion and enter the mines in the work of rescue, but they are training thousands of miners and mine foremen in the use of the life-saving apparatus.

The Geological Survey is less than a third of a century old. It was started with an appropriation of only $100,000, and its main purpose then was to gather data and to study fundamental problems with reference to the geology of the public domain. Since then it has expanded its work in many directions, was the forerunner of the conservation movement in the United States, and has made itself one of the most useful of all the bureaus of the American Government. It now spends approximately $1,500,000 a year in carrying forward its activities.

CHAPTER X.

THE DEPARTMENT OF AGRICULTURE.

No branch of the executive service of the United States has contributed more to the welfare of the people of the country than the Department of Agriculture. Under the influence of the gospel of progressive farming the yield of wheat has increased from 10 bushels per acre in 1866 to an average of 15 bushels under present farming conditions. Corn now yields about 30 bushels to the acre during an average year, as compared with 25 bushels a half century ago. Throughout all the list of plant and meat crops the same ratio of expansion has taken place.

But great as has been the growth in the past 50 years, it is believed by the experts of the Department of Agriculture that this expansion will be much more than duplicated during the coming 50 years. A good farmer to-day is able to produce an average of 25 bushels of wheat to the acre, 60 bushels of corn, and a bale and a quarter of cotton. If the average farm crop of a half century hence is no better than that produced by the good farmer of to-day, the total value of the crops at that date will be many millions of dollars greater than it is to-day.

The increased value of cotton on the basis of a bale and a quarter to the acre as compared with the present yield of two-fifths of a bale would show an increase in value in the cotton crop alone amounting to more than $1,250,000,000. Secretary James Wilson thinks there will be little difficulty in increasing by half the yield of every staple crop grown in the United States, and that the remarkable progress in educational work among the farmers of the country made during the past decade will grow in amazing proportions during the coming quarter of a century.

While the Department of Agriculture is developing the farms and vegetable crops, it is not overlooking the importance of expanding the live-stock industry. The live-stock interests of the Nation are looked after by the Bureau of Animal Industry. This bureau has charge of meat inspection, national quarantine regulations for live stock, the study of animal diseases and their relation to the human race, and investigations in stock raising and dairying.

One-fourth of the dairy cows of the United States do not pay market price for their feed. If the average cow on the American farm can be induced to furnish just 5 pounds of butter more a year, it will add $30,000,000 annually to the productive capacity of the American dairy. If the hens of the country each can be induced to lay

1 dozen eggs more a year, they will increase the annual value of the egg supply to the extent of $50,000,000.

The Government expends about $3,000,000 a year on meat inspection, inspectors being maintained at about a thousand establishments in 237 cities and towns. Each year about 50,000,000 live animals are examined before slaughter, and approximately 7,000,000,000 pounds of meat is inspected after slaughter. Nearly a million animals are condemned annually, either in whole or in part. Tuberculosis is the cause of about 46 per cent of the condemnations of cattle products and 96 per cent of the condemnations of hog products.

The Bureau of Animal Industry also maintains an experiment station at Bethesda, Md., for investigations in animal diseases, and has an experimental farm at Beltsville, Md., where work in dairying and the breeding and feeding of live stock and poultry is carried on.

This bureau also has charge of the work of eradicating animal diseases. It has been fighting the Texas fever tick for years, and is gradually succeeding in exterminating this dangerous foe of the beef industry. The bureau recently found that over 18 per cent of the cattle in the District of Columbia were affected with tuberculosis. A quarantine was established after the elimination of the affected cattle, with the result that in a year or two dairy stock in the District have been practically freed from the ravages of this disease.

The bureau has also produced a highly effective serum treatment for the prevention of hog cholera, by means of which it is believed that the tremendous losses from this disease may be greatly reduced and in time entirely prevented. In one experiment there was a lot of 35 pigs. Twenty-two of these were vaccinated with the preventive serum, four were inoculated with virulent hog-cholera blood, so as to give them the disease, and nine were untreated. The four inoculated pigs contracted the disease and died, as did all nine of the untreated ones. Every one of the 22 vaccinated pigs remained well. The bureau also prepares and distributes vaccine for the prevention of blackleg in cattle, to the extent of about a million doses a year. Likewise it distributes tuberculin for the diagnosis of tuberculosis in cattle, and mallein for the diagnosis of glanders in horses.

The Bureau of Animal Industry has also had an important part in the work of sanitary improvement of milk supplies, and has cooperated with the authorities of many cities to that end.

One of the most interesting bureaus in the department is that of Plant Industry. This bureau studies the diseases of plants as carefully as physicians study the diseases of men. It not only disseminates information with reference to the diseases, but is constantly experimenting in its efforts to produce specific remedies. For instance, it formerly was the custom of apple growers to spray their trees with copper compounds. These were found to be injurious, and the Bureau of Plant Industry worked out a new method of spraying with noninjurious sulphur compounds. In its investigation of the fruit spot-and-leaf disease known as cedar rust or orange rust of the apple, a remarkable fact has been discovered. The fungus which causes the disease must have each alternate generation on the red cedar. If the red cedar is eliminated from the vicinity of apple orchards this disease is easily stamped out. This method finds a parallel in the mosquito theory of yellow fever in the human race.

One of the most interesting activities of the Bureau of Plant Industry is its work in ransacking the world for new crops for the American agriculturists. It has brought dates from Egypt and the oases of the Sahara, durum wheat from Russia, millet from Siberia, wild peaches from China, and many other plants from every region of the world. In addition to this, it has been carrying on a process of cross-breeding in plants which has been of inestimable economic value to the American people. It has been estimated that the introduction of durum wheat is worth millions of dollars. One of the remarkable successes of the bureau in cross-breeding has been the development of an orange hardier than the Florida orange by crossing that variety with a worthless but hardy orange tree from Japan.

That the bureau has a wide field of research in

the adaptation of plants for the needs of the American people is shown by the fact that there are more than 100,000 different species of plants in the world, of which less than 5,000 are utilized by mankind. The people of the United States use only about 300 kinds, except in the most limited way. One needs to go no further than the rice industry to find what wealth may be produced by an introduced crop. There are now upward of 700,000 acres of rice grown annually in the United States and the farm value of the crop amounts to $16,000,000.

In its efforts to eliminate "bad burners" from cigar stands, the Bureau of Plant Industry has constructed a mechanical smoker, consisting of a series of glass tubes so arranged that each smokes a cigar just as a man would, except that the "puffs" are of exactly uniform strength in each tube. A carefully adjusted aspirator draws the proper intermittent current of air through the cigar, and accurate observations are made to determine the rapidity with which each one burns. Each cigar is carefully scored upon the several points which go to make up a good record. Some burn evenly, some rapidly, and some down on one side. In others the wrapper puckers ahead of the fire, and a black, metallic-looking ring forms around the cigar. These are undesirable. The character of the ash is also tested, and if it flakes badly, or is dark and dull, the cigar is not a good one.

The bureau also has charge of farming experiments and investigations. It is claimed that by intelligent methods of cultivation millions of acres of arid land can be made to produce the finest kinds of crops, and that without irrigation. The important essential is to plow very deep, and to plow very often, thus keeping loose soil at the surface, through which the moisture below cannot escape.

The work of mapping, classifying, and investigating the soils of the agricultural districts of the United States is intrusted to the Bureau of Soils. This bureau is engaged in making detailed maps of important areas throughout the better developed sections of the country, and reconnoissance maps, showing less detail, of the Great Plains region and other sparsely settled districts. It also studies fertilizer requirements and the relation of different types of soil to crops, with a view to determining what crops can be grown most advantageously. Seven hundred different types of soil have been found in the areas so far surveyed.

The United States is the third largest forest owner in the world, being outranked only by Russia and Canada. The area of the National Forests of the United States is almost 200,000,000 acres, and they contain more than 500,000,000,000 feet of merchantable timber. All this is watched over by the Forest Service of the Department of Agriculture, which has a corps of 2,000 trained men. Each National Forest is in charge of a supervisor, and is patroled by forest rangers, who are stationed at points where they may best attend to the needs of the public and protect the forests from injury by trespass or fires. In addition to the regular ranger stations, there are also fire lookout stations, and these are connected with central stations by telephone lines; where it is not possible to build such lines they are provided with the heliograph and other systems of signals. It is the aim of the Forest Service so to protect and utilize the forests of the country that there may be a continual supply of timber for use in the industries and that the land may add most to the public welfare.

The insects of the country annually destroy farm property worth a billion dollars. The Texas fever tick in a year kills cattle worth $60,000,000, and the ravages of the Hessian fly and the joint worm may cut the value of a wheat crop to an even greater extent. The work of combating the insect and similar pests in the United States is assigned to the Bureau of Entomology. This bureau, so to speak, has set the dogs on insect pests by bringing from all parts of the world other insects which will eat them and destroy their eggs. One of the principal fights this bureau has on its hands at the present time is the effort to kill out the gypsy moth and the brown-tail moth.

One of the methods of combating these two moths has been to bring from other countries parasites and predaceous insect enemies which will attack the moth caterpillars and destroy them. A predatory beetle from Europe has multiplied rapidly and in some localities has been able to give the gypsy moth a tussle for supremacy. A parasitic fly was brought over in 1906, and in four years has increased fiftyfold a year, and has spread a distance of from 10 to 12 miles in every direction. It has not only gone after the gypsy and brown-tail moths, but it has turned its attention to the fall web-worm and the tussock moth, which through the autumn afford food for generations of parasites at a time when the gypsy and brown-tail moths are not available as a food supply. Still another species has been found to attack the caterpillars of the cabbage butterfly, in addition to gypsy and brown-tail moths. Another parasite attacks the eggs of the gypsy moth. Some of the insect allies introduced by the bureau make a business of destroying the larvæ of the offending moths, making their own nests in the cocoons of the moth.

The bureau also conducts an unrelenting campaign against the codling moth, the orange thrip, and every other kind of insect enemy of the cultivated crops and the trees of the United States. It is one of the leaders in the campaign against the house fly and the mosquito.

The bureau renders services to other countries in return for their favors in furnishing parasites which prey upon the insect pests of this country.

Lately it has sent ladybug beetles to Spain to eat the Spanish mealy bug, dog-tick parasites to South Africa for combating the dog tick, and bumblebees to the Philippines for improving the clover crop.

The bureau known as the Biological Survey employs itself in investigations concerning the economic relations of birds and mammals to the work of the farmers and stockmen of the country. The rat is now known to be responsible for the dissemination of the bubonic plague, and, in addition, it annually destroys millions of dollars worth of products in the granaries and storehouses of the United States. The Survey has shown how to destroy this pest effectively and economically. It is now studying the native animals which harbor the ticks by which the dreaded spotted fever is transmitted to human beings.

The survey has been cooperating with the Forest Service in the destruction of chipmunks and mice, which are so destructive to the seeds planted in reforestation work. It has likewise assisted in the California crusade against the ground squirrel. A preparation of barley covered with starch containing strychnine is used for destroying the squirrels. More than 50,000 acres were baited in this way in one season and the squirrels were destroyed at a cost of from 2½ to 6 cents an acre. It has been demonstrated that 35 prairie dogs will destroy as much vegetation as is necessary to maintain a sheep during a season. The Biological Survey is trying to find a method of poisoning these little rodents without endangering the lives of valuable birds like shore larks and longspurs. The survey has charge of the enforcement of the law prohibiting animal and bird pests from being imported into the United States. Not long ago a mongoose, one of the most prolific animals known, and a very dangerous species, was surreptitiously brought into the country at Everett, Wash. It was discovered and killed a few weeks later. About the same time it was disclosed that the eggs of the tern were brought into the United States at New York and sold there in a half-decomposed state under the name of Australian booby. This fraudulent traffic was promptly suppressed. Some years ago a lot of starlings were liberated by private parties in Central Park, New York. They now range as far north as Springfield, Mass., and as far south as central New Jersey. The starling is a pest in foreign countries, and, fearing a duplication of the history of the English sparrow, the Biological Survey is planning to prevent further distribution of the bird if it proves to be a pest here. The survey is also engaged in an effort to promote international cooperation in regulating traffic in plumage birds.

The work of spreading the gospel of good farming has reached enormous proportions. During the last year, more than 25,000,000 copies of bulletins, circulars, and reports were distributed to the farmers of the country. After nearly a million copies of the Farmer's Bulletin on the economical use of meat in the homes had been distributed gratis, nearly 50,000 copies were sold. The Bureau of Statistics gathers and publishes information with reference to the crops of the country. It has a corps of 135,000 crop reporters. Their reports are summarized monthly by a board of the highest officials of the department, and the work is guarded with the greatest care in order to prevent the information from getting out ahead of time, to be used in speculation.

There are about 60 agricultural experiment stations in the United States which are engaged in cooperating with the department in disseminating agricultural instruction. They issue annually some 500 publications which are sent to nearly a million addresses. Each of these stations conducts some particular line of investigation, and at the end of the year their aggregate work has resulted in the addition of a vast amount of valuable information to the literature of agricultural science.

More than 2,000,000 farmers annually attend the farmer's institutes which are held jointly by the State and National Agricultural Departments. Field demonstrations are also given, and the Corn Clubs, in which school boys are awarded premiums for the best results in growing corn, have resulted in creating an unprecedented interest among the youths of the country in farming operations.

The department also maintains a Good Roads Bureau where everything pertaining to progressive road construction and maintenance is studied and experimented with, and where a campaign of education is waged which, it is hoped, will serve in a quarter of a century to free the American people from an annual mud tax estimated at $200,000,000.

CHAPTER XI.

THE WEATHER BUREAU.

No other country has such an extensive system of weather investigation and forecast as the United States. Spending more than a million and a half dollars a year to be weatherwise, Uncle Sam is learning many secrets of the atmosphere that have never been known before. The Mount Weather station of the Weather Bureau, situated in the Blue Ridge Mountains of Virginia, has been equipped with every sort of instrument human ingenuity can devise to pull down the secrets of the upper air.

The Weather Bureau gets reports from more than 3,500 land stations, 2,000 ocean vessels, and some 50 foreign stations. The information which comes to the Weather Bureau from all these places enables the forecaster to venture a prediction about what the weather will be for the next 36 to 48 hours, and in a general way for a week in advance.

It is said that more than 80 per cent of the winds, rains, and storms follow beaten paths, behaving upon established principles, and doing just as the weather man expects them to do. Some-

THE WEATHER BUREAU

times, however, a storm will refuse to follow the beaten paths and it is then that the weather man fails. The average man remembers the one failure rather than the five good forecasts in which the weather man correctly predicts the weather. The weather forecasts are based upon simultaneous observations of local weather conditions taken daily at 8 o'clock in the morning and at 8 o'clock in the evening, Eastern time, at about 200 regular observing stations throughout the United States and the West Indies, and from the reports received daily from various other places in the Western Hemisphere. The results of these observations are telegraphed to the Weather Bureau at Washington, where they are charted for study and interpretation by experts.

A complete telegraphic report includes data describing the temperature, atmospheric pressure, precipitation, direction of the wind, state of the weather, wind velocity, the kind and amount of clouds, and the direction of their movement. From these data the forecaster, by comparison with preceding reports, is able to trace the path of the storm area from the storm's first appearance to the moment of observation, and approximately to determine and forecast their subsequent courses and the occurrence of other weather conditions. Forecast centers are also established at Chicago, New Orleans, Denver, San Francisco, and Portland, Ore.

Within two hours after the morning observations have been taken the forecasts are telegraphed from the forecast stations to more than 2,300 principal distributing points, where they are further disseminated by mail, telegraph, and telephone. The forecasts are mailed to 135,000 addresses a day and delivered to nearly 4,000,000 telephone subscribers within an hour from the time the prediction is made.

In addition to this service there is what is known as the climatological service, which collects data with reference to temperature and rainfall and crops season conditions. During the winter months a publication known as the Snow and Ice Bulletin is issued, showing the area covered by snow, the depth of the snow, the thickness of ice in rivers, and other matters reported upon from every section of the country. This publication is of especial interest to those interested in the winter wheat crop, to ice dealers, to the manufacturers of rubber goods and other articles, the sale of which is largely affected by the presence or absence of snow and ice.

The extent to which the work of the Weather Bureau affects the daily life of the people is very great, and is said to be increasing yearly. Perhaps the most directly valuable service rendered is that of the warnings of storms and hurricanes issued for the benefit of marine interests. These warnings are displayed at nearly 300 points along the Atlantic, Pacific, and Gulf coasts, and the shores of the Great Lakes, including every port

OBSERVATION TOWER AT WEATHER BUREAU.

and harbor of any considerable importance. Scarcely a storm of marked danger to maritime interests has occurred for years of which ample warnings have not been issued from 12 to 24 hours in advance.

The warnings displayed for a single hurricane are known to have detained in port on the Atlantic coast vessels valued with their cargoes at more than $30,000,000. The warnings of sudden and destructive changes in temperature are issued from 24 to 36 hours in advance, and are disseminated throughout the threatened regions by Weather Bureau flags and otherwise. The warnings issued for a single cold wave are said to have saved over $3,000,000 of property from injury and destruction. The warnings of frost and freezing weather are of great interest to the growers of fruit, tobacco, cranberries, and market-garden products. The value of the orange blooms, vegetables, and strawberries protected and saved on a single night in a small district in Florida was estimated at more than $100,000.

The publication of river and flood forecasts based upon reports issued by the 500 river and rainfall stations upon one occasion resulted in the saving of live stock and other property to the estimated value of $15,000,000, when the approach of a flood in the Mississippi was forecasted by the Bureau a week in advance. Railroad companies make continued use of weather forecasts in all their shipping business. Perishable products are protected against extremes of temperature by icing or heating. Oftentimes shipments of perishable goods are hustled forward when it is found possible to get them to their destination in advance of expected unfavorable temperature conditions. When this can not be done, goods in transit are run into roundhouses for protection. Bananas require very careful handling and must be kept at a temperature ranging from 58° to 65°, and the banana shipper keeps close watch on the weather map. The meatman tries to ship his products in cold weather, while the movement of live stock by freight is avoided when a hot wave is forecasted.

Temperature forecasts and cold-wave warnings are closely watched by brewers, winemakers, and manufacturers of soft drinks. Wine shipments are usually withheld until danger from cold is passed, as a slight frosting causes the tartaric acid in wine to crystallize and precipitate. Many brewers hold beer shipments when the distance is more than 60 miles and a minimum of 20° is expected. With notice of an approaching cold wave, greenhouses are closed and boilers fired. Large stockyards drain their mains. Gasoline engines are drained. Work in concrete is stopped. Brewing companies and ice factories take care of exposed ammonia condensers. Railway companies arrange for more heat in fruit cars. Natural gas companies turn a large amount of gas into their pipe lines. Merchants curtail their advertisements. Coal dealers supply partial orders to all customers instead of full orders to a few. Ice factories reduce their output. The dredging of sand and gravel ceases, and iron ore piled up for shipment is placed in the holds of vessels to prevent the wet masses from freezing solid. Charity organizations prepare to meet demands for increased food and fuel, and thus minimize suffering among the poor.

Rain forecasts protect the raisin crop, enable the fruit grower to pick his fruit in advance of rain, the vegetable grower to dig his vegetables in dry weather, the grower of alfalfa to bale his crop in the field, the maker of lime, cement, brick, draintile, and sewer-pipe material to protect it from rain during the process of manufacturing, photographic firms to make special arrangements for large orders; indeed, one might continue almost interminably to cite the practical uses of the work of the Weather Bureau.

The meteorological institutions of the world have entered into a sort of an agreement to record upon every favorable day the radiation of the sun and the related problem of the polarization of sky light. These observations are exchanged by the different institutions, and once they have been taken for a long term of years and are compared with the weather records of those years, it is hoped that weather forecasting at long range will become a scientific reality. In this work the Weather Bureau uses an instrument known as the pyrheliometer. Used in connection with an electrical resistance thermometer it is so sensitive to heat that it can register a difference in temperature a million times more minute than can be recognized by the average person. The pyrheliometer is made of two blackened disks fitted on a rod, like pulleys on a shaft. These disks are immersed in water, the sun's rays are concentrated on them, and the amount of radiation is determined by the varying temperature of the water at different exposures.

One of the most interesting phases of the work of the Weather Bureau is that part which is being carried on at the Mount Weather Observatory. This institution is making all sorts of investigations into the whys and wherefores of the weather, and utilizes all kinds of ingenious and delicate instruments in making these studies. One of these instruments consists of a woman's hair and a pen which writes with unfreezable ink. The oil is extracted from the hair, and in this way it becomes extremely sensitive to all variations of moisture in the air. Great care is taken to prevent the accumulation of foreign matter on the hair, and it is washed once a week with clean water applied with a camel's-hair brush. The expansion and contraction of the hair moves the tiny pen and automatically makes a written record of the humidity of the atmosphere. One of the houses of the weather station is built without windows. Another had to be constructed without iron or steel, not even excepting nails. Even the work horses about the place can not wear iron shoes when the magnetic laboratory observations are being made. The rooms in this laboratory must be maintained at a temperature of such constancy that it does not vary more than one-tenth of a degree the whole year round.

The observers at Mount Weather fly kites and release captive balloons in a way that would make the heart of any small boy turn green with envy. These kites are sent up into the air every favorable day. Each of them contains a full set of instruments for registering the heat, the direction and velocity of the wind, and other weather conditions in the upper air. The average height to which the kites and captive balloons attain is about 2 miles, although some of them go much higher. On days when kites and captive balloons can not be sent up other balloons are liberated, either singly or in tandem. They carry a set of automatic instruments which record the weather conditions in the atmosphere through which they pass. Some of them travel hundreds of miles before they are found and returned. Nearly all of these are eventually sent back by the people who discover them.

The investigations at Mount Weather have revealed conditions differing widely from those supposed to exist before these researches were begun. The accepted rule that the temperature decreases as altitude increases is found to have many exceptions, a great layer of warm air frequently floating upon a layer of cold air, while the thickness and horizontal extent of the warm air layers vary greatly. Again, temperature inversions have been recorded by instruments at the time the kite or balloon was sent up, whereas no trace of these phenomena remains when the kite is brought down again a few hours later. Likewise it has been found that a given mass of air changes with its onward movement past the line of ascent, and the wind direction varies with different levels. Sometimes, when the wind at the ground is from the south, the direction a half-mile up may be from the southwest and a mile up it may be blowing directly from the west.

Cloud movements indicate that in this hemisphere the wind direction changes to the right with increasing altitude, but kite and balloon observations show that it may at times change toward the left. Observations seem to show that temperature changes at the ground and at altitudes of 1 and 2 miles occur simultaneously, thus contradicting the hitherto accepted theory that the changes high up precede those at the surface. Hot waves are seldom felt more than half a mile above the surface of the earth, and they do not advance abruptly with a solid front like a wall, but start at the ground and pile up layer upon layer.

The application of the Mount Weather data to practical forecasting has proven of great assist-

THE WEATHER BUREAU 139

ance. This data serves to reverse some theories formerly held. Sometimes a storm passes eastward without being followed by expected clearing weather, because a second storm was developing off the middle or South Atlantic coast. This new development is not indicated by observations at the surface, but the Mount Weather flights show north winds at high altitudes in advance of such a formation. Again, when an atmospheric depression is approaching from the southwest, and the kite records show winds turning to the right as they go up, the usual warming up is retarded in the Atlantic States about 24 hours. Likewise, the turning of the winds to the left as the kite ascends into the upper air shows the depth of the cold, northwest winds, from which inferences may be drawn as to the probable fall in temperature at the surface of the earth within the ensuing 24 hours.

The instruments used by the Weather Bureau to make a continuous record of weather conditions are extremely ingenious and interesting. One of these is an automatic pen which records on paper the state of the weather as to cloudiness and sunshine. It consists of a straight glass tube with a bulb at each end. These bulbs are filled with dry air, the chambers being separated by a small quantity of mercury and alcohol. Platinum wires are inserted in the middle of the tube. The lower bulb is blackened with lampblack, and is always turned toward the south. It is so mounted that whenever the sun shines it will start the recording pen to writing and as soon as the sun ceases to shine, the pen ceases writing. A chart is placed upon a revolving roller operated by clockwork, and by this means the Weather Bureau is securing year in and year out a record of the amount of sunshine at the point of observation.

Another instrument records the velocity and direction of the wind, while others make a record of temperature conditions, barometric pressure, rainfall, etc. The rain gauge, which records automatically the amount of rain falling, consists of a receiver and a little bucket with two compartments in it, mounted on trunnions in such a way that one of these compartments is always under the receiver. When a compartment becomes full it tips over and empties its contents into a tank, and in the act of doing so brings the other compartments into position to be filled. When the bucket tips it closes an electric circuit, and the automatic recording pen attached writes down the number of bucketfuls thus discharged.

To the United States belongs much credit for the development of the science of meteorology. Joseph Henry, of the Smithsonian Institution, who had aided in the perfection of the telegraph, by the use of that instrument began to draw weather maps, and as early as 1856 he displayed them each day at the Smithsonian. In 1870 the United States began to issue daily weather maps.

Many weather superstitions have been proved to have no foundation whatever in fact. One of these was the theory that our forefathers were healthier than we because of their "old-fashioned" winters and summers. An examination of systematic temperature and rainfall records shows that there has not been an appreciable change in a century. Some winters are colder than others, and some summers hotter, but they average up about the same as in the "good old days."

The maps and bulletins of the Weather Bureau are utilized in many ways by the public. Grain and cotton brokers are guided largely by the forecasts in their operations. Data of atmospheric pressure are used in tests of boilers, radiators, and automobiles, and in studies of the amount of fuel required to drive engines under varying atmospheric pressures. Statistics of wind force and direction assist in the installation of water-supply systems to be operated by windmills, in determining the origin of fires resulting from flying sparks, the pressure to which large buildings will be subjected under stress of heavy storms, and the surface movement of lake waters in connection with the disposal of city sewage. The humidity records are used by silk and candy manufacturers, in tuberculosis investigations, and in studies of the loss of electric current in high voltage transmission. River data are utilized by filtration plants in guiding their methods of chemically purifying the water used for drinking purposes, as the conditions of the raw water supply as regards bacteria content and turbidity are greatly affected by the height of the river and the amount of rainfall. Maps are used by business men generally, by aero clubs in studies for flights, and by school-teachers in class instruction.

The miscellaneous climatological data are used in medical and scientific studies of the relation of weather to diseases and other conditions of health, life, or human pursuits; by railroad companies in the adjustment of claims and demurrage charges; by homeseekers; by invalids in search of health resorts; by irrigation investigators; by contractors and builders in settling labor accounts; by gas and electric light companies in showing their customers the relation of their monthly bills to the varying hours of daylight at different seasons of the year; as adequate testimony in court proceedings; in dry-farming investigations; in studies of soil culture, practical agriculture, and the life and migration of insect pests; in plans for the development of the arid regions; in preparation of historical records; by bond and investment companies in determining the loan values of farm lands in newly opened countries.

CHAPTER XII.

THE DEPARTMENT OF COMMERCE AND LABOR.

The Department of Commerce and Labor covers a wide range of governmental activities. The scrutiny of corporations, the regulation of immigration and naturalization, the gathering of census statistics, the regulation of standards of measure, the propagation and distribution of fishes, the maintenance of lighthouses, the supervision of navigable waters, the Coast and Geodetic Survey work, and the Steamboat-Inspection Service are among the affairs with which the department deals. Among the most interesting phases of its activities are the census and the maintenance of standards of measure, which are treated in separate chapters.

The Bureau of Immigration and Naturalization has charge of the work of receiving aliens into the United States and of the enforcement of the laws by which they may become American citizens. One person out of every three in the United States is an immigrant or the child of an immigrant. Frequently more than 5,000 immigrants arrive in one day at the port of New York, and on some occasions the average is 5,000 a day for a full month. This gives the inspectors only two minutes to each immigrant, and a question must be asked and answered nearly every second. Only one immigrant out of a thousand is excluded, although the restrictions are being multiplied each year. The head tax of $4 collected from each immigrant more than supports the Immigration and Naturalization Service of the country.

Immigrants coming to the United States should possess enough money to take care of themselves for a sufficient time to permit them to secure employment. During a recent year the incoming tide of humanity exhibited to the officials of the Immigration Service more than $28,000,000, an average of more than $27 per person. Fully 86 per cent of these had less than $50 when they came in. The bulk of the immigration into the United States to-day comes from southern Europe.

It has been proposed in Congress that all male aliens between the ages of 16 and 50 shall be required to stand a physical test equal to that undergone by recruits for the Army and Navy, this test, of course, to be applied to manual laborers only. Approximately four out of five of the immigrants who come into the United States come through the port of New York. Of the 1,041,570 immigrants arriving in 1910, 786,004 came through that port.

One of the greatest difficulties which the immigration authorities have to face is that of distributing this flood of humanity over the entire country rather than allowing it to concentrate around the port of entry. There is a provision in the immigration law which provides that contract laborers shall not be brought into the United States. A striking illustration of the ease with which conscienceless persons or corporations can violate the spirit of this law without putting themselves within reach of its letter, is the case of a large concern which arranged with a philanthropic (?) society to keep it supplied with common manual laborers, offering them fair wages. The wages would usually be paid for the first week, and then the aliens were placed on "piece-work," at a wage, and under conditions, barely affording an existence. This would result in their leaving the concern as soon as, by starving economy or otherwise, they could raise a sufficient sum to take them to some other place. Then their places would be filled with other unskilled and ignorant men piloted by the society. Thus the concern maintained a constant supply of cheap foreign labor, the supposedly philanthropic organization earned a rich financial reward, and the aliens were outrageously exploited.

The heavy immigration from southern Europe is accredited mainly to the promotion methods of steamship agencies and professional money lenders. They make large profits out of the immigrant business, and even if they have to carry some of the immigrants back, it still leaves enough profit to make the business very much worth while.

The hardest problem which the Immigration Service has to solve is that of enforcing the Chinese immigration laws. Sometimes the Chinese slip into the United States from Canada or Mexico in sealed freight cars, or even in the refrigerators of dining cars. At other times they come hidden in coal-bunkers, chain-lockers, forespeaks, and other secluded parts of ocean-going vessels. It is stated that many of the Chinese in the United States to-day have reached here in violation of the Chinese immigration law.

A typical case of evasion of the law was that of a Chinaman who recently arrived at San Francisco accompanied by an alleged son. So well were they coached that on examining them the officers became satisfied that their claims were bona fide and instructions were given for their landing. If the Chinaman had been satisfied to perpetrate only two frauds and lay the basis for later similar operations, success would have attended him. But he overreached himself. As he started ashore one of the watchmen noticed something about him that excited the suspicion that he was carrying coaching letters, and a search of his person revealed the fact that he had consented to be the message bearer for a number of the detained Chinese, who, their cases being fraudulent, wished to get letters ashore to the smugglers interested in them, showing how they had testified in order that corroborating witnesses could be produced. A reexamination of this Chinaman showed that he and his son were not even members of the same family, and that their cases were manufactured out of whole cloth.

When an immigrant lands in the United States, if he be a steerage passenger, he must undergo a minute examination. Physicians, expert on diseases prohibited from entry, are stationed a distance of 25 feet apart, and the immigrants are marched past in single file. As they walk across the 25-foot space, each one 25 feet behind his predecessor, he is eyed minutely from head to foot by the physician, and if there is any reason whatever for suspecting the presence of any disease prohibited by the immigration laws, the suspected alien is sent back for further observation and investigation. An alien must reside in the United States for a period of five years before he is entitled to become a full-fledged citizen.

A branch of the Department of Commerce and Labor which has figured prominently in the public eye is the Bureau of Corporations. It is this bureau that investigated the Beef Trust and asserted that the packer's profits on dressed beef amounted to about $1 per steer. It has also investigated the Standard Oil Co., the Cotton Exchanges, the tobacco industry, and the lumber industry. It declares that its Standard Oil investigations caused the railroads concerned in carrying oil to cancel every rate declared illegal by the investigators and to remove most of the other causes of complaint as to inequitable traffic regulations. It is asserted that when the exposure of the American Tobacco Company's methods was made it promptly abandoned the use of secret subsidiary concerns which had posed as independent, but which in reality were trust concerns engaged in breaking down competition. Still later this bureau made a report on the billion-dollar Steel Trust.

The Bureau of Labor devotes its activities to the work of gathering information about the condition of the laboring classes of the United States, and of all matters which affect them. Some of its recent publications include bulletins on the increase in the cost of food and other products, civil-service retirement in Great Britain and New Zealand, railroad-pension systems in the United States, strike conditions at the Bethlehem Steel Works, a compilation of laws relating to compensation for industrial accidents in foreign countries, condition of woman and child wage-earners in the United States, and phosphorus poisoning in the match industry. This bureau is simply a gatherer of information and has nothing to do with the enforcement of laws relating to labor conditions. However, it does adjudicate claims for compensation growing out of injuries received by Government employees.

The Bureau of Manufactures is engaged in making available for the manufacturing establishments of the country the information gathered with reference to trade opportunities in foreign lands by the Consular Service of the State Department. In four years there were published over 5,000 separate items, each representing an opportunity for the sale of a certain machine or commodity by an American manufacturer. Business men directly interested are furnished letters in business detail to create new or to extend old lines of trade. The bureau is engaged in an effort to educate the American exporter in the art of properly packing goods. In addition to these things it has prepared an International Commercial Directory containing accurate and reliable information as to buyers in foreign countries. This Directory is published for distribution at a price which will relieve the Government of any expense in connection with its publication.

The Bureau of Statistics deals largely with the gathering and publication of data concerning the commerce of the United States. In addition to this it issues one of the most useful publications published by the Federal Government. This is known as the Statistical Abstract, which contains annual statistics about every line of activity in which the Government is interested. If one wishes to know how many telegrams are sent in the United States in a year, the Statistical Abstract brings that information down to date. If he desires to ascertain how much wine and liquor are consumed during each fiscal year, the Statistical Abstract answers the question. If he desires to ascertain how many tons of freight were carried in the United States, he consults the Statistical Abstract. It tells him how many boys and girls go to school in the United States, how faithful they are in their attendance, and what it costs to educate them. It informs him how many farms there are in the United States and how much the average farm is worth. It tells him how many women there are who are breadwinners, how much taxes the average man pays, how many fires there are in each State in the Union in a year, and practically everything else anyone wishes to know of a statistical nature concerning the Government and its activities.

The Bureau of Fisheries is one of the busiest in the department. It distributes over 3,000,000,000 eggs and fish every year. Of these over 2,500,000,000 are tiny little fish known as fry. Of the fish and eggs distributed, the flatfish ranks first with nearly a billion, the pike perch second with half a billion, the white perch third, and the yellow perch fourth, each with over 300,000,000. The shad and the cod are distributed to the extent of a quarter of a billion each. The importance of fish as a food product is not appreciated by the average American citizen. The waters of the United States annually contribute more than $60,000,000 worth of food products to the American people.

One of the most interesting phases of the work of the bureau is its efforts to acclimatize fish from

COMMERCE AND LABOR 151

the Pacific in the waters of the Atlantic. For nearly 40 years it has tried to establish the chinook salmon in Atlantic coast waters, but it is only recently that success has marked its efforts. Specimens of this fish have lately been found in Lake Sunapee, N. H., weighing from 3 to 5 pounds. Encouraged by this outcome, the bureau has recently planted 40,000 fingerling chinook salmon in Lake Champlain. Around the salmon there is a cloud of impenetrable mystery. It is hatched in fresh water, goes out to sea, and returns to its birthplace to die. Beyond this, little is known of its habits. How far it goes out to sea, what it lives upon, and how it finds its way back to its birthplace are questions that no man can answer. Great schools of them have been sighted in the ocean hundreds of miles from land, but when seen they were always headed for the shore and fresh water. They travel in such numbers that often the smaller streams are literally choked with them. They follow closely along the shore in search of suitable spawning grounds. In an effort to establish the age of the salmon little tin tags have been fastened to the tails of minnows turned loose, in the hope that they would show up later. This experiment has been tried in the case of cod, off the coast of Massachusetts, and some of the tagged fish have been caught several hundred miles away from the place where they were liberated.

The propagation of the oyster and the study of

its diseases and its other natural enemies engage a considerable portion of the work of the Bureau of Fisheries. The oyster lends itself admirably to efforts for its conservation. As an egg producer it beats the American hen as badly as an express train beats the slowest snail that crawls. Some of the best layers produce as many as 50,000,000 eggs a season, while an average of 16,000,000 eggs is maintained. Under natural conditions only one egg in ten million is likely to develop into a mature oyster. Under methods of artificial propagation this ratio may be lowered perhaps a hundredfold. There are many enemies which prey upon the oyster. The drumfish delights to find a planted bed, for there oysters are smoother and their shells are more easily crushed. The starfish travels in great schools at a speed of about 500 feet a day. It begins its work of destruction when it is no larger than a pinhead, and keeps it up all through life. It attaches itself to the oyster, and by persistence finally succeeds in worrying it out and forcing its stomach into the oyster's shell, through which it absorbs the life juices of the oyster. The Bureau of Fisheries has devised a dredge consisting of about a dozen mops arranged like the teeth of an old-fashioned harrow. This is dragged across the oyster bed and when it is filled with starfish they are brought to the surface and scalded to death.

The oyster has all the organs common to animal life, nearly all of them centered in its gills. In these gills are the pumps which maintain a proper circulation of the water supply, the food collectors, which strain the oyster's bread and meat from the water, the hands that carry the food to the mouth, and the nursing chamber where the eggs are brought to that maturity which enables the baby oysters to go out into the ocean and seek homes for themselves. After a very short period of free existence spent mainly in looking around for a desirable place to build a permanent residence, it settles down and lives there the rest of its natural life. The food of the oyster is tiny diatoms, little specks of plant life which live in the water. The Bureau of Fisheries has established a system of feeding the oyster by providing a liberal supply of diatoms. It inclosed a shallow lagoon at the south end of Chesapeake Bay and dumped several tons of ordinary commercial fertilizer into the marshes along the shore of the lagoon. As this was washed into the water it produced a tremendous crop of diatoms, and the oysters grew fat upon them. In order to widely distribute the diatoms a screw propeller was attached to a windmill and in this way a continuous current through the lagoon was established.

The bureau is also engaged in studying the pearl mussel supply of the rivers of the United States and in trying to discover a method for their artificial propagation. Sponge culture by artificial methods, the study of fish diseases such as thyroid tumor or cancer, the control of the seal fisheries of Alaska, and the investigation of the diamond-backed terrapin, the stone crab, the quahog or hard clam, and seaweed, are among the other activities of the bureau.

The Lighthouse Board has charge of the maintenance and construction of lighthouses and other aids to navigation along the coasts and in the rivers of the United States. It maintains all sorts of aids to navigation from the painted buoy up to the big lightship tenders, and the lighthouse keepers have some of the most thrilling experiences of any people in the Government service. Some of the buoys maintained are provided with whistling apparatus, others with fixed lights, and others with alternating lights. The use of acetylene gas in the light buoys is becoming more extensive, and a most unique method of automatically lighting them is resorted to. A mineral substance known as selenium possesses the property of being a nonconductor of electricity when the light does not shine upon it, and a conductor when it does. By the use of this the buoy is automatically lighted as soon as the sun goes down, and the light is extinguished as soon as sunlight appears the next morning.

The Bureau of Navigation has charge of the enforcement of the law requiring all ocean-passenger steamers carrying 50 passengers or more on routes of 200 miles or more to be equipped with efficient wireless apparatus and operators. It also has charge of the enforcement of the law for the regulation of motor boats. It maintains shipping commissioners at 17 seaports.

The Steamboat-Inspection Service inspects all of the steamboats of the United States and those clearing from American ports. Owing to the efficiency of this work less than 400 lives were lost out of the 300,000,000 passengers carried in one year. This bureau has officers stationed wherever excursion steamers handle passengers to insure that no steamer is overloaded. The bureau tests the boilers, the hulls, and all life-saving apparatus aboard every steamship carrying American passengers, and no vessel can engage in such business unless it receives a clean bill of health from the Steamboat-Inspection Service.

Another interesting activity of the Department of Commerce and Labor is the work of the Coast and Geodetic Survey. This bureau is charged with the making of surveys of the coast of the United States and coasts under the jurisdiction of this country. This includes the measuring of bases, triangulation, topography, and other matters along these coasts. It also makes surveys of rivers to the head of ship navigation, and studies the depth, temperature, and current movements in the waters along the coast and throughout the Gulf and Japan streams. It is engaged in a study of the magnetic properties of the earth, and the variations of terrestial magnetism. It also determines the precise levels in the United States and geographic positions by astronomic observations and triangulation in order to furnish the reference points from which all State surveys begin. The granite post with its metal bench mark, showing the exact geographical position and height above the sea is a familiar sight in many parts of the country.

CHAPTER XIII.

THE CENSUS BUREAU.

THE Census Bureau is perhaps the world's greatest gatherer of statistical information. Once every 10 years it puts an army of 75,000 people into the field for the purpose of gathering the data which will afford a great national snapshot of the United States as it is, and furnish a basis for ascertaining what progress the country has made during the decade. After these decennial inquiries are made, the bureau disbands its army of 75,000 enumerators. It takes a force of 3,000 two years to digest the statistical information gathered. The permanent bureau maintains a force of 800 for the gathering and publishing of statistical data between census periods.

When the Census Bureau begins the work of taking the decennial census, the first question which confronts it is that of making out the schedules of questions which are to be asked by the census enumerators. It is by no means a simple matter of writing down every question that happens to suggest itself to the schedule maker. Upon the number and the character of the questions contained in a schedule depend the accuracy and value of the returns. There are two principles which must govern those who frame a census schedule. Enough questions must be asked to get the information desired, and yet the fewer and simpler these questions are, the greater will be the accuracy of the data they bring out. So the schedule maker tries to find a happy medium between the large number of questions which would call forth much information, and the small number of simple questions which would secure the greatest accuracy. Many different schedules of questions are submitted to different classes of people. The population schedule, of course, goes to everybody. This schedule for the Thirteenth Census contained 33 questions. The next most important schedule has to do with the farms. It contains some 600 questions. The schedule of the manufacturing industries contains several hundred questions. The population schedule is always the most important. The census is primarily a matter of counting noses to determine the population of the country for purposes of apportioning representation in Congress.

All the other inquiries have come about as an incidental matter, a sort of by-product, as it were. Upon the count of population may depend the political complexion of the Nation. The population schedule for the Thirteenth Census contained a number of new interrogatories. One of these was for the purpose of finding out what proportion of the people are employees. Another new question

THE CENSUS BUREAU 159

related to whether the person was a Union or Confederate soldier during the Civil War. This question was asked with reference to service in the Union Army at the Eleventh Census, the names of survivors and their service being gathered. No provision was made for the publication of this data, which would have filled eight large quarto volumes of a thousand pages each. The returns were deposited in the Pension Bureau and never have been printed.

It required more than 70,000 people to gather the population and agricultural statistics of the country in 1910. In the taking of the census a careful tab is kept on every enumerator's work every day he is in the field. He is supplied with two cards for each day's work. At night he fills them out, forwarding one to the supervisor of his district and the other to the Census Bureau in Washington. He must give a list of the places he has visited, the number of people he has enumerated, and, in short, a general history of the day's work. The supervisor and the central office both check his cards, and if there is the slightest reason to suspect that he has not been doing his work properly he will be asked to explain. His final report must balance exactly with the sum of his daily reports.

The cost of the Thirteenth Census was approximately $14,000,000, of which about $7,000,000 went to pay for the enumeration in the field. The census law requires that every person shall make true and faithful answer to the enumerator who calls upon him, and provides a fine and imprisonment for willful failure to give such answers. At the same time it is equally careful to insure the people that their confidence shall be protected if they answer well and truly. The enumerator is required to hold in sacred confidence everything he learns in the discharge of his duties, and a jail sentence stares him in the face if he divulges any of the information he obtains. No matter if he unearths the biggest tax dodger in the country, or the most notorious criminal in the land, his mouth must be forever closed. That he does unearth a vast amount of tax dodging is disclosed by the fact that during a recent year the people of the country informed the tax assessor that they were worth $35,000,000,000. When the enumerator came around, with expanding chest and swelling pride they informed him that they were worth more than a hundred billion dollars.

One of the things which the Census Bureau has to guard against is frequent attempts at padding the lists. In one census a negro enumerator in Mississippi made returns for all the farms in his district, and then duplicated these returns for every member of the family on each farm. This padding was for the purpose of increasing his own pay. In another case a Maryland enumerator visited the cemeteries in his district and returned the names upon the tombstones. Sometimes ambitious cities engage in campaigns of census padding. In a recent census two rival cities undertook to pad their population returns. Each was watching the other. The one went at it in a crude sort of way, and was soon detected. The other handled the situation with a finer hand and might have succeeded in its efforts but for the watchfulness of the rival city.

Bitter disappointments often follow the announcement of census returns. Ambitious cities hope to make a better showing than their rivals. For instance, as Los Angeles and Seattle were both ambitious to be written down as the second city of the Pacific coast by the Thirteenth Census, a great campaign of city booming was carried forward by each of them. Los Angeles won out.

But for the invention of machines capable of arranging and adding figures more accurately than can be done by the human hand and the human brain, and much more rapidly, the taking of a Federal census under present conditions would be utterly impracticable. It would require so long to tabulate, digest, and publish the returns that it would be time for another census to be taken before the one in hand could be completed. Electricity has solved the problems of digesting the returns which come from the enumerators in the field. Prior to the Eleventh Census all returns were tabulated by hand; and a long, tedious task it was. In 1890 the electrical punching and tabulating machine came into use, having been invented by a former employee of the census.

Speaking of this machine Director Merriam of the Twelfth Census declared that it "has proved a boon to the Census Office. It needs only be said that if, at the Twelfth Census, the tallies of age and sex, nativity and occupation had been made by hand, it would have required the time of a hundred clerks nearly twelve years." He also estimated that the electrical machinery does the work in a tenth of the time, at a third of the cost, and with a greater degree of accuracy than could be accomplished by hand, and that it saved the Government $5,000,000 in the work of the Twelfth Census.

This machinery is remarkable for its ingenuity. Symbols are prepared which represent the various items of data as extracted from the schedule. Editors take the schedules and insert the symbols over the item in the various columns and form divisions. A separate card is devoted to each person in the United States, and on each of them is set down the facts relating to the sex, age, race, birthplace, etc., and a machine is used to punch holes through the symbols which tell the story of each individual. Each machine has a capacity of about 1,800 cards a day, and there are 300 machines in the Census Office.

The 90,000,000 cards which represent the 90,-000,000 people in the United States would make a stack 10 miles high. A careful check is kept upon the accuracy of the operators of the punching machines, so as to make sure that they are not hitting

THE CENSUS BUREAU

the wrong keys. While it is not possible to compare all of these 90,000,000 cards with the schedules from which they are punched, a certain number of cards are selected at random from each operator's work and compared with the original. If the operator is inaccurate she must mend her ways or turn the machine over to some one else.

After the cards are punched they are fed into what is known as the tabulating machine. This machine is so arranged that as the card passes through, an electrical connection is established by a blunt needle passing through the card wherever there is a hole punched, into a cup of mercury, and the fact of this connection is automatically recorded. The machine automatically prints the total results for each unit of area, such as districts, townships, wards, cities, or States. This machine has almost human intelligence. Whenever a card fed into it is properly punched it gives an approving ring and passes the card through. If the card does not have the proper number of holes punched in it the tabulating machine stops and refuses to budge until the offending card is withdrawn.

One may get a striking lesson of the costliness of small errors from a statement made recently by Director Durand, of the Census Bureau. In the case of farm statistics the enumerator sometimes makes the mistake of adding or leaving off a cipher in reporting the number of bushels of grain raised on a given farm. To follow up all these errors and check off the obvious ones, after the method of the Twelfth Census, would cost, he estimates, several hundred thousand dollars. By the use of the typewriter-adding machine, such errors in a column of figures were so patent that the trained eye detected them without the necessity of editing by individual schedules. At the last census the statistics of agriculture were tabulated by means of punched cards of which some 200,000,000 were used. These cards would have made a stack over 25 miles high. The typewriter-adding machines have served to expedite the work of tabulating the returns of the 7,000,000 farms from which statistics were gathered.

The work of publishing the returns of the census is a very large one. For many years the reports were published by private contract, but at present the Government Printing Office does the work. The reports for the Thirteenth Census are much more compact than in the case of any preceding census. Heretofore the decennial census reports have taken up almost as much room in a library as Dr. Eliot's famous section of lineal literature. Director Durand has scaled down the size of his reports considerably. He had an excellent example to guide him. The Federal Blue Book, or register of Government employees, formerly was published in two volumes, each of them larger than an old-fashioned family Bible. The latest one issued by the Census Bureau, without omitting a single essential fact, has been squeezed

THE CENSUS BUREAU 165

down to two volumes whose aggregate size is considerably less than that of the smaller of the two former volumes.

In addition to the statistics of population, agriculture, and manufactures, the decennial census gathers like information with reference to mines and quarries in the United States. In this work it has an agreement with the Geological Survey. There is also provision for smaller investigations to be made in decennial years. One of these relates to the enumeration of inmates of institutions for criminals, paupers, feeble-minded, and juvenile delinquents. Another consists of the enumeration of benevolent institutions, and the third is a special inquiry with reference to the deaf and dumb and the blind of the United States. Irrigation statistics are also gathered. This is being done by a special field force in cooperation with the division of irrigation investigations of the Department of Agriculture.

When the Census Bureau finishes the big decennial inquiry it undertakes other lines of work during the years intervening between census periods. Each year it gathers statistics of the financial and municipal activities of cities having a population of more than 30,000. It also gathers annual statistics concerning the ginning, consumption, and the stock of cotton. Its other annual work includes the gathering of data concerning births and deaths in the registration States and information concerning forest products. Every five years the bureau makes an investigation of all manufacturing industries. The Thirteenth Census has made the first nation-wide investigation as to the prevalence of race suicide, as indicated by the number of children born and the number living in comparison with the number of women of different classes, their age, and the duration of married life.

The history of census taking in the United States is an interesting one. The Federal Government has conducted these inquiries 13 times since the foundation of the Government, and in doing so has spent some $75,000,000. Starting out in 1790 with but four questions, all of them upon the single subject of inquiry—population—the work expanded in a hundred years to such a remarkable extent that in 1890 there were 31 different subjects of inquiry, carrying over 13,000 questions.

The most remarkable expansion in the work took place at the Tenth Census, in 1880. At the preceding census there had been but 12 subjects of inquiry, embracing only 156 questions. In 1880 the number of subjects had increased to 26, and the number of questions to 1,310. These inquiries were so top-heavy that in 1900 Congress decided to reduce the number of subjects to four—population, agriculture, manufactures, and vital statistics. It is indeed a far cry from the 17 marshals and 200 assistants, with their quill pens and saddlebags, who gathered and prepared the returns of the First Census in 1790 to the 70,000 census takers of 1910 with their electrical tabulating machinery.

The First Census cost $44,000, and it is calculated that the one which will be taken in 1920 will cost more than $20,000,000. There was much disappointment over the showing of the First Census. Many thought it made the population too small, on the ground that it was supposed to be for purposes of taxation. Thomas Jefferson unhesitatingly expressed his belief that it was erroneous, and as Secretary of State notified the representatives of the United States abroad that the returns were far short of the truth. He was careful to supply many omissions in red ink. Subsequent events indicate that the First Census was, as a matter of fact, a very accurate one, and that the trouble lay in the overestimates of colonial populations which had been made previously. One of the most interesting publications ever issued by the Government is that containing a list of the heads of families as disclosed by the census of 1790. This work was undertaken only a few years ago, and is a publication of surpassing interest to the genealogists of the United States.

Once the Census Bureau completes its count of the population of the country it announces the results to Congress. That body takes the figures and from them determines the number of Representatives who shall constitute the House of

Representatives in Congress during the ensuing decade. It has the constitutional right either to increase the number of Representatives, or to increase the number of people to be represented by the average Member. The aim usually is to strike such an apportionment so that no State loses a Representative by the procedure. Under the apportionment of the Thirteenth Census the House consists of 435 Members, one Member to each 211,877 of population. The Senate usually allows the House to determine the matters involved and then agrees to the House apportionment measure.

After Congress has passed the apportionment bill, providing the number of Representatives from each State, it devolves upon the legislatures of the States to divide them into districts and to provide for the election of the requisite number of Representatives. Usually party politics controls this work. The party in power in a legislature nearly always tries so to lay off the congressional districts that in the election the opposing party shall be at a great disadvantage. It tries to crowd all of the counties with big majorities to the opposite party into a few districts, leaving all the other districts in a position to return Representatives of their own political persuasion. Sometimes it so lays off a congressional district as to make it resemble a shoe string more than anything else. Elbridge Gerry first practiced this art as a political leader, and it has been known as "gerrymandering" ever since. Con-

THE CENSUS BUREAU

gress itself often plays politics when a reapportionment measure comes up for consideration. If a political wave has swept the party then in power in the House out of power in the legislatures, it holds up the apportionment bill in the hope that its fortunes may again be in the ascendant in the legislatures of the States where the gerrymander is the deciding factor as to which party shall have control of the State delegation in Congress.

CHAPTER XIV.

THE BUREAU OF STANDARDS.

At the National Bureau of Standards one may have ocular demonstration that truth is stranger than fiction. In one room of this remarkable institution is a giant testing machine, powerful enough to pull asunder a great steel shaft. In another room the visitor may behold by optical means the bending of tool-steel shafting, 3½ inches in diameter, beneath the weight of a visiting card. Across the hall is a weighing machine with balance so sensitive as to register the decrease in weight of a piece of metal when moved 2 inches farther from the earth. In another room are to be found length measures so delicate that their scale can be read only by the aid of a microscope magnifying 50 diameters, and which, when being used, are packed in ice so that the variations of heat may not affect their accuracy. In still another room the visitor may study the ultra-violet rays of light, such as the unaided human eye has never seen. At another place he may see men testing thermometers which register a temperature below the freezing point of pure hydrogen; and others which will accurately meas-

THE BUREAU OF STANDARDS 171

ure heat up to approximately 7,000°, a heat so intense that no earthly substance can survive it.

The layman can hardly appreciate how close home to him comes the work of the Bureau of Standards. His groceries are bought by standard measures, the imported sugar in his coffee at breakfast has been tested by the bureau for the Customs Service. The electric light by which he reads at night conforms to the standards of this bureau. The clinical thermometer by which the doctor ascertains his temperature when he is sick, and the apothecary scales by which his medicines have been measured, owe their accuracy to the work of this bureau.

The Bureau of Standards is the home of precision, but not of undue precision, for the bureau aims to assign to each case the order of accuracy it deserves. A clinical thermometer, correct to a tenth of a degree, is tested in a few minutes. If, however, a standard of length, yard or meter, is for some great manufacturing plant where measuring instruments are made, weeks are spent in testing a single standard, while fundamental national standards take years to establish. The modern metric standards of length and mass took 15 years to prepare, verify, and distribute to the Governments of the world.

The unique facilities for scientific work at the bureau attract visitors from every land. A liquid-air plant affords freezing temperatures almost to absolute zero; electric furnaces give heat enough to melt rock; machines are at hand to freeze the moisture from the air and provide a new dry climate wherever required; through large tunnels run a multitude of pipes and wires, carrying not merely hot, cold, and iced water, but steam, vacuum, and compressed air to the various laboratories. Every room needing special time service can be wired to beat second intervals from that marvel of precision—the Riefler clock, which runs correct to within a half second a month. There are ice-making machines, gas-making machines, ventilating systems, and remarkable switchboards where all kinds and strengths of electric current may be sent to any room as easily as a telephone connection is made. In the glass-working shop, wonderful tubes are made for vacuum lamps, elaborate apparatus of glass for regulating temperature of tanks of oil to the hundredth part of 1°, and many other intricate works of skill. Then there is the glassworker, who grinds true lenses and flat surfaces to marvelous accuracy for optical research.

Respect for the infinitesimal is a cardinal virtue in the bureau's work; no factor is too small to be ignored, no labor too exacting, no expense too great, when national standards are involved. Scientific discovery now rests upon that refined scrutiny of things which marks precision measurement. With more exact measurement of the moon's distance, Newton might have announced his discoveries many years earlier. Accurate

MACHINE THAT TESTS STANDARD WEIGHTS.

weighings of the nitrogen of the air showed a slight excess weight due, as Ramsay found, to five new gases which we inhale with every breath, but which were till then unknown. So with the precise manipulation of testing and measuring, radium was discovered. Nearly every important scientific discovery of modern times has been in whole or in part the result of measuring instruments of remarkable refinement.

One of the most impressive sights to be seen in this institution is its new giant testing machine, which has a compressive power of 2,300,000 pounds, and a pulling power of 1,150,000 pounds. This latter power is sufficient to pull asunder a great steel shaft measuring 5 inches in diameter, or to break a huge structural column more than twice as large. It is able accurately to register this great strain. Immediately after exerting a pressure of more than 2,000,000 pounds, and registering this degree of pressure with great accuracy, it will crush an eggshell and register the pressure required in that operation with equal fidelity.

This great machine may be likened roughly to a huge hydraulic jack with a pair of registering scales attached. It will test any piece of material from a few inches in length to 30 feet. Two huge screws, some 40 feet long, 12 inches in diameter, and with threads five-eighths of an inch deep, are used to apply the power. Oil is used instead of water, in great cylinders, to furnish the power for pressure or tension. Only a small part of the great pressure which the machine exerts falls upon the weighing instrument. Great springs are distributed through the parts of the machine to bear the strain and absorb any shock which might result from the breaking of the material being tested. Although this great testing machine is vast in proportions and powerful in its strength, a still more powerful machine is installed in the Bureau of Standards' testing plant at Pittsburgh. This machine is able to exert a force of 10,000,000 pounds, which is more than sufficient to break the shaft of the biggest war vessel afloat.

It would be a long story to describe the variety of materials whose properties are measured by the bureau to ascertain their quality. They range from the horseshoe nail of the army mule to the steel and cement for the great Isthmian Canal; from the single strand of silk to steel rails; bookmaking materials, paper, type, ink, glue, cloth; structural materials for building skyscrapers, bridges, and houses, including also paints, varnishes, protective coatings; office supplies—such as writing papers, sealing wax, mucilage, ink, paste, typewriter ribbons, including even red tape. The permanency of public records depends upon the ink and the paper, and until recently both were doubtful.

In the material-testing section a self-acting twine tester unwinds the balls, measures the yardage, and rewinds them while samples are tested for breaking strength. Uncle Sam's twine each year costs a quarter-million dollars, and must be full measure of strength and length. The cloth in the national flags and that used in bookbinding and other purposes is tested as to as many qualities as required, sometimes the threads to the inch, sometimes as to the wear, sometimes as to strength, but always to select the best, or ascertain whether goods are of the quality specified. The quality of paper was once expert guesswork. The paper was felt with the fingers and tongue, torn, crumpled, even chewed, and the expert was then supposedly able to guess the quality. Now every element is measured by the bureau—fiber, sizing, mineral; the dye, its color and fastness are studied; while the bursting strength, weight and thickness, folding durability, are measured on automatic machines more accurately than the paper is uniform. So thorough is this work that the "recipe" by which the paper was made can be reproduced from the tests.

The amazing electrical progress of the past half century is due largely to the wonderful improvement in methods of measuring electricity and to the single world system of units of electrical measure. The Bureau of Standards has had experts working for years to fix the world's electrical units and standards. Some of these researches are of astonishing precision, and, while they can be appreciated only by the expert, everybody will profit by the general electrical advance made possible by the greater exactness of the standards. The standard cells which fix the value of the volt as a laboratory standard are kept constantly in oil baths regulated to a constant temperature, not varying by so much as the hundredth of a degree. The standard of voltage is now the mean of six standard cells selected as the best of several hundred. The standard ohm, the unit of resistance, is determined by the resistance which a tube of mercury of minutely specified dimensions and construction offers to a current of electricity.

The bureau is investigating how electricity corrodes iron and steel in underground pipes and structures. The danger is such as seriously to imperil city water and gas mains, great buildings, bridges, etc. The problem is being studied throughout the United States by the bureau's experts.

In one of the buildings is a unique dynamo used for wireless work, which gives electric current of 100,000 waves a second for use on the great wireless mast just outside the building, whose top reaches almost as high as the Washington Monument. This is connected with the laboratories of the bureau, where experimental research is in progress under the Army and Navy wireless experts.

In the room where precise weighing is done, the temperature is under strict control, for if it rises

THE BUREAU OF STANDARDS

or falls by even half a degree while accurate work is being done, or even for several hours beforehand, air currents would move the scale pans and hinder the work. Even the heat from the body would cause trouble, hence in precise weighing, the expert is 10 feet away and by rods with ingenious mechanisms changes weights from pan to pan and adds V-shaped weights of fine wire to either side to effect a balance. The motions of the beam are read by a telescope using a mirror on the beam, in effect, an optical pointer 20 or 30 feet long.

One balance operates in a vacuum to eliminate the buoyant force of the air. If one pan of the balances were higher than the other, the weight would appear lighter, because it is farther from the center of the earth. If a 2-pound weight is raised 2 inches, these balances would show the difference in weight due to the increased distance from the earth.

The weights are kept covered in glass cases, and the least dust is carefully brushed off with a soft camel's-hair brush. Chamois-covered lifters are used to handle the larger weights, for the finger-prints of even the cleanest hands would vitiate them.

The smallest weights in actual use are one-twentieth milligram or one-sixth-millionth of an ounce. They are of aluminum, thinner than tissue paper, and would have much room to spare if set on a pinhead. The balance on which they are used weighs easily to within one-thirty-millionth of an ounce.

The fundamental standards on which all weights depend are made of platinum-iridium alloy prepared after a decade of investigation and testing by an international commission of scientists. These standards are kept under double glass covers, in a fireproof vault, and are rarely used, and then only to check up the best working standards.

In some of the rooms of the weights and measures section are to be seen portable outfits, such as city sealers would carry, charts showing how much we pay per pound for the commodities, such as foods, done up and sold by the package, and other evidence of the investigations that have been made in all the States of the Union. These investigations have done much to show the need of regulating the size of packages.

The unit of length of the United States is the meter, the standard measure of which was brought from Paris in 1890. The original standard bar has been reproduced many times in platinum iridium. This new standard resembles, in section, the capital letter "H," with the two upright lines bending out at both the top and bottom. The lines which constitute the scale on this bar are so finely cut that they are almost invisible to the naked eye. Two of these bars are on deposit in the Bureau of Standards and one of them was taken back to Paris several years

THE BUREAU OF STANDARDS 179

ago and compared with the original. It was found that in 15 years there was less than the fifty-thousandth part of an inch difference in its length.

When a measure is compared with this prototype meter bar, the two are packed side by side in ice in a trough-like comparator mounted on independent piers. The observers measure the position of the minute marks with remarkably accurate micrometer screws and strong microscopes. Under one of the buildings of the Bureau of Standards is a tunnel in which standards of length are compared. There is a series of piers, independent of the floor, with which, by means of the meter bar and a 5-meter bar, any bar or tape up to 50 meters may be accurately measured. This comparator is used for the standardization of the invar tapes which are used by the Coast and Geodetic Survey and the United States Geological Survey in their work of accurate base measurements. On the opposite side of the tunnel is a long steel bench, 164 feet long, in which platinum-iridium plugs are set at intervals. On each plug a cross line has been ruled and the distance between the lines is determined.

A whole floor of one of the largest buildings is fitted up for precise determinations of temperatures by means of the melting points of various elements; for the standardization of clinical thermometers, of which many thousands are tested annually; for the accurate measurement of temperature by means of resistance thermometers in which the liquid resists freezing. The range extends down far below the temperature of liquid air and up as high as solar temperature. At higher temperatures optical means must be used, for all the elements melt in the intense heat. The work of this division underlies all metallurgy. The instruments used to measure the heat value of fuels are standardized here. This is of growing importance, since large contracts now pay for coal on the basis of heating value, rather than by gross weight. Pyrometry, another branch of this work, is devoted to measuring high temperatures, and devices of extraordinary ingenuity have been invented to cover heat ranges where ordinary thermometers fail.

The optical experts use waves of light as units of measure; they analyze colors, study transparency of many materials and their power to reflect the various colors and even the light invisible to the unaided eye. With the ultramicroscope, the motions of invisible particles of silver are studied, particles which, though too small to be seen directly, vitiate the measurement of electric current in precision work. Radiation, meaning light and heat energy, is measured by a marvelous instrument called the bolometer, in which a millionth of a degree of temperature is easily registered. The bureau ascertains the quality of lenses by testing the focus, curvature, and other properties. Most scientific facts have reached us

DR. WILEY AT WORK.

THE BUREAU OF STANDARDS

through glass, and in the form of a lens it is the eye of science. A defect in curvature would mar every view taken or seen through it.

The sugar laboratory receives samples of sugar from all parts of the world at the ports of entry. The impurities are measured by the twist which a solution of the sugar gives to light waves passing through it. This laboratory also supplies perfectly pure sugar for $18 a pound. This sugar is used to test the instruments with which the heating value of fuels is measured, as well as to fix the 100 per cent point in sugar testing.

In one room the visitor's watch must be removed, for here is the strongest magnet in the world, which will draw nails held loosely in the hand from a distance of a foot; so strong, too, that if a nail is placed in the closed fist the hand can be turned only with great effort. This magnet is used to study the strange effects of magnetism on light waves, not merely twisting, but actually lengthening or shortening the light waves themselves.

In minute measures of length a remarkable optical instrument is used, in which light waves are the units. The interferometer measures wave lengths which would take 75,000 to cover an inch. One may step up to the demonstration interferometer and measure for himself with wave lengths of light. To illustrate, a bar of steel, 3 feet by $3\frac{1}{2}$ inches, may be bent by a visiting card, and the infinitesimal bending perceived by this remarkable instrument. The bar is supported at its ends, and bears upon its middle a small mirror. Above the bar is a yoke upon which is fixed another interferometer mirror only partly silvered. When the shaft is bent downward ever so slightly, he sees reflected a series of concentric bright and dark circles, resembling a target, and as the shaft is bent the circles expand outward like the circles in water when a stone is dropped in. As each new circle forms, the bar has been bent one one-hundred-thousandth of an inch. With this instrument, five or six new circles may be seen to form at a touch, so that the total flexure would be, say, one twenty-thousandth of an inch. The interferometer is used in many refined researches, particularly in fixing standards of length and measuring light waves.

The results of scientific research during the past quarter of a century have been far-reaching. But the scientists to-day declare that the lessons of these 25 years have demonstrated that more wonderful results lie ahead than have been achieved in the past, and that no man is able to predict what strides toward ideal living conditions and racial betterment may be made in the half century immediately ahead. It is to the pioneering work of such institutions as the Bureau of Standards that these results will be due.

CHAPTER XV.

THE PUBLIC HEALTH.

THE Federal Government deals with problems relating to the public health through five separate bureaus under the administration of five of the executive departments. Foremost among these bureaus, by reason of the wide range of its work, is the Public Health and Marine-Hospital Service, which is under the Treasury Department. Through the Bureau of Chemistry, which protects the national food supply, the Bureau of Animal Industry, which inspects the Nation's meat products, and the Bureau of Entomology, which is leading the country-wide fight for the abolition of the fly and the mosquito, the Department of Agriculture has a large share in health conservation in the United States. The War Department is represented by the Medical Corps of the United States Army, having to its credit the final proof that the mosquito is responsible for yellow fever, and the additional credit of demonstrating the possibilities of modern sanitation and preventive medicine. The Navy Department is represented by the Medical Corps of the Navy.

After these have all done their work, along comes the Department of Commerce and Labor, and, through the Census Office, gathers the statistics which show the effect of the work of all the other departments in their efforts at conquering disease, reducing mortality, and promoting longevity.

That the health of the people is a problem of prime importance, and that it can be promoted, cutting down the death rate and lengthening the span of life, is abundantly attested by vital statistics in every civilized country. It is estimated that more than a million preventable deaths occur each year in the United States and that these inflict an economic loss upon the Nation of more than a billion dollars. Between the census years of 1890 and 1900, the average American saw his journey from the cradle to the grave lengthened from 31 years, 1 month, and 6 days, to 35 years, 2 months, and 12 days. The census of 1910 probably will show an additional four years added to the span of the average life.

According to insurance statistics, the mortality rate among the industrial classes is nearly double that among the well-to-do. In Austria and Spain, where ignorance of the laws of health is widespread, the death rate is nearly double that obtaining in the United States, where ideal conditions are still far from being realized, and in India the average life is but little more than half as long as the average life in America. The death rate from tuberculosis has fallen off one-half since Koch discovered its germ. The death rate from diphtheria is only a third as great in Chicago to-day as it was a generation ago. Every time the world's death rate is cut down one per thousand, it means the saving of a million and a half lives a year.

From these statements it will appear that the activity of the Federal Government in the promotion of the national health is one of its most important concerns. In the promotion of these ends the bureaus concerned with the public health find a vast deal of interesting work to do. The Public Health and Marine-Hospital Service, presided over by that eminent sanitarian, Dr. Walter Wyman, has a wide field of activities. Its work in putting down yellow fever in the South a few years ago, its labors in protecting San Francisco from a threatened outbreak of pestilence after the great earthquake, its services in stamping out bubonic plague in California, its epoch-making investigations of the hookworm disease, its work of artificially growing the bacillus of leprosy, its labor toward uniting the Western World in international sanitary work, and its successful resistance of the threatened cholera epidemics which stormed the shores of America in 1892 and 1893, and again in 1910 and 1911, are a few instances where it has come prominently into the public eye. But it does a thousand things in the course of a year which enable the average American to feel a greater security against the dangers of disease than he otherwise could.

All through every day and night of every year it stands guard at the ports of the country to see that no loathsome or dangerous diseases are permitted to come into the country through those ports. The first person who boards an incoming steamer after it takes up its pilot is the quarantine officer, who is a representative of the Public Health and Marine-Hospital Service. He examines the officers of the ship and only when they are able to show a clean bill of health will he allow the ship to go to its dock. Every one of the aliens who come into the United States must undergo an examination by its officials.

The service also has charge of interstate sanitation and the suppression of epidemics, cooperating with the States by lending its experts to them for the ascertainment of the cause of epidemics and for planning campaigns to check them. It has its finger upon the pulse of the country, collecting data regarding contagious and infectious diseases with the view to advancing our knowledge regarding their prevention and suppression, which is a fundamental duty of the Federal Government in its relation to the public health.

In the supervision of the sale of viruses, serums, toxins, and similar products, the Public Health Service renders great assistance to the sick of the country. Without some central agency to adopt certain standards for these materials, and to see

THE PUBLIC HEALTH

that they are maintained, people might be in danger of all sorts of infection. All vaccine virus, diphtheria antitoxins, and the like, must measure up to the standards of strength and purity set by the service or they can not be sold in interstate commerce. The Hygienic Laboratory has prepared standard units for antitetanic and antidiphtheric serums, and sends out to the laboratories making these serums a standard unit for comparison. The Belgian Government and the great Wellcome Laboratories of England are using the standards set by this Hygienic Laboratory, as is also the Brazilian Government.

Another interesting activity of the service is the standardization of all heroic remedies. Digitalis and other remedies have varied much in strength, and no doubt thousands of people have lost their lives by overdoses of these remedies administered ignorantly, on account of the lack of uniformity of strength. One of the most notable contributions that has yet been made to the literature of sanitation was made by the Public Health and Marine-Hospital Service in the course of its studies on milk and its relation to epidemic diseases. There are more than 20,000,000 milch cows in the United States, and they give perhaps a billion gallons of milk a year. If milk is a disease carrier, ignorance of the fact might cost untold thousands of lives, so the service started out to find just how far milk may act as the transportation system of the germ kingdom.

When its investigators set to work to trace down epidemics of typhoid fever, they found that milk is one of the greatest known disseminators of the disease. In Savannah, Ga., only 19 cases of typhoid occurred during a recent year from January to May. During May 95 cases were reported. Sixty-three of these cases were traced to a single dairy, and a majority of the remainder of the cases were thought to have been infected from these other cases. The infected dairy sold milk at wholesale, as well as retail, among its wholesale patrons being a bakery, over which a typhoid patient lived. The dairy had been infected by the use of the milk cans, which had been returned unsterilized from this bakeshop.

Another great benefit following research work was the discovery of hookworm infection, which was sapping the vitality of large numbers of people in an important section of the country. The knowledge thus acquired is now being applied in an extensive campaign against the disease. Other investigations of equal importance relating to typhoid fever have been conducted during the past five years, and will ultimately contribute to a reduction of this disease in the United States.

The service is also at the head of the nation-wide campaign against rabies, and has pointed out how the dreaded disease may be completely wiped out. It furnishes the virus which is used for the administration of the Pasteur treatment to State boards of health, and administers it to

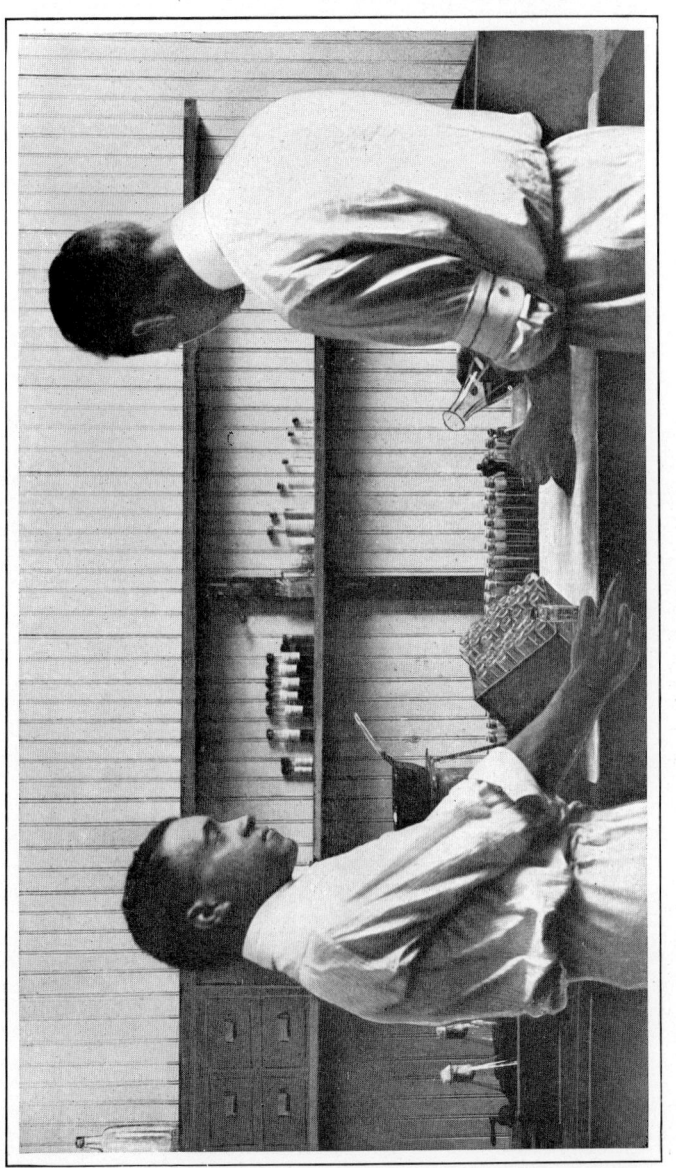

PREPARING TUBERCULIN FOR SHIPMENT.

patients who have been bitten by animals suspected of having hydrophobia. In the Hygienic Laboratory the experimenters make use of many dogs, cats, guinea pigs, and mice. Many a human life has been saved by the experiments thus made. In 1853 two water companies experimented with a half million people in London, with the result that there were 3,476 deaths. The same year a Leipsic scientist experimented with 56 mice, and had the lessons he learned by those experiments been heeded, the cholera epidemic in London would have been averted. Using monkeys for the purpose, similar studies have been made in the Hygienic Laboratory with respect to measles. This disease has been transmitted to these animals, and it is the hope of the laboratory authorities that a curative serum will soon be found which will save the lives of large numbers of children.

It costs less than a million dollars a year to run the Bureau of Chemistry of the Department of Agriculture, yet this bureau is charged with the duty of guaranteeing the quality of the manufactured foods and drugs of the United States, so far as they cross State boundary lines. It is estimated that these foodstuffs and drugs cost the people at least $6,000,000,000, so that the insurance of the quality of the things the people take into their stomachs is the cheapest insurance in the world. While the protection afforded by the pure food and drug laws can not reach its maximum without an intelligent public sentiment behind it, yet the growing interest of the Nation in pure-food regulations is tending toward that end. While in former years it was estimated that very little of the manufactured foodstuffs was properly made, or at least properly branded, Dr. Harvey W. Wiley now estimates that at least 90 per cent of the food and drugs of the country are made and sold in compliance with the law.

So effective has been the work of the bureau that France has established a pure-food system modeled after our own, and other nations are borrowing ideas from it. The bureau has over 20 branch laboratories, scattered among the principal cities of the country, and wherever its experts have reason to suspect that the pure-food law is being violated, they take samples and analyze them. If the samples do not measure up to the requirements of the law, either in the matter of branding them or in their quality, the stock from which they were taken is seized and held pending the action of the courts. This usually is favorable to the bureau; in fact, nearly 95 per cent of the cases turn out that way.

The seizures cover almost every kind of food and drug in the United States. Some time ago a widely advertised skin food was examined and found to be nothing more than Epsom salts, with a little pink coloring matter added. In another case, some strawberry jelly was seized, and upon examination it was found to be made up of glucose, timothy seed, and coloring matter. Dozens of kinds of patent medicines have been seized, and in nearly every instance bottles which sold for at least a dollar retail, contained only a few cents' worth of material, and that not particularly meritorious. One of the chief endeavors of the bureau is to put out of business that lot of human vampires who would fatten upon the very flesh of those afflicted with incurable diseases. With their fake cures for cancer, tuberculosis, drug addiction, and other diseases which bring so much woe to the human race, they extract millions of dollars from the pockets of those who can least afford it, and leave them in a last state that is worse than their first. Cancer cures that have been advertised as possessing wonderful properties, and carrying with them a long list of seemingly good testimonials, upon examination by the bureau have been found to contain nothing more curative than water. Others which were declared to be able to draw out the worst cancer had nothing more astringent in them than charcoal. In drug habit cures the bureau has found that in most cases they contain other habit-forming drugs as bad as the one for which they claim to be a cure. Hundreds of these "cures" have been denied the use of the mails through the activities of the Bureau of Chemistry, and thousands of poor, distraught mortals suffering from incurable diseases, or who have dear ones suffering from them, are protected from the schemes of impostors who would grow rich upon their misery without the slightest attempt to alleviate it.

The Bureau of Chemistry has other functions to perform than those of inspecting foods and drugs, although about 90 per cent of its activities are concerned with the enforcement of the pure-food law. It is engaged in extensive researches in the field of nutritive value of foods, and is making a detailed study of the deterioration of eggs and poultry in shipment and storage. An investigation of the fish and oyster supply is also under way. It is the aim of the Bureau of Chemistry to be able to afford the people protection in their food, and also to give them such information as will give them refuge from the reign of high prices by pointing out those foodstuffs which possess the happy combination of high nutritive value, low price, and palatable taste.

One of the greatest difficulties the bureau had to face in the beginning of its work was the elimination of coal tar, or analine dyes in coloring foodstuffs, candies, and drinks. A half century ago a young English chemist was engaged in trying to find a new process of making quinine. An accidental combination gave him a color known as "mauve." That accident resulted in opening the way for the making of analine dyes, of which there are now more than 2,000 colors in use. Before the days of pure-food laws, these dyes were used widely in the preparation of food supplies.

Few agencies of the Federal Government have

ever been able to work such reforms in such a short time as the Bureau of Chemistry. It has been a storm center since the enactment of the pure-food law, and will remain so as long as men are interested in making money by selling questionable food products. Its fights on the question of "What is whisky?" and in the matter of bleached flour were memorable combats with powerful interests. When the pure-food law was pending, Representative Stanley, of Kentucky, showed his fellow Members of the House how some of the whiskies of that day were made. Holding up a concoction which he had prepared before their eyes, he remarked that it would make a howling dervish out of a monk and a rabbit to spit in a bulldog's face.

It has been estimated that if the flies and mosquitoes of the country could be banished from the United States at one fell swoop, and if all the people of the country could be induced to observe the principles laid down in antispitting ordinances, it would result in the saving every year of enough lives to make an army as great as ever marched to a single battle in the history of America. One authority goes even further than this, and declares that a quarter of a million deaths annually in the United States are to be laid at the door of the mosquito and the fly alone. The principal prosecuting attorney in the case of the fly and the mosquito to-day is the Bureau of Entomology of the Department of Agriculture.

A most remarkable case it has made out against the fly.

The bureau caused 414 members of the fly tribe to be captured in various parts of the country, and they were searched for incriminating evidence. Stored away on the fuzzy bodies and legs of the culprits were found untold millions of germs. In some instances, a single fly carried more than a million. These were flies caught in carefully sterilized nets, so that none of the germs found on them could be laid at the door of the nets. Then each fly was placed in a separate sterilized bottle, and an accurately measured quantity of sterilized water was put into the bottle with it. Mr. Fly was allowed to swim around until exhausted, and a drop of the water was extracted and the germs on it counted. A careful record was kept of the showing made by each fly, and the lowest number was 500, while some of them showed 6,000,000 germs. And then there has been an untold amount of other evidence gathered. During the Spanish-American War lime was used in the latrines, and the flies that swarmed around the mess tents would have lime plainly visible on their feet. In New York filth was dyed with red ink and put on the streets. Flies soon showed up in the house with red on their legs. The Bureau of Entomology, as prosecuting attorney against the fly, has prepared several pamphlets relative to the case, and is ready to make any reader the sitting judge who will take time to write for these briefs in the case of The People v. The Fly. It also is ready to submit evidence to any reader in the case of The People v. The Mosquito.

CHAPTER XVI.

THE SMITHSONIAN INSTITUTION.

When James Smithson wrote his will making a bequest of half a million dollars for the founding of an institution for "the increase and diffusion of knowledge among men," he builded better than he knew. Perhaps never in history has a half million dollars yielded such splendid returns as that with which James Smithson endowed the institution which bears his name. Many of the most portentous discoveries in the history of science have been made through the activities of the Smithsonian Institution. The foundations of the telegraph and the telephone were laid by its first secretary, Joseph Henry, as was also the understructure of the science of meteorology. Its second secretary, Spencer F. Baird, instituted the work of fish culture, without which the food fishes of this country, preyed upon by their natural enemies, and gathered in by the millions by man, must have had such great inroads made upon them that the commercial value of the Nation's fisheries would be vastly less than it is under scientific propagation. Its third secretary, Samuel P. Langley, is credited with the begin-

GOVERNMENT TAXIDERMIST.

THE SMITHSONIAN INSTITUTION

ning of the transmission of time signals as applied to railroad operations in the United States. It was his work, also, which demonstrated the remarkable fact that the firefly is forty-nine times as efficient as a lighting agent as the average gas jet, and which laid the foundation of a series of investigations, which may yet prove vastly important to mankind. He also planned first a systematic effort toward mastering the problems involved in the transmission of the heat and light of the sun to the earth, and initiated the investigations which are being made by all of the meteorological agencies of the civilized nations to find out the relation existing between the sun and the weather. Further than this, it was his research into the field of aerodynamics which made possible the flying machine of to-day. The Wright brothers have both testified that it was upon the work of Secretary Langley that they founded their efforts to solve the problem which the birds have mastered from the beginning.

The present secretary of the Institution is Charles D. Walcott, who was for many years Director of the United States Geological Survey, and organizer of the United States Reclamation Service. Mr. Walcott is one of the leading American geologists and has borne an important part in the development of the natural resources of the United States.

Perhaps the most interesting undertaking in which the Smithsonian is engaged to-day is the effort of Director C. G. Abbot, of the Astrophysical Observatory, to solve the problems of the heat and light of the sun. All life, all being, everything with which humanity is concerned, depends upon this heat and this light. Decrease the amount of heat which comes from the sun by a few degrees, and the world would become a frozen sphere, enshrouded in impenetrable darkness.

Prof. Abbot, who succeeded Dr. Langley as Director of the Observatory, after a series of investigations, declared it probable that there were certain variations in the amount of heat received from the sun at different times, and that these variations probably lie at the bottom of all weather changes on earth. So he set to work to study sunbeams. From that day to this all manner of traps have been constructed in which to catch these sunbeams and to compel them to add their mite to the sum of human knowledge about the great source of our light and life. All sorts of remarkable instruments have been made to study the sunbeams, and to measure their relative intensity. One of these is known as the bolometer, a device of Dr. Langley. His earlier instruments would record a difference of temperature as minute as a hundred-thousandth part of a degree. Later its sensitiveness was so increased that it was able to record a change as minute as the millionth part of a degree. This has been increased still further from time to time, until now the bolometers of the Astrophysical Observatory are able to detect changes in temperature even down to the hundred-millionth part of one degree. How much more sensitive this is than the human body is disclosed by the fact that few men are able to guess the temperature within five degrees.

The manner in which the bolometer is used and constructed is most interesting. It is operated upon the principle that a wire will carry less electricity when warm than when cold. Therefore, the end sought is to concentrate the light or heat waves upon a wire and register the change of the amount of electricity passing through it. The light and heat from the sun is received first by a plain mirror, which throws the beams of light into another mirror, concave in shape. This in turn concentrates the beam, which has meanwhile passed through a great prism of rock salt, as clear as glass, onto a platinum thread smaller than a spider's filament, through which a current of electricity is kept passing. The prism serves to analyze the beam into its different component colors.

Then the bolometer, placed successively in these different colors, measures their temperatures. The current is measured by a galvanometer or little balance made of a thread of spun glass, 5 inches long and as fine as a human hair. This is fastened to a support by suspending it on a thread of spun quartz, 2 feet long and a five-thousandth part of an inch in diameter. In the exact middle of the spun-glass beam is fastened a mirror as small as a pinhead, so perfectly made that every point of the mirror's side will touch when placed on a 6-foot globe. The mirror weighs no more than the hind leg of a fly.

With this instrument a change of heat no greater than that given off by a candle 5 miles away is easily recognized. By the use of a spectroscope in connection with the bolometer, Director Abbot is able to study the heat of the invisible rays of light known as the infra-red and the ultra-violet. The Astrophysical Observatory makes use of pyrheliometers and other extremely sensitive instruments in its investigations. It has constructed a standard pyrheliometer which will be recognized as such by all of the investigating agencies of the world. It maintains a station on the summit of Mount Wilson, Cal., 6,000 feet above the sea level; does occasional work upon the summit of Mount Whitney, 14,500 feet above sea level, and at Washington, near the sea level.

The work which has been done during the past two or three years leads to the belief that Dr. Langley's theories of solar radiation will be worked out, and that in the years to come mankind will be able to forecast the weather with far greater accuracy. How important the mastery of weather conditions would be can not be appreciated at first blush. The farmer would never need to plant a crop and have it overtaken by a destructive drought. Knowing what the season would be in advance, he would sow crops requiring little moisture in dry seasons, and those requiring a great deal of it in wet seasons. The railroads could make their business conform to future weather conditions, and could run their excursions at such times as rain would not interfere. No one would ever need to be caught napping by a cold wave or a great flood. Political conventions could always be held when the weather was seasonable. In a thousand ways such a system of accurate weather forecasting would prove of inestimable value to the human race.

The foregoing instances of the activities of the Smithsonian Institution in the direction of the increase of human knowledge show how effectively it has wrought in the past in increasing such knowledge as may be applied for bettering the conditions of the human race, but the officials of this Institution believe its usefulness is only well begun. They point out that the Institution is well fitted to organize and supervise investigations and explorations on which the income of $20,000,000 could be spent wisely and effectively. Its activities are not limited to investigations in the field of science and art, but it is able to make historical and ethnological researches, and statistical inquiries with reference to physical, moral, and political subjects.

One of the things it hopes to do in the future, if funds can be raised for that purpose, is to make a world-wide study of earthquakes through a national seismological laboratory under its direction. The immense destruction of life and property by large earthquakes emphasizes the importance of investigations which may be able to bring about a reduction of the damage of these great disturbances. The science of seismology is in its infancy, but enough is known to show that the hope of the successful prediction of earthquakes is not a chimera. The accurate surveys of the Coast and Geodetic Survey in California demonstrated that the great earthquake of 1906 was due to forces set up by slow movements of the land which probably had been going on for a hundred years. Having learned that such slow movements precede many large earthquakes, monuments are now being set up in California to enable scientists to discover future movements of the land which will enable them to predict the approach of the giant earth tremors.

In its efforts to increase the sum of human knowledge, the Institution aids investigators by making grants for research and exploration, supplying books, apparatus, laboratory accommodations, etc. It advises the Government in many matters of a scientific character, supports a table at the Naples Marine Zoological Station, and coöperates with all scientific bodies of national importance, such as the National Academy of Sciences and the American Association for the Advancement of Sciences. In its work of spreading knowledge, the Institution maintains three regular series of publications. One of these is its annual report, which presents a review of scientific progress during the year it covers. Another is the "Smithsonian Contributions to Knowledge," consisting of frequently issued works in each of which is published to the world some original contribution to its information, based on research. The third series is known as the "Smithsonian Miscellaneous Collections," which contains much information of great direct value to the scientist, and indirect value to the public at large. The endowment of the Institution amounts approximately to $1,000,000, from which an annual income of $58,000 a year is received.

In addition to the work of the Institution carried forward with its own funds, it has charge of activities of the Government besides the Astrophysical Observatory, which are supported by congressional appropriations. One of these is the National Museum. No better museum for scientific research is to be found anywhere in the world. Scientists from everywhere come here to study the various collections. The Division of Economic Geology contains more than half a million different exhibits, and is the world's foremost collection of its kind. One may find any sort of exhibit, from a huge meteorite weighing thousands of pounds to a few grains of sand.

No collection in the Museum is more interesting to the visitor than the anthropological exhibit.

Here one may trace human progress from the stone age down to our own twentieth century civilization. He may trace the development of the arts and sciences all through the centuries, from the day when man first became the master of fire and made his first hollowed-out log boat, down to the time when he studies the invisible rays of light and heat and crosses the ocean on a *Mauretania*. One may see the skeletons of extinct animals so large that those of the elephant seem small in comparison. He may stand under the skeleton of a huge whale, more than 80 feet long, and look through a microscope at sea shells so small that to the naked eye they seem but specks of dust.

The collection of birds contains over 180,000 specimens, nearly 70,000 eggs, and many nests. Of the 18,000 or more kinds of birds the National Museum possesses a goodly share, from humming birds to ostriches, only two families of living birds being unrepresented. Among eggs, the Museum possesses a perfect one of the giant Æpyornis, an extinct bird much larger than the ostrich, and whose eggs are occasionally exposed in the sands of Madagascar.

The collection of insects is one of the largest in the world, and here one may see various forms from all regions, as well as insects with curious habits. One of the latter is the bombardier beetle, which, when attacked, as a means of defense discharges with a distinct report an offensively smelling liquid.

ROOSEVELT LIONS IN NATIONAL MUSEUM.

THE SMITHSONIAN INSTITUTION 205

The mammal collection contains about 150,000 specimens, ranging from the smallest shrew, barely one-fourth the size of a house mouse, to the largest elephant and whale. The large skins are tanned and kept in dark cases where they will not be injured by the light, and where they can be easily examined by persons interested in their study. A few representing the more characteristic kinds are mounted. A collection which has excited much popular interest is that brought home by the naturalists of the Smithsonian African Expedition under the direction of Col. Theodore Roosevelt. It numbers about 5,000 mammals, including the giant eland, an antelope as large as an ox, never before brought to this country, and the square-lipped rhinoceros, which is now confined to regions not easily visited by sportsmen, as well as several thousand specimens of birds, reptiles, fishes, mollusks, etc.

The National Museum contains a collection of exhibits which enables the visitor to read the story of American history and American progress at a glance. Here he may see the relics of George Washington, among them his army coat and his camp kit. In another case one beholds the relics of Grant, in another those of Lincoln, and so on all the way down through the line of American men of fame. In other rooms he may behold the whole story of American railroad transportation, from the old John Bull engine down to the present day. Here is the first clumsy typewriter ever invented, and there one of the latest models of the combined writing and adding machine. A National Gallery of Art has also been established and large collections are being gathered.

An interesting work of the Smithsonian Institution, carried on under Government appropriations, is the exchange of publications authorized by Congress for those of other Governments. The proceeds of this exchange constitute an important addition to the Library of Congress. The Institution also acts as intermediary for an exchange of publications between the learned bodies and literary and scientific societies of the United States and those of other countries. Even individuals are allowed to share in its benefits. Since its establishment the Institution has handled more than 3,000,000 packages.

The work of the Bureau of American Ethnology is also directed by the Smithsonian. This bureau has been engaged in preserving for the future the languages, songs, customs, and traditions of the Indians. It has collected data concerning 60 linguistic stocks of Indians and upward of 300 tribes. It has done much in the exploration and preservation of American antiquities and their protection from vandalism. The National Zoological Park, at Washington, with an area of 167 acres and a collection of nearly 1,500 animals, is maintained under the supervision of the Smithsonian.

One of the most interesting works in which the Smithsonian is engaged, as the agent of the Government, is that of acting as the regional bureau of the International Catalogue of Scientific Literature. This great catalogue began with the beginning of the present century, and each year there are published 17 volumes, in which are catalogued every contribution to scientific knowledge made in every country of the world. Over 10,000 pages are annually required to list these contributions according to authors and subjects. To have one consolidated index of all the doings of mankind in the field of science is to possess one of the most valuable of all aids to human endeavor. The International Catalogue aims not only to cite the title and the author of every scientific book and paper published in the entire world, but briefly to supply an analytical digest of the subject-matter of each. This is accomplished in a most ingenious way. Letters are made to represent heads and figures subheads, and by these figures the users of the index can determine at once what subjects are treated in each contribution cited. This great publication, growing at a rate that will make 1,700 volumes by the end of the present century, is not a money-making scheme. In fact, there is no provision whatever for the use of any surplus that might accrue from its publication and sale. It is purely a permanent establishment of world cooperation, with no other aim than to support itself and to become invaluable to the human race. It has commanded the active cooperation of nearly every civilized Government. Each nation prepares the index of its current scientific literature for the year. The work of the United States is done at the Smithsonian Institution. After these national indexes are prepared they are sent to London, where the central bureau is located, and there they are each year consolidated into the one huge index of 17 volumes. In the regional bureau of the United States every scientific publication in the country is gone through as with a fine-tooth comb for scientific matters. Then recourse is had to every published index, to make sure that nothing has been overlooked. Every stone of literature that may cover some scientific truth is turned in the patient search for new matter.

The bureau at the Smithsonian furnishes between 25,000 and 30,000 references a year, which cover approximately one-eighth of the scientific work of the world. Millions of dollars are being spent every year in scientific investigation and many of the foremost men of the day are devoting their entire time to such work. It has remained for this index to make all of this endeavor available to scientific men and the world at large. It is interesting to note that this great undertaking is the result of a suggestion made in 1855 by Professor Joseph Henry, the first secretary of the Smithsonian Institution.

CHAPTER XVII.

THE PANAMA CANAL.

No other engineering undertaking in the entire history of the world compares with that of digging the Panama Canal. It required 100,000 men 20 years to build the pyramid of Cheops; a hole deep enough to bury 12 such pyramids is made in a year at Panama. It required nearly a score of years to build the Suez Canal; as much dirt is excavated at Panama in 12 months. The Manchester Ship Canal was a number of years in building; that task is duplicated in 15 months at Panama.

It took the French as many years to discover that they could not build a 15-foot canal as it will take the United States to make it a finished waterway 40 feet deep; and it cost the French as much to make a failure of their project as it will cost the United States to make a success of its undertaking.

Chief Engineer George W. Goethals has made himself the greatest digger in history. In four years he excavated enough material to make a monument of dirt with a base larger than the height of the Washington Monument and towering far into the regions of perpetual snow. This material would fill a modern dirt train long enough to girdle the globe two-and-a-half times. When Uncle Sam took hold of the work of building the canal it was figured that it would require nine years to excavate 105,000,000 yards of dirt; at the rate the work is now progressing he will have moved 165,000,000 yards in five years. The cost of excavating a yard of dirt in Culebra Cut has been reduced from 11.5 cents to 8.88 cents. The distance the excavated material is hauled increased from 8 to 12 miles in two years, but the cost of hauling it was reduced from 18.54 cents a yard to 15.22 cents.

Measured in the results which will follow the completion of the undertaking, the work at Panama stands in a class by itself. Cities which are to-day mere way stations on the international routes of trade will grow into rich world centers. The East will be brought 8,000 miles closer to the West. Eighty million tons of freight a year may be carried through the canal without overtaxing its facilities.

The most extensive part of the work of constructing the Panama Canal is that of actually digging the big ditch. The material which must come out of it represents an amount equivalent to that which would be required to make a canal through level ground from Washington to New York large enough to float a *Lusitania*. The two ends of the big waterway are simply sea-level ditches from deep water in the Atlantic and the Pacific, a distance of 7 miles to Gatun on the Atlantic side and 8 miles to Miraflores on the Pacific side.

Think of a single landslide, with a superficial area of 47 acres, slipping foot by foot into the canal! Yet the canal diggers, when they encounter such an unexpected difficulty, simply redouble their efforts and declare they will not permit it to delay the opening of the canal one single hour! Think of loading a 20-car dirt train with 800 tons of material with less than a hundred shovelfuls of dirt! Think of exploding a single blast of 20 tons of dynamite and tearing loose 70,000 yards of earth and stone! These are some of the things which show how gigantic is the undertaking.

The middle section of the canal, 34 miles long, has a water level 85 feet higher than the sections from Gatun and Miraflores to the sea. The canal diggers are damming up the Chagres River at Gatun so as to make a great lake, cutting a great ditch through the Culebra Mountain so as to permit the water of this lake to back up to a depth of 40 feet through the mountain. This requires a dam at Gatun which will make the lake 85 feet deep at that point. This dam is approximately a mile-and-a-half long, a half mile wide at the bottom, 400 feet wide at the water line, and a hundred feet wide at the top. Its total height will be 115 feet, or 30 feet higher than the surface of the water in the lake it creates. It covers 288 acres of land.

Its slope is so gradual as hardly to be noticed in the landscape. Take a yardstick and raise one end 3 inches higher than the other, and the resulting slope will be considerably steeper than the average slope of the Gatun Dam. When completed the dam will contain some 20,000,000 yards of material, which is being put into place at the rate of more than 5,000,000 yards a year. Construction was begun by building two parallel lines of stone retaining walls across the valley, 1,200 feet apart. Between these two walls millions of cubic yards of sand and clay are being pumped into large ponds maintained at the crest of the dam. The water deposits its load of solid matter and flows off to be pumped up again with another load. The natural cement held in suspension by the dredged water tightens up every tiny space as a brick mason might close a hole in the wall.

One of the problems which the engineers have had to encounter in building the Gatun Dam is that of disposing of the vast amount of surplus water which comes down the Chagres. This is a moody stream, sometimes quiet and shallow and at other times a torrential river with a sustained flow of 137,000 cubic feet of water a second. How to build a spillway that will pass such an enormous amount of water from the lake surface to the sea level, 85 feet below, has been a difficult problem to solve. The lake has been made so big, covering 164 square miles of superficial surface, that the Chagres on its greatest rampage might flow into it for more than five hours and yet raise its level only 1 foot; the water level may be raised 7 feet without doing damage.

The Chagres now crosses the line of the canal 23 times on its 23-mile journey from Gamboa, where it first strikes the big waterway, to Gatun. When the Gatun Dam is completed the river will lose itself in the waters of the lake at Gamboa. The spillway over which the surplus water of the Gatun Lake will flow consists of a huge crescent-shaped dam of concrete surmounted by 13 large piers and 2 big abutments, which divide the dam into 14 openings, each of which will be opened and closed by giant gates.

Almost every method of excavating known to the engineering world is brought into use in digging the Panama Canal. At the entrance on each side of the Isthmus giant seagoing suction dredges collect the material and carry it out to sea. On each side of one of these dredges are huge 20-inch suckers, operated by centrifugal pumps, which work with such tremendous suction power that they pick up such things as pieces of anchor chains.

In the Culebra Cut the steam shovel is king, and dynamite by the carload is used. More than a million pounds of explosives are fired off every month in the canal works, the major portion of which is used at Culebra. In some of the big blasts 25 or more wells are dug by machines operated by the largest air-compressor plant in the world, and into each of these holes the major portion of a ton of dynamite is placed, and then the whole thing is touched off by pressing an electric button.

In another place hydraulic excavation is resorted to. Here one sees a great pumping station capable of forcing 30,000 gallons of water a minute through a pipe which tapers from 40 to 16 inches in diameter. To this are attached four or five flexible water nozzles through which are forced streams of water from 4 to 6 inches in diameter, with a pressure of 130 pounds to the square inch. These streams of water literally eat the dirt away.

The canal would be of no use were there not a method of getting ships from the sea level to the lake level, 85 feet above, and vice versa. To accomplish this purpose giant marine stairways are being built. These are constructed like a double-track railway, so that one ship may be going up while another is going down. There are three steps in the stairway at Gatun on the Atlantic side. On the Pacific side there is one step at Pedro Miguel and two at Miraflores. At each step a ship is lifted up or down slightly more than 28 feet. The two side-by-side locks, including the outside walls, are approximately 380 feet wide. They are separated by an inside wall or partition, which is 60 feet thick. Running lengthwise through the outside walls and the middle partition are great culverts, or concrete pipe lines, which are almost large enough to serve as tunnels for a double-track railroad. Connecting with these three huge tunnels are a series of smaller ones, 8 feet in diameter, which run across the locks under their floors. These open through the floors of the locks in a series of holes, each 2 feet in diameter.

The water is first admitted into the big tunnels, and passes from them into smaller ones beneath the floors of the locks, and from them into the lock itself. When a ship seeks to pass out of Gatun Lake to the sea level, the upper gates are opened and electric towing locomotives pull it into the first lock. Then the gates are closed behind it, and the valves in the tunnel are so arranged that the water passes out of the upper lock, down through the holes in the floor, then through the small tunnels, then through the large ones, and then into the next lock below. As soon as the water in this lock rises to the level of the water in the lock above, the gate between them is opened and the ship is towed into the lower lock. This operation is repeated until the vessel finds itself 85 feet lower than it was when the process of lockage began.

The lock machinery is operated by electricity generated at Gatun Dam. The world's most elaborate system of protecting the locks from injury has been resorted to. When a ship approaches the upper lock, it encounters a huge steel chain, each end fastened to a giant hydraulic jack. After the vessel is stopped, it will be met by four large towing locomotives on narrow-gauge racktracks. Two of these will hitch to its bow and two to its stern, the two in front pulling it forward and the two behind preventing it from moving too rapidly. At every vital point in the lock system there will be a duplicate set of gates, their weight varying from 300 to 600 tons. Each gate is composed of two leaves, hinged to the side walls of the lock like an ordinary pair of one-way double doors, except that they do not shut straight across the stream, but come together like a flattened V, with the apex pointing upstream. They will be opened and closed by a huge arm weighing 130,000 pounds and having a diameter of 16 inches.

In addition to all the other precautions to insure the safety of the locks, there is an emergency dam provided. It consists of a large cantilever bridge mounted on a pivot base on the side wall of the upper end of the uppermost lock. In case everything went wrong and the water in the lake should begin to rush out through the locks at the destructive speed of 28 feet a second, this bridge would be turned across the lock, and a set of girders made of the hardest nickel steel, would be let down, one end fast to the bridge, and the other engaging an offset in the lock floor. Each of these girders would make a sort of inclined rail-

THE PANAMA CANAL 217

way, on which huge sheets of steel, mounted on roller bearings, would be let down to check the current.

The work of building the six locks required for the canal is proceeding with unexampled dispatch. It requires over 2,000,000 barrels of cement, and as many cubic yards of stone and sand, to build the locks at each end of the canal. The concrete handling plants are the largest of their kinds in the world. At Gatun clamshell buckets, carried on big cableways and operated entirely by machinery, unload the rock and sand from the barges. It is then loaded on automatic electric cars in exact portions, and is carried to the big concrete mixers which handle more than two 2-horse loads at a time. The cars on the double-tracked circular electric railway need no motormen. The current is so regulated that their speed is kept constant at about 3 miles an hour. Boys cut off the switch of each car as it reaches its stopping place. When the concrete is mixed it is dumped into big buckets mounted on flat cars drawn by small electric locomotives. These haul two buckets to a point under a big cableway, by which they are carried to the place where the material is to be dumped.

One of the remarkable circumstances connected with the construction of the canal is the great increase in working efficiency that has taken place. A ton of dynamite is now made to do twice as much work as it did two years ago. Expert attention given to the use of the lubricating oil alone has resulted in the saving of $6,000 a year. By shaking the cement out of the empty bags and returning them to the manufacturers, $50,000 a month is saved. In a hundred ways efficiency has been developed with the result that the canal army has a record of an average annual excavation of 32,000,000 cubic yards, as compared with a predicted average of less than 12,000,000 yards.

The United States owns, in connection with the work of building the canal, the Panama Railroad, which is 47 miles long and has net earnings, including the steamship line it operates, of nearly $2,000,000 a year. The French bought the road for $18,000,000 and sold it to the United States for $7,000,000. The road has been relocated and has a larger number of embankments in proportion to its length than any other railway in the world, one of them being 82 feet high, more than a mile long, and containing nearly 3,000,000 yards of dirt and rock. This railroad carries nearly 2,500,000 passengers a year.

Nine thousand Americans live on the Canal Zone, of whom more than half are in the actual employ of the Canal Commission or the Panama Railroad. They command wages 50 per cent higher than those obtained in the United States; their clothes cost much less; their food is bought at cost; they get houses rent free, free light, free medical service, free transportation to free schools for their children.

THE PANAMA CANAL 219

The bulk of the manual labor on the canal is performed by West Indian negroes who are paid 90 cents a day. These negroes are given the privilege of free lodging and are furnished three square meals a day for 10 cents each. Often one sees one of these negroes with nothing in either hand and carrying an umbrella or a letter on his head. Once a new gang of them were set to the work of hauling away dirt with a wheelbarrow. Three of them filled up the wheelbarrow, after which one stooped down and the other two placed it upon his head to be borne away.

Arrangements are now being made for the fortification of the canal. This will consist of large forts at each end of the canal, in each of which will be placed four 14-inch rifles, six 6-inch guns, and twelve 12-inch mortars. Twelve companies of Coast Artillery, four regiments of Infantry, one battalion of Field Artillery, and a squadron of Cavalry will be stationed here in time of peace. The fortifications are expected to cost $12,000,000.

Chief Engineer George W. Goethals is already making arrangements for the operation of the canal. It is thought that the tolls will be fixed at a dollar a ton, which will be cheaper than going through the Suez Canal, around Cape Horn, or the Cape of Good Hope. The cream of the present force will be retained for the operation of the canal. It is intended to utilize the present laundry facilities, baking establishments, coaling plants, machine shops, and everything else now in operation which will promote traffic through the canal after it is built.

One may gather some idea of the cost and of the magnitude of the operations at Panama from the statement that it requires over 200 tons of silver and 9 tons of gold to pay off the canal force. The employees are paid monthly, and payments are made wholly in gold and silver.

The Canal Zone affords the finest example of preventive medicine and public sanitation in the world. The death rate has been cut more than in half since the beginning of the American occupation. Something of the excellence of the work of sanitation may be inferred from the statement that if the United States spent as much for sanitary purposes in proportion to population as is spent in the Canal Zone and in the cities of Panama and Colon, it would spend $1,200,000,000 a year for such purposes. If we spent as much at home in proportion to area as we spend at Panama, the annual outlay would approximate $12,000,000,000.

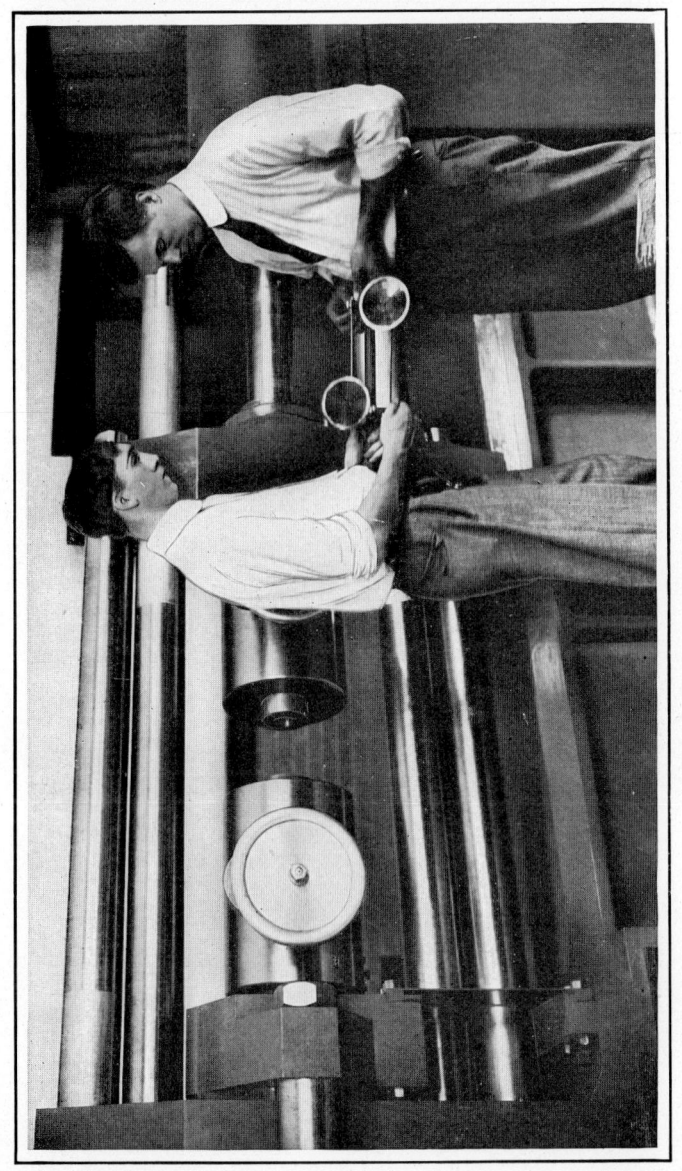

TESTING STEEL FOR THE PANAMA CANAL.

CHAPTER XVIII.

THE INTERSTATE COMMERCE COMMISSION.

REGULATING as it does the affairs of common carrier corporations having an annual income of approximately $4,000,000,000, the Interstate Commerce Commission is one of the most important of the independent branches of the Government service. It has governmental supervision over all of the common carriers of the United States which do an interstate-commerce business, and which are included in the definition of common carriers written in the interstate-commerce law. This not only includes the railroads doing an interstate business, but also such steamboat lines as operate in interstate commerce in connection with railroads, under common control, management, or arrangement. It also includes the interstate operations of the express companies, sleeping-car companies, telegraph, cable and telephone companies, wireless-telegraph companies, and pipe lines carrying other commodities than water and gas. The railway lines which it regulates have an aggregate mileage of more than 250,000 miles. They carry annually some 900,000,000 passengers and more than 1,500,000,000 tons of freight. The distance which these passengers are carried is equivalent approximately to 30,000,000,000 miles for one passenger, and the freight transportation is equivalent to the task of carrying 1 ton of freight more than 200,000,000,000 miles. The average ton of freight is moved 1 mile for less than 1 cent.

Much of the time of the Commission is taken up in the interpretation of interstate-commerce laws for the benefit of shippers and carriers. A court will not answer a hypothetical question or decide an imaginary case, but the Interstate Commerce Commission will turn aside from the red tape of legal procedure and give all parties interested the best information it possesses with reference to matters over which it has jurisdiction. If a question arises which involves matters of common interest or frequent rulings, general rules are published informally and the opinions of the Commission are printed and placed in the hands of all who need them. By this means a comprehensive code of rules is in process of development, the observance of which will operate to promote just and impartial conduct on the part of both shippers and carriers.

One of the principal functions of the Commission is to settle differences between the common carriers and their patrons. In doing this, it receives two kinds of complaints—formal and informal. Informal complaints are largely in the majority. About 4,000 complaints of this nature are filed annually. These complaints may be filed by any citizen having a grievance against a common carrier. They may reach the Commission simply in the form of a letter stating the grievance. If the complaint is found to be justified, after an informal investigation, the offending carrier receives a recommendation from the Commission that it remove the ground of complaint. These complaints range all the way from an alleged overcharge for a railroad ticket to an unsatisfactory method of handling thousands of tons of coal. They involve no expense to the persons filing them, and usually result in a satisfactory adjustment of the matters at issue.

Formal complaints cover every sort of subject from a claim for reparation involving a few dollars, to a complaint against the entire tariff of a railroad, involving millions, or the practices and regulations of a large number of carriers. Sometimes individuals and corporations make these complaints. At other times cities and towns make them.

During an average year approximately 800 formal complaints are filed with the Commission, and a like number are disposed of. Every one of these complaints is made public at the time it is filed. The chief clerk of the Interstate Commerce Commission has a table in his office, and as the complaints come in they are placed there for inspection by the representatives of newspapers all over the country who visit the offices of the Commission to daily obtain information. After the complaints have thus been made public, and notice served on interested parties, the Commission sets a date for hearing both sides of the questions involved. During a recent year over 700 hearings and investigations were made. A large number of these were held in Washington, though the Commission or certain of its members go to various parts of the country to hold hearings when it is not convenient for the interested parties and their witnesses to come to Washington. During a single year as many as 70,000 pages of testimony are taken, exclusive of voluminous exhibits. If the pressure of business requires it, the duty of holding hearings may be performed by special examiners designated by the Commission. After these hearings have been held and the testimony is printed, the commissioners study it and then announce their decision. Since the establishment of the Commerce Court, the decision of the Interstate Commerce Commission may be appealed from to that court by either party to the controversy, although in many cases the action of the Commission is taken as final.

Every common carrier subject to the act is required to file every interstate freight and passenger rate it makes with the Interstate Commerce Commission. During an average year the tariff publications so filed may amount to more than 175,000. The law provides that no tariff shall become effective until 30 days after notice is given, except with the permission of the Interstate Commerce Commission. Sometimes it is desirable that a certain rate may be established upon short notice, and during an average year about 4,000 such applications are acted upon by the Commission.

Perhaps the most far-reaching and fundamentally important power conferred on the Commission is the authority to suspend proposed advances in rates pending investigation of their reasonableness. The Commission must constantly be on guard to see that rate changes of contemplated orders do not adversely affect contests in great cases. In order more readily to determine all rate matters, the Commission is trying to secure a standard or uniform classification of all freight. Many thousands of articles must be described in order that a complete system of uniform classification may be put into use.

The Commission is required by law to report to the Attorney General all cases that come to its notice of violations of the criminal sections of the interstate-commerce laws. During an average year there are about 50 such prosecutions, in four-fifths of which pleas of guilty are entered. The penalties assessed range from $100 to $120,000, and the aggregate amounts to more than $200,000 a year. In the case of the Hocking Valley Railroad and the Sunday Creek Coal Company it was found that the railroad extended credit to the coal company to an unprecedented extent, more than $2,000,000 of freight bills being left unpaid.

The Government indicted both the shipper and the carrier on the theory that such an extension of credit was in itself a departure from the published tariff, and also, that when given to some shippers and not to others, it is a discrimination.

Another duty of the Commission is that of supervising the accounts of the railroads and other common carriers of the country, and of gathering statistics relative to their operation. Realizing that unless a uniform system of accounting be adopted, it would be impossible for the Commission to do its work efficiently, Congress clothed it with authority to require the institution of a uniform system of accounting. All accounts of every common carrier subject to the act must be kept according to classifications prescribed by the Commission, and it is a punishable offense for any carrier to keep any other record whatever than those prescribed or approved by the Commission. This uniform system of accounting requires common carriers to enter all records of their operation in such a way that the Commission may know all about every dollar they receive, where it comes from, and where it goes.

This provision is intended to prevent such unfair and unlawful practices as charging up to operating expenses money used in making a common carrier's property more valuable. Every common carrier subject to the act must file a monthly statement of all its operations, and a final annual statement, which must agree entirely with the sum of the monthly statements for the year. In its investigations of the express companies of the country the Interstate Commerce Commission has produced some interesting facts concerning their operations. The figures show that more than 70,000,000 pieces of express matter were handled in 3 months, that the average weight per piece was slightly less than 33 pounds, and that the average revenue per pound was 1.54 cents.

Among the more important duties of the Interstate Commerce Commission is that of fixing rates. This is a most difficult problem, and one on which a vast deal of conflicting evidence is produced in every case. The railroads themselves often make very contradictory statements concerning this question. In a recent State controversy the railroads affected declared that it would cost $100,000 a mile to reproduce their property. Only a few months before they had sworn to the tax collector that these properties could be reproduced for $25,000 a mile.

The law requires that the railroads shall not charge an "unreasonable rate," and what would be a reasonable schedule of rates if the road cost $25,000 a mile might be an unremunerative schedule to the railroad company if it cost $100,000 a mile. It is believed by many that nothing but an actual physical valuation of railroad property can furnish a satisfactory basis for declaring what a reasonable rate is, and until such a valuation is possible, the next best thing is to maintain a current compilation of all significant facts bearing upon the construction of railroads, and upon their operating, financial, and other relations. This work is being done by the Division of Statistics of the Commission. The Commission also gathers independent information concerning cases in which witnesses for the plaintiff and the defendant have testified, so as to be able to determine for itself the truth of the testimony.

The Commission requires all railroads to give adequate reports of accidents, and has power to investigate upon its own initiative all collisions, derailments, or other accidents. During a recent year there were 450 passengers killed and 15,000 injured. During the same year there were upward of 3,000 employees killed and nearly 70,000 injured. Congress has gradually been forcing the railroads to adopt safety appliances which tend to reduce the dangers of railway operation. In 1893, 77 out of each thousand men engaged in coupling and uncoupling cars, in the employ of the railroads of the country, were injured, as compared with 16 fifteen years later. The railroads long opposed the proposition that they should be required to equip their trains with power brakes and automatic couplers. The importance of requiring automatic couplers is disclosed by the fact that during a recent year 207 deaths and 3,002 injuries to employees were caused by coupling accidents. During the same year nearly 600 deaths and more than 13,000 injuries resulted from employees falling from cars. The requirements that train crews shall mount cars to operate hand brakes still prevails upon some railroads to a greater or less extent. The Commission has the power to designate all safety appliances that shall be used and the manner of their placing such as grab irons, ladders, hand brakes, and running boards.

One of the problems with which the Interstate Commerce Commission is now dealing is that of investigating all safety devices in the way of block signals and train control. More than a thousand different plans of devices intended to promote the safety of railway operations have been submitted for examination to the Block Signal and Train Control Board organized by the Commission. These devices apply to signals, automatic train control, ties, rails, switches, and other plans for making railway transportation safer. One of the things which the board is looking for is a really efficient and always reliable block signal. There are hundreds of signaling devices which will warn a train crew when everything goes right, but as soon as something becomes wrong with their own apparatus they are likely to give the train crew a track-clear signal when they ought to display the danger sign. In other words, the really safe block signal is the one which will warn of its own defects, as well as of dangers ahead. The average block-signal device puts up the danger signal when there is another train in the block, and works all right so long as there is no break in its mechanism. In devices of this kind the danger signal goes up only when there is a current of electricity passing through the wire. When the current is cut off or the wire is broken by accident or malicious design, the semaphore shows clear. Thus, if a malicious person were to tamper with the apparatus or if it should in any other way get out of order and fail to carry the current of electricity through, the semaphores would signal clear, no matter what dangers might be ahead. The closed-circuit apparatus overcomes this. In such apparatus the semaphore always stands at danger when there is no current on, and can be placed at clear only by the application of a current. If anything goes wrong with this apparatus, the semaphore automatically sets itself at danger, and warns the oncoming train. No matter what goes wrong, as soon as the electric current ceases to pass through the apparatus it can be depended upon to stand guard at the block with its danger signal in view. It may sometimes stop a train when there is no real danger ahead, but it is certain never to advise an engineer that the track ahead of him is clear when it is in reality obstructed. The engineer of a fast-moving train must accept the instructions of the signal, and with the open-circuit signal has no means of knowing whether it is telling the truth or not when showing clear.

In addition to the block-signal investigation, there is the proposition of controlling trains by automatic agents. It is hoped a device may be found by which a train can be stopped on the safe side of the danger line even though the engineer be asleep or dead at his post. Such an apparatus must not only work well on paper, but it must show up satisfactorily under practical tests. Hundreds of different devices have been submitted to the Train Control Board, but few of them have had merit enough even to warrant a trial. One of the most interesting devices which has been studied and tried out provides an automatic record of the movement of all trains within each 10 or 20 blocks, and in addition to this provides automatic protection locally for all the trains. In each locomotive cab there is a bell and a light, giving both an audible and a visible danger signal. Besides this there is an automatic recording device, which registers the action of the engineer in response to this signal and the time of that action. If he reverses his engine and puts on the emergency brake, that action is automatically registered. If he fails to do so, that fact is shown, and the brakes are automatically applied by the apparatus. The device also provides a means of interlocking manual control, which is so arranged as to make any false movement improbable. There is a little lever projecting up from the track when in position, which comes into contact with another lever on the engine, and automatically puts on the air brakes and stops the train if the engineer fails to obey the signals.

The outcome of the investigation of the Block Signal and Train Control Board will probably be that as soon as the inventions which stand the test of practical operation prove their merit, a report will be made to Congress favoring the enactment of a law requiring all railroads to equip their trains and lines with these protections against the element of human error, which is always present in railroad operations. There will be opposition on the part of the railroads to the enactment of such a law, as a matter of course. There was opposition to the enactment of the safety-appliance law, but it is probable that the number of lives that have been saved by this law and the consequent falling off in the number of damage suits against the railroads have more than reimbursed the railroads for their expenditure in equipping their trains with air brakes and automatic couplings.

A law was enacted a few years ago compelling all railroads doing an interstate business to equip their engines with ash pans such as would overcome the necessity for firemen to go under their locomotives to remove ashes. Another law which is of recent enactment is the one that requires all locomotive boilers to be inspected. Many people have been killed and much property has been lost by the explosion of the boilers of engines in the yards and on the roads. The new law is similar to the one which provides for the inspection of all steamboats carrying passengers and of their boilers. The country is laid off into a number of districts, with an inspector for each of these districts. The chief of the inspection service is appointed by the President, and he has considerable assistance besides the district inspectors throughout the country. It is probable that a careful list of specifications will be drawn up, and that the locomotive manufacturer will have to submit the materials entering into the construction of the boilers to the boiler inspectors. In addition to this, engines in service will be inspected at frequent intervals and tests will be made to determine whether or not they may be safely used. When a locomotive is condemned by the inspectors, it will be sent to the scrap heap or to the repair shop.

Another activity of the Commission has to do with the enforcement of the provisions of a law which forbids railroad employees connected with the movement of trains to be on duty more than a specified number of hours in any 24. This law will not allow a railroad man to work extra hours, even though he desires to make the extra pay such extra work carries with it.

Any member of the Commission may be named by the President, under what is known as the Erdmann Act, to cooperate with the Commissioner of Labor in any effort to settle any differences which may arise between railroads and their employees. This measure has resulted in the arbitration of many disputes between the railroads and the men in their employ.

It seems certain that as the years go by stricter regulation of the common carriers of the country will be the policy of Congress. The duty of supervising the enforcement of the laws regulating them will fall upon the Interstate Commerce Commission, and as nothing affects the people more intimately than transportation, the work of this Commission will be felt by every citizen more or less directly.

CHAPTER XIX.

OUR INSULAR POSSESSIONS.

FEW Americans realize the fact that the United States owns and exercises jurisdiction over more than 3,000 of the islands of the sea, whose aggregate population is upward of 10,000,000, and the combined area of which is more than 700,000 square miles.

The Philippine Islands and Porto Rico are largely autonomous, framing their own laws under the liberal provisions of their respective organic acts passed by Congress, subject to review by Congress. The affairs of these islands are administered by the Bureau of Insular Affairs of the War Department, through which information respecting them is disseminated.

The islands of the Philippine group number 3,141, and have a total land area of nearly 125,000 square miles, approximately that of the six New England States, New York, and New Jersey. There are some 8,000,000 people in the Philippines, about seven and one-half million of whom are civilized, Christian people, the Filipinos being the only Christian people in the Orient. The remainder of the inhabitants of the islands are Mohammedans and pagans who maintained autocratic forms of tribal government until recently.

The whole of the Archipelago is now under civil government, but in some of the islands the civil offices are occupied by military officers. The Central Government is composed of the Governor General, and eight commissioners, four of whom are Americans and four Filipinos. This Commission is the upper house of the Philippine Legislature, the lower house being the Philippine Assembly, elected by the people and composed at present entirely of Filipinos. This legislature has general legislative authority in the islands, except over that part inhabited by Moros or other non-Christian tribes, over which the Philippine Commission has sole legislative authority. The legislature elects two Resident Commissioners to the United States, who have seats in Congress. The United States has gradually extended to the people of the Philippine Islands such participation in the government of the islands as they have shown themselves able intelligently to exercise.

At the beginning of each session of the Philippine Legislature, the Governor General sends a message to that body, which corresponds to the message of the President of the United States to Congress, concerning finances, pending matters, and desired legislation. A summer capital is being built at Baguio, such as that at Simla, India. All progressive tropical countries maintain a resort at an altitude which insures a cool and recuperative climate to which the offices of the Government may be temporarily removed during the heated season, which is beneficial not only to those suffering from disease, but also to those enjoying good health. Construction on the Government buildings was started in 1909 and has continued as rapidly as the finances of the Philippines would permit. The other improvements include a large number of cottages and two large dormitories. With the extension of the railroad into Baguio, now contracted for, the value of Baguio will be greatly enhanced to the Filipinos. It is one of the possibilities of the future that a university may be built there.

The annual report of the Philippine Commission makes a number of recommendations to Congress respecting enabling legislation which it deems necessary for the islands, and the Governor General in his annual message to the legislature calls attention to the fact that Manila is one of the few large cities of the world of great importance which has no gas plant and recommends that the legislature grant a properly guarded franchise to parties who, he understands, are ready to construct such a plant.

The Governor General has oversight of the administration of all public affairs in the islands. He has under his executive control and supervision the Executive Bureau, the Bureau of Audits, the Bureau of Civil Service, as well as the provincial and municipal governments, including the city of Manila. He has the power of parole and pardon, may change the boundary of any province, municipality, or other political subdivision, and may close or open certain ports of entry.

One of the chief officials directly under the Governor General is the executive secretary, who has duties assigned to him which are combined in no one official in our Government. The executive control vested in the Central Government of the Philippine Islands over provincial and municipal governments is exercised directly by the Governor General through the executive secretary. He also conducts much of the correspondence of the Governor General in his name.

The man who has some of the most arduous work of the whole governmental service in the Philippine Islands is the secretary of the interior. One of the problems which confronts him is that of control over and development of the more or less uncivilized tribes, all of which widely differ in customs, dialect, and pursuits, and even in race. With more than half a million of these people, many of whom formerly practiced head-hunting and had little respect for justice or right as it was practiced on them, the problem of winning their friendship and cooperation has been a most difficult one. Until the advent of the Americans, these people were exploited commercially by the Spaniards and more intelligent Filipinos, but under the present form of civil government they have come to look upon the Americans with genuine regard as friends who will protect them in their rights as well as sternly punish them when they offend. Through this means of attraction, impartial justice, and the gradual growth of confidence, the American influence is being extended farther and farther into the hitherto trackless and inaccessible regions, bringing more and more of them into peaceful occupations, and lessening every day the depredations and intertribal conflicts of the past. The sharply drawn tribal lines of old are disappearing, and Igorots, Ifugaos, and Kalingas now visit each other's territory in peace and meet in friendly contests of strength and skill. The practice of head-hunting as a method of settling quarrels or gaining prestige is lessening, and the use of the courts and appeals to the American governor are becoming more and more the method of settling disputes. In many instances, these people are being successfully employed to police their own country. Unspeakably filthy towns have been made clean and sanitary, and they are learning to come to a physician when injured or ill.

The Filipinos feel that they ought to be permitted to govern the uncivilized tribes. The Americans reply to this by saying that there is no basis for this claim, either in justice or expediency, and by calling attention to the fact that wherever the people of these tribes have been under the jurisdiction of the local Filipino government, they have not been protected in their rights or helped to a higher plane of human existence. These tribes even hint at offering armed resistance to any attempt to take them from under the direct supervision and control of the American officials.

The Interior Department of the Philippines covers a large range of activity. One of the bureaus under its charge is that of Health. It operates the Philippine General Hospital, the civil hospital, and a number of other hospitals throughout the Archipelago. It is now engaged in using the moving-picture show as a method of bringing a knowledge of the necessity of sanitary surroundings to the people of the Philippines. It is also engaged in taking care of the public cemeteries of the islands, by enforcing regulations with reference to their establishment and proper maintenance. Under these regulations one no longer sees in the Provinces a local cemetery assuming the form of a tropical jungle partially inclosed by broken fences which permit hogs and dogs to despoil the shallow graves of the dead. The Bureau of Health also maintains free dispensaries, and otherwise looks after the health of the people.

Owing to incomplete returns, vital statistics are yet restricted to Manila. The death rate per thousand among Filipinos in Manila is very high, being 47.65 for 1910, as against 12.05 for Spaniards, 13.27 for Americans, 14.32 for other occidentals, and 16.64 for Chinese. Two-thirds of this shocking Filipino mortality is among children of less than 5 years of age, and if it were not for the remarkably high birth rate they would eventually die out. In Manila nearly 50 children to every thousand of population are born annually. While complete and fairly reliable vital statistics are not yet available for the Philippine Islands as a whole, the facts relative to Government employees are definitely known. The death rate among them for the fiscal year 1910 was but 5.82 per thousand. Insurance companies now write insurance for residents of these islands on the same terms as they would give them in the United States.

Cholera epidemics in the Philippines are growing fewer each year, and leprosy is being rapidly wiped out. The total number of lepers in the islands to-day is placed at 2,272, as against approximately 4,700 when the work of segregating them began. The bureau maintains a leper colony on an isolated island, in which the patients are given all possible liberty and diversion, and every possible effort is being made to find some method of successfully treating this dread disease. The real plague of the Philippines is said to be tuberculosis, and a widespread campaign is being instituted to put an end to its ravages. A Marine Quarantine Service is also maintained under the direction of the Interior Department, as are also a Forestry Service, a Bureau of Science, a Weather Bureau, and a Bureau of Lands.

Millions of acres of public lands are subject to homesteading in the Philippines, but the homesteads taken up amount to less than 2,000 a year. One of the principal ailments of the Philippines in an economic sense is that they are "land poor." Under the legislation now existing, no individual may homestead or purchase more than 40 acres of public land from the Government. The average area of all applications for free patents received is only approximately 8 acres. A corporation may now purchase not more than 2,500 acres of public land. The commission has recommended to Congress that the limit for homesteading be increased to 125 acres, and that the limit purchasable by an individual be increased to 1,250 acres, and by a corporation be increased to 15,000 acres, in order to encourage the establishment of large plantations with modern equipment and permit the development of the country.

Another of the departments of the Philippine Government is that of Commerce and Police. It has supervision over the bureaus of Constabulary, Public Works, Navigation, Posts, Coast and Geodetic Survey, and Labor, and the offices of Consulting Architect and the Supervising Railway Expert In addition to this, it is charged with the general supervision of all corporations other than building and loan associations, banks, and trust companies.

The Philippine Constabulary is one of the most interesting bodies of police in the world. A large number of men who constitute the constabulary were head-hunting savages only a few years ago. They are thoroughly loyal to the United States, and are of immense aid to the American Government in maintaining peace and prosperity in the islands.

A postal-savings bank and an insular telegraph and cable system are maintained in connection with the postal service of the islands. The postal-savings bank had 13,000 active accounts in 1910, and the number of depositors is increasing at the rate of over 4,000 a year. Nearly two-thirds of the depositors are Filipinos.

The Bureau of Public Works awards large prizes to the Provinces maintaining the best road systems. A prize of $5,000 is awarded to the Province having the best maintained and most complete system of first-class roads, and a similar prize is given for the second-class roads and for the greatest expenditure for roads and bridges proportionate to revenue receipts.

The Department of Finance and Justice has charge of the courts, the enforcement of the law, the collection of internal revenue and of customs receipts, together with the other financial operations of the islands.

The Department of Public Instruction is training the Filipinos to use the English language. A larger proportion of the population is now speaking English than were speaking Spanish at the time the Americans entered the islands. The Bureau of Agriculture and the prison administration are also under the direction of the Department of Public Instruction. Bilibid Prison, at Manila, is one of the largest in the world. It is regarded as one of the most progressive prisons possessed by any country.

A penal colony is maintained on a reservation of 360 square miles on the island of Palawan, in the south, where there are about 1,000 convicts, many of whom have their wives with them. Firearms are not permitted on the reservation, and there are no guards, jails, or prisons, yet peace and order are maintained as satisfactorily as in any ordinary community. These convicts have a sort of government of their own and are given considerable liberty, being permitted to engage in agriculture and other pursuits. Almost without exception they have not abused the liberties given them.

All of the various services in connection with the conduct of the Government in the Philippine Islands are paid for entirely out of Philippine revenues.

The island of Porto Rico is another possession of the United States. It is governed by a governor appointed by the President of the United States, and a legislature which consists of two houses, one elected by the people and the other appointed by authority of the President. It has a Resident Commissioner in the House of Representatives of the United States.

The island is prospering under the form of government which it has been given, but at the same time the people are dissatisfied with their political status. They are very anxious to have the Executive Council, which constitutes the upper branch of the legislature, abolished, and an elective senate substituted in its place. They also feel that they are entitled to become full-fledged citizens of the United States, and insist that their form of government shall be so changed that the executive branch is entirely divorced from participation in the affairs of the legislative branch. The expenses incident to conducting the Government of Porto Rico are borne entirely from Porto Rican revenues.

The Philippines are not the only islands in the Orient in the possession of the United States. The island of Guam, with a population of nearly 12,000, was ceded to the United States by Spain, and is used as a naval station. The commandant of the naval station is also governor of the island. It has a circuit court, an island court, and a court of appeals. The Spanish colonial laws are in force in Guam, except as they are modified by executive orders issued by the governor. A compulsory school system is now in operation, and the children are being taught the English language, carpentry, and other handicrafts.

The United States also owns those of the Sa-

moan Islands which lie east of longitude 171°
west. The commandant of the naval station at
Pago Pago is governor of the islands and has
power to appoint officers and frame laws or ordinances, but native customs which are not inconsistent with the laws of the United States are
not changed without the consent of the people.
The natives have very little money, so they usually pay their taxes in trade.

Hawaii, now a Territory of the United States,
formerly known as the Sandwich Islands, sustains
a different relation toward the United States from
that of the other insular possessions. This comes
about by reason of the fact that the islands were
annexed by Congress, and are as much a part of
the country as is Alaska, or as Arizona or New
Mexico ever have been. The Philippines, Porto
Rico, and the other islands are simply possessions
of the United States; Hawaii is a part of it. The
Territory has a legislature of two houses—a senate of 15 members elected for four years, and a
house of representatives of 30 members elected
for two years. The people have a chance to govern themselves in a large measure. In 1910 they
held a prohibition election which went wet, 3 to 1.

Forestry is carried on in Hawaii, and bulletins
of instructions printed in English and Hawaiian
in regard to planting and caring for fruit trees
are distributed among the people. The second
Friday of November in each year is set apart as
Arbor Day, and it is said that the young Hawaiian

is as much of a forest enthusiast as any other young American. A Federal experiment station is maintained in Hawaii, and experiments of all kinds with reference to Hawaiian products are being made. It is probable that one of the outcomes of the work of the experiment station will result in the establishment of many cotton plantations. In one locality an acre of sea-island cotton planted on coral limestone soil yielded an average of 700 bolls per plant within six months.

The investigations with reference to leprosy which are being carried on in Hawaii are among the most remarkable yet attempted. They have shown that the mosquito plays no part in the transmission of the disease, but that, under certain conditions, the fly conveys the germ in large numbers. It has also been shown that heredity is not a factor in its spread, and that it can not be received except by infection. The experimenters are now trying to find a vaccine to be used in the treatment of the disease. There are yellow-fever mosquitoes on the islands, but none of these are able to do any damage so long as yellow-fever is kept out. The malarial mosquito has never been introduced, consequently malaria is unknown in the islands.

CHAPTER XX.

HOW CONGRESS LEGISLATES.

THE procedure by which the two Houses of Congress take up the 45,000 bills introduced by their Members, select from them the ideas which are to be incorporated into law, and work them over into perfected legislation, is most involved and complicated, but nothing is left undone to insure the successful operation of the legislative machine at all stages. The misplacement of a comma may involve the constitutionality of a law or change the purpose of a million-dollar appropriation.

It is evident that comparatively few of the bills which are introduced during the life of a single Congress have any chance of being enacted into legislation or even of being considered by the two Houses. If only four minutes were given to the consideration of each of the bills introduced, it would require Congress to stay in session 300 days in the year to dispose of them all.

This discloses the reason why the House and the Senate must be subdivided into committees which can consider these matters and report their conclusions to their respective bodies. Sometimes the action of a committee may be reversed, but this is the exception rather than the rule. In order for the reader to get a proper idea of the operation of the legislative machine in the taking of a bill introduced by a Member and working it over into a Federal statute, let us take an actual bill and follow it through all of its stages, from its introduction to its approval by the President and its enshrinement as a law.

On March 23, 1909, Representative John J. Esch, of Wisconsin, introduced a bill requiring railroads and other common carriers engaged in interstate and foreign commerce to make full reports of all accidents to the Interstate Commerce Commission, and authorizing investigations thereof by the Commission. He placed this bill, with many others, in what is known as the "hopper" of the House, a large basket in which Members place all bills which they introduce. The Parliamentary Clerk at the Speaker's table, acting in behalf of the Speaker, and in accordance with the rules of the House, wrote on the bill a statement referring it to the Committee on Interstate and Foreign Commerce. The bill was then sent to the Journal Clerk and other clerks of the House, where records of its introduction were made. At this stage of the journey the newspaper men had an opportunity to read it and to report it to their papers.

After the House records of the introduction of the bill were completed, it was sent to the

Government Printing Office, and 625 copies of it were printed. These copies were deposited in the document room, where files of all bills are kept. Two copies of the bill were delivered to the bill clerks of the two Houses, and two copies to the distributing clerk, one of them going to the committee to which the bill was referred.

The Committee on Interstate and Foreign Commerce holds frequent meetings, and at one of these meetings it considered this bill. In the consideration of the bill the committee decided that it ought to be amended, and by a majority vote an amendment was adopted.

On December 14, 1909, the committee voted to report the measure to the House with its amendment and to recommend its passage. When the hour for making committee reports arrived, Mr. Esch announced that his committee, having considered the bill, had decided to report it favorably with amendment, and that it was accompanied by a written report of the committee. Thereupon, the Speaker ordered the bill and the report referred to the House Calendar.

It then went on another trip through the hands of the recording clerks of the House, and was sent to the Government Printing Office, where 1,000 copies of the bill and report were printed. On the following day, which was known as Calendar Wednesday, the Speaker directed the call of committees, and when the Committee on Interstate and Foreign Commerce was reached, Representa-

HOW CONGRESS LEGISLATES

tive James Mann called up this bill from the House Calendar, he being chairman of the committee.

The Speaker announced that the Clerk would report the bill. This meant that the Clerk would read the bill in full, together with the amendment proposed by the committee. Thereupon, Mr. Mann announced that he would yield to Mr. Esch such time as he required to discuss the provisions of the bill and the amendment made by the committee. Each side of the House, Republican and Democratic, is given an equal length of time in which to debate any bill, when the pending matter is a party question; when it is not a party question, the proponents and opponents of the measure divide the time for debate equally. After the Esch bill was debated, the question was taken on its passage, and there being no strenuous opposition to it, it was passed without division.

The Clerk of the House thereupon certified that the measure had passed the House, and again it went through the process of being recorded and printed, and a certified copy was carried by the Clerk of the House to the Senate Chamber. Upon entering the Senate Chamber, the Sergeant at Arms of the Senate announced to the Vice President the arrival of a message from the House. Upon being recognized, the House Clerk stated to the Senate that he had been directed to announce that the House had passed this bill. Thereupon the Vice President took the bill and referred it to the Senate Committee on Interstate Commerce.

When the Senate Committee on Interstate Commerce received the bill, its clerk sent notices to the various members of the committee that a meeting would be held for the consideration of this and other measures. When the meeting was held, the members gathered around a long table, seated in the order of the length of their service on the committee, the chairman at the head of the table. They discussed the measure and decided to amend it so as to make it differ from the bill which passed the House. Later, on February 18, 1910, Senator Cullom reported the bill to the Senate with the amendments the committee had added, and with a report from the committee thereon. On February 23 the bill was taken from the calendar and consideration of it begun. Thereupon Senator Aldrich declared that there were some changes which ought to be made and requested that it be referred back to the committee for further consideration. The Vice President called for a vote on that proposition, and it was so referred.

The committee reported it back to the Senate with further amendments on March 15. On March 21 the bill was brought up before the Senate, and was debated by that body, sitting as a Committee of the Whole. The various Members of the Senate discussed it, and then postponed further consideration because of the absence of Senator Cul-

A VIEW IN WASHINGTON.

HOW CONGRESS LEGISLATES

lom. On April 7 Senator Cullom asked unanimous consent that the bill be taken up for consideration, and the Senate, sitting as a Committee of the Whole, resumed consideration of the measure. Senator Heyburn had objected to a certain passage in it and upon this objection Senator Cullom moved that the passage be stricken from the measure. This was agreed to. Then Senator Cullom moved another amendment to make the measure effective 60 days after its passage. This amendment also was carried. Then the Committee of the Whole was through with its work and reported the bill to the Senate as amended. The Senate thereupon ordered the amendment to be engrossed and the bill to be read a third time. The Reading Clerk then read out the title of the bill, and the Senate passed it without division.

Then the measure was printed again as passed by the Senate, and its Clerk carried a certified copy of the amended measure back to the House with the announcement to that body that he was directed to announce that the Senate had passed the bill with amendments. On April 9 the Speaker laid before the House the bill with the Senate amendments, and a motion was made that the Senate amendments be disagreed to and that the House ask for a conference. This motion prevailed and the Speaker appointed the two senior Republican members and the senior Democratic member of the House Committee on Interstate and Foreign Commerce as conferees on the part of the House. Then the Clerk of the House went back to the Senate and informed that body that the House had disagreed to the Senate amendments and desired a conference with the Senate on the disagreeing votes of the two Houses. The Senate thereupon voted to insist upon its amendments and agreed to a conference, and the Vice President appointed Senators Cullom, Aldrich, and Foster as conferees on the part of the Senate. They thereupon met with the conferees from the House, and smoothed out and compromised the differences between the two bodies upon this bill. They then drew up a conference report, which was presented in the Senate and the House, and both bodies agreed to it.

Thereupon the completed measure was referred to the Committee on Enrolled Bills, which examined it and reported to the Speaker that it had found it truly enrolled, after which the Speaker signed it and sent it to the Senate with the announcement that he had done so. Then the Vice President signed it and then the Committee on Enrolled Bills sent it by messenger to the President, who approved it with his signature, and announced to the Senate and House that he had done so, through a message in writing borne to those bodies by one of his secretaries.

Of course there are many variations in the procedure of carrying a measure through Congress from the introduced bill to the approved law. It happens in many instances that the bill comes out of the committee having it under consideration without amendment, passes the House without amendment, goes to the Senate, and is there reported by the committee without amendment and is accepted in its original form by the Senate. In such cases, no conference committees are appointed, and the act goes to the President in its original shape. In other cases the Senate originates the bill and passes it and allows the House to follow its lead. Each branch has equal authority in the origination of legislation except that the Constitution gives the House the exclusive right to originate revenue measures.

Another exception has grown up in the practice of allowing all of the big appropriation bills to originate in the House. When one of the big appropriation bills is being prepared, the officials of the Government, with whose activities the bill is concerned, are heard by the committee having the measure in charge. Most of these measures are prepared by the House Committee on Appropriations, although some of them are prepared by other committees. The hearings, under which the appropriations are recommended by the committee, are printed for the information of both branches of Congress, so that every Member shall be able to inform himself upon them. After the committee makes its report, the bill is placed on the calendar, and at the proper time the chairman of the committee arises, addresses the Speaker, and makes a motion that the House go into the

Committee of the Whole House on the state of the Union for the consideration of bill numbered so-and-so, making such-and-such appropriations. The motion for the House to go into Committee of the Whole is put and agreed to. Thereupon the Speaker calls some member of the majority to the chair, turns the gavel over to him and retires. Also, the mace, which is the emblem of the authority of the House, is taken from its pedestal and free debate is begun.

It is while the House is in Committee of the Whole on the state of the Union that the Members talk upon all topics under the sun, more frequently than not germane to anything else than the pending bill. The Presiding Officer is no longer addressed as "Mr. Speaker," but as "Mr. Chairman." After debate has continued until time for adjournment or until other matters claim the attention of the House, the Representative in charge of the bill addresses the chair and moves that the committee rise. Thereupon the Speaker returns and takes the chair. The Chairman of the Committee of the Whole then addresses him and announces that the committee, having had under consideration the pending bill, has come to no resolution thereon. This process is repeated from day to day until the consideration of the bill is completed.

A motion is then made that the committee rise and report the bill with such amendments as have been decided on, with the recommendation that the

House pass it. The committee thereupon rises, the Speaker resumes the chair and the Chairman reports the recommendation of the committee. If a separate vote is not demanded upon each amendment they are all voted on at once, the Chairman demands the previous question upon his motion that the bill shall pass, and if that motion prevails, no further debate is in order. Procedure in the Senate is in large measure the same, with the exception that the previous question, cutting off further debate, is never in order. Oftentimes, in fact usually, each House puts certain provisions into a bill which it does not expect the other House to approve, but which it thinks will serve a good purpose in negotiating compromises which are necessary before the disagreements of the Senate and House can be adjusted.

On questions involving political considerations there are occasions when every sort of strategem known to parliamentary law is resorted to both in the House and Senate. The rules of the two Houses are full and complete, and the Senator or Representative who would make the most of the parliamentary situation when a great political battle is being fought over pending legislation, must be a master of parliamentary usages in general and the rules of the body of which he is a member in particular. There are three ways in the Senate to get a matter before that body. One is by unanimous consent, the second by making it a special order, which requires two-thirds vote, and the third is by taking it up in its due course on the calendar. In the House there are three calendars, one known as the Union Calendar, the second as the Unanimous Consent Calendar, and the third as the House Calendar. It is much easier to get a matter through the Senate on an appeal for unanimous consent than through the House. The rules of the House enable the majority, as long as it can hold its forces together, to pass or defeat any measure without much difficulty.

Less than one-fiftieth of the bills introduced in Congress ever reach the stage of enactment in law. A larger proportion of bills for the relief of individuals are passed than those of a public nature. Only a few hundred public laws are passed by a single Congress. If every amendment to the Constitution which has been proposed in the last 10 years had been approved by Congress and ratified by the States no one important provision of that ancient document would be now effective. In three weeks at the beginning of the first session of a Congress joint resolutions were introduced which would have postmasters and Federal judges elected by the people, the ancient punishment of civil ostracism revived, the independence of the Philippines declared, the prohibition of a protective tariff ordered, a censorship for advertisements created, the enacting power of Congress taken away, and the printing of market quotations forbidden.

HOW CONGRESS LEGISLATES

The work of Congress requires an adequate plant as well as a capable force of lawmakers. Such a plant is now possessed by the Congress of the United States. It is estimated that the group of buildings which constitute the national law factory represents a total cost of $30,000,000. The Capitol itself has cost, exclusive of repairs, a total of $15,000,000. The Library of Congress represents an expenditure of $7,000,000 more, while the cost of the Office Buildings and the heating plant brings the total up to more than $30,000,000. The plant of the British Parliament cost only half as much, while those of the German Reichstag and the French Parliament cost even less. Many improvements yet await installation. One of these is an air-cooling plant for keeping the Capitol cool in summer just as a heating plant is used to keep it warm in winter. The British Parliament has installed an air-cooling and filtration plant in the Parliament buildings.

The Office Buildings of the House and Senate are sumptuously, yet tastefully, furnished. The restaurant plant in the Senate Office Building is elaborately equipped. The kitchen is fitted with an electric dishwasher, an electrical ice cream making plant, an ice crusher, and everything else a palatial restaurant needs. Both of the Office Buildings are equipped with expensive baths, and a Member may have anything he wishes in the way of a bath, from a needle spray to a seance with a professional masseur. A large tank for a cold plunge is also in use, and there is nothing to excel the congressional baths this side of the perfumed ones of Rome and Pompeii. One begins to realize the immensity of the American legislative plant when he is told that the buildings constituting it contain some 1,400 rooms and some 40 elevators.

CHAPTER XXI.

THE HOUSE OF REPRESENTATIVES.

As the branch of the American Congress which is closest to the people, receiving its authority directly from them, and going back to them every two years to give an account of its stewardship, the House of Representatives stands as the nearest approach to a reflection of the will of the people that is to be found in the American governmental system. Senators are elected for a term of six years, and are therefore less subject to the fluctuation of public opinion than Representatives. The President is elected for a term of four years, and public opinion may swing as a pendulum to one extreme and back again before the country has a chance to pass upon his administration. Only the House reflects every change of sentiment which comes over the people.

The House of Representatives in the Sixty-third Congress will be made up of 435 Members, not counting Delegates from the Territories and Resident Commissioners from the Philippines and Porto Rico. The membership of the House is fixed by Congress. The Constitution provides for a decennial census to determine the population of each

State in the Union, in order to determine exactly what proportion of the total membership shall be assigned to each of the several States. After the census returns at the beginning of each decade are in hand, Congress takes up the problem of determining the size of the House during the 10 years to follow. So long as the population of the country continues to grow as rapidly as it has in the past, it is inevitable that either the number of Members must be largely increased, or else that the number of people who shall constitute the average congressional district shall be correspondingly increased. To increase the membership of the House in proportion to the growth of the country would result in that body becoming so large as to be unwieldy. On the other hand, to maintain it at the same number would result in such a large increase in the number of people who would constitute a congressional constituency that States with slowly expanding populations would lose members, while States with rapidly growing populations would gain a corresponding number of members. So Congress faces the problem of determining upon a membership which is not excessive and a representation which does not too greatly cut down the existing representation of any State. Therefore it has nearly always increased both the membership of the House and the ratio of the population entitled to one representation. For instance, the House under the apportionment of 1901 had a membership of

THE HOUSE OF REPRESENTATIVES

391, as compared with the membership of 435 under the apportionment of 1911, while the ratio of population was 194,182, under the census of 1900 as compared with 211,877 for the census of 1910.

Not all congressional districts have the same population in practice, although theoretically they should have. This is due in part to the fact that congressional districts usually follow county lines, town lines, or ward lines in cities, so that the population can not therefore be divided with exactness. Congress simply apportions representation among the various States, and allows each State to fix the limits of the congressional districts to which it is entitled. In fixing these lines the State legislatures frequently resort to what is known as gerrymandering. That is, if the Republicans happen to control the legislature of a State when a redistricting bill is pending, they aim to crowd all of the strongly Democratic counties into as few districts as possible, thus insuring Republican representation in the greatest possible number of districts for the decade ahead. On the other hand, if the Democrats are in power, they try to crowd as many of the Republican voters into one district as they can. This sometimes results in remarkable variation from the ratio of representation fixed by Congress. For instance, under the 1900 census the ratio was 194,182. Yet in the fourteenth district of Pennsylvania there was a population of only 146,000, while in the third district there was a population of 251,000.

The House of Representatives is not a continuing body. Each House dies with the fall of the Speaker's gavel at noon on the 4th of March of every alternate year. The new Members are elected in November before the old House dies, and they go upon the payroll on March 4, the day of the death of the old House. Except when an extra session of Congress is called, the new Members do not begin their real duties as legislators until the first Monday of the following December.

Just before a new House of Representatives assembles the members of each political party hold a caucus to nominate candidates for the elective officers of the House, the Speaker, Clerk, Chaplain, Sergeant at Arms and Doorkeeper. Of course it is known long in advance which party will control the House and elect its officers, and the nominations made by the other party are merely perfunctory.

When the House convenes it is called to order by the Clerk of the preceding House, and no other business is in order until a Speaker is elected. Once the Clerk acted as presiding officer from the first of December to nearly the middle of February, while the House could do nothing but ballot for Speaker, none of the political factions in the House being able to muster a majority for its candidate for the Speakership. When the Clerk of the former House calls the new one to order, the chairmen of the party caucuses nominate the caucus candidates for the Speakership and a ballot is taken to determine which shall be chosen. Of course, the candidate of the party which has a majority in the House wins. A committee is then appointed to notify him of his election, and to escort him to the Speaker's chair. Amid loud and long applause, the waving of thousands of flags, and the click of dozens of cameras, he accepts the gavel from the Clerk, and in a few words thanks the Members and pledges himself to fulfill the duties of Speaker. After this the caucus chairmen bring in their respective resolutions, naming the minor elective officers of the House, and, of course, the resolution of the majority party is adopted. The House is then organized.

The next step after the House has chosen its staff of officials is that of holding the great biennial lottery to determine the choice of seats in the House for the Congress then beginning. When a new Congress comes into being all of its Members are supposed to be equal and no Member is entitled to advantage over others in the choice of seats. The names of all the Members of the House are arranged alphabetically and numbered according to their position on the list. Then a small page is blind-folded and told to draw a ball out of a box. There are exactly as many balls as there are Members of the House, and each ball contains a number corresponding to that of a Member. An official shakes the box and the boy draws out a ball and hands it to this official. He reads the number on it, and then refers to his alphabetical list. If Representative Smith is 320th on the list and the ball bears the number 320, Mr. Smith gets first choice of a seat. This is continued all the way down through the list. Before the drawing begins, the entire floor of the House is cleared, the Members retiring to the area behind the railing, and going forward in the order their names are called by the officers conducting the drawing. It is usual to exempt former Speakers of the House, a few of the oldest Members, and the chairmen of the Committees on Ways and Means, Rules, and Appropriations, all of these being permitted to select their seats before the drawing begins. The only limitation upon the choice of seats is that the Republicans take one side of the center aisle and the Democrats the other.

The next question which comes up is that of a code of rules for the regulation of the procedure of the House during the life of the Congress then beginning its career. Each of the two parties offers a code of rules, usually that it has adopted in caucus. For more than a generation after the Civil War these rules gradually grew more and more restrictive, placing the power of the House more and more in the hands of the Speaker, and giving greater and greater sting to the lash of the party whip. It was always a favorite assertion of former Speaker Cannon, the last of the line of Republican Speakers who reigned in the House from 1895 to 1911, that the Speaker was the creature of the House, and that it could put him out of his position any hour it chose to do so. Yet he always knew his party associates would put up with almost any kind of application of the party lash rather than dethrone him. Theoretically he was absolutely right; practically he was wholly wrong.

After the adoption of the rules—and it is always made possible to suspend them when political or other exigencies require it—the next question is the selection of the committees of the House. For a century it was the custom for the Speaker to name all of the members of the various committees. In late years he usually consulted the minority leader as to the personnel of the minority members of the committees, but this was an unofficial act of grace. When the Democrats came into power in the Sixty-second Congress, they decided that the power to appoint committees should be taken from the Speaker and that all standing committees should be elected by the House. The Democrats selected majority members of the Ways and Means Committee in caucus and then made them a Committee on Committees for the purpose of nominating members of the standing committees. Its selections for the majority representation on committees were ratified by the Democratic caucus. The Democratic majority permitted the Republican minority to nominate its representation in its own way, and the Republican caucus delegated the duty to the minority leader. The nominations were then all confirmed by formal election in the House.

There are 56 committees in the House of Representatives. Of these perhaps less than half are of much importance except upon rare occasions. Theoretically the Ways and Means Committee is the greatest committee of the House. In the years before the Civil War this committee not only had charge of all legislation for the raising of revenue, but also that of making all appropriations. It was then decided to separate the work of the committee, allowing the Ways and Means Committee to continue in charge of revenue matters, and creating an Appropriations Committee in charge of legislation carrying appropriations. At that time Thaddeus Stevens was chairman of the Ways and Means Committee. He decided that the Appropriations Committee would become the more influential, and took the chairmanship of Appropriations in preference to that of Ways and Means.

A few years ago a contest came up in the House which disclosed the attitude of its Members with reference to the question of the relative standing of these two committees. When the House took up the matter of determining which committee should remain in the Capitol and which should go to the new House Office Building, neither the Ways and Means Committee nor the Appropriations

BEARING THE MACE.

Committee wished to move, and there was room for only one of them to stay. They couldn't agree on the matter themselves and so referred it to the House, which, by a large majority decided that the Appropriations Committee should be allowed to retain its quarters in the Capitol Building. Since the Democrats came into power in the Sixty-second Congress, their course in making the majority members of the Ways and Means Committee a Committee on Committees has served to make Ways and Means beyond all question the most important committee of the House and its chairman the actual as well as the titular floor leader.

The relative importance of the various committees varies with the character of the issues before the country. When the tariff question is uppermost the Ways and Means Committee is by far the biggest committee in the House. When the coinage question was uppermost the Committee on Coinage, Weights, and Measures was the most important of them all, although in recent years it has had almost nothing to do. Twenty years ago the Committee on Interstate and Foreign Commerce was a comparatively unimportant one. Since that time the large number of problems of one kind and another affecting interstate-commerce matters, the public health, and the Panama Canal, have served to make it probably the most important legislative committee of the House. The Committee on Post Office and Post

Roads has increased in importance so rapidly that it now ranks as one of the "Big Four" committees—Ways and Means, Appropriations, Interstate and Foreign Commerce, and Post Office and Post Roads.

New Members arriving in Washington sometimes astonish those who know the ropes by their expression of preference in the matter of committee assignments. Some years ago, when John Sharp Williams was the minority leader in the House, a new Member came out of Texas who said he had only one request to make of Mr. Williams, and that was that he be permitted to become a member of the Committee on Railways and Canals. He was told that this committee had next to nothing to do and would be a very undesirable assignment, but he insisted that that committee would write the most important legislation of the ensuing decade and that he wanted to be one of its members. His wish was gratified, but from that day to this the Committee on Railways and Canals has done little else than organize at the beginning of each Congress.

The House of Representatives requires an efficient staff of officials and clerks to serve it. The Speaker has a personal staff of about half a dozen clerks and messengers. One of these clerks is known as the clerk at the Speaker's table. He is always an expert on parliamentary law and one who has the precedents of the House procedure ever at his finger tips. Under the Republican

Speakers from 1895 to 1911 this position was held by Asher C. Hinds, of Maine, who came to know more about House procedure than any other man in the country, and his compilation of House Precedents, published by the Government Printing Office and contained in a half dozen large quarto volumes, is the most exhaustive compilation of parliamentary law in the world. Mr. Hinds was elected a Member of the House in 1910, and, the Democrats coming into power, he was succeeded as chief parliamentarian by Judge Charles R. Crisp, who had held the office before when his father, Charles F. Crisp, was Speaker.

The House has a Chaplain, who invokes Divine guidance for its deliberations every time it meets. For years this Chaplain has been a minister who is blind as a result of a wound received in the Civil War. He is a Republican, but when the Democrats came into power they unanimously agreed that he should be reelected.

One of the most interesting things in the House is the mace, the emblem of its authority. If a Member refuses to obey the orders of the Speaker or of the House, the Speaker orders the Sergeant at Arms to bring the offender to order. This official takes the mace, which is a variation of the old Roman symbol of power—the fasces of the lictor—except that a silver eagle is substituted for the battle ax, and marches to the seat of the offender. A Member always dreads a visit from the Sergeant at Arms bearing the mace and usually subsides before it is taken from its pedestal near the Speaker's chair.

The House has its own post office, its own restaurant, a folding room from which documents are sent out, a document room where all sorts of legislative documents are on file, and other facilities which leave nothing to be desired in expediting legislation. It is when a session of Congress comes to a close that one of the most interesting scenes of congressional activity is enacted. For several days before there is usually a great crush of business with perhaps an all-night filibuster on top of it. An all-night session is a strenuous affair and the Members try to keep awake by singing, smoking, telling jokes, and quarreling—in fact, everything else but legislating. There are usually some rather strong candidates for operatic honors in the House and when they sing such songs as "We Won't Go Home Until Morning," "For He's a Jolly Good Fellow," "Old Kentucky Home," and "Old Black Joe" there are high times in the House.

The House of Representatives is perhaps the most expensive lawmaking institution in the world. Beginning with the Sixty-third Congress the annual expense of maintaining it will approximate $6,000,000 a year, which does not include its large printing bill. The salaries of its Members aggregate nearly three and a half million dollars. Each Member is allowed $1,500 for clerk hire, and this aggregates nearly $700,000. The

House has a large staff of officers and clerks, the aggregate of whose salaries is more than $500,000. There are other items to be considered, such as an allowance of 20 cents for each mile traveled by each Representative in coming to his duties by the nearest route, stationery bill, etc., all of which bring the total cost of maintaining the lower branch of the National Legislature well up to $6,000,000.

CHAPTER XXII.

THE SENATE.

The Senate of the United States, called by George Washington "the saucer in which the tea of the House brew is cooled," is a legislative body differing in many respects from any other in the world. It is the most powerful factor in the American governmental machine. There are things which the President and the Senate may do without the assent of the House of Representatives; and things which the House and the Senate may do without the assent of the President, yet the President and the House can do nothing without the assent of the Senate. The Senate is vested with a measure of all of the three powers of the Federal Government—legislative, executive, and judicial. It exercises legislative power as one of the branches of Congress and its concurrence is necessary to the perfection of all kinds of legislation. It exercises executive power under the constitutional mandate requiring its advice and consent to make the nominations of the Federal officers by the President effective. It is further exercised by the constitutional requirement that no treaty shall become effective except it be ratified by a two-thirds vote of the Senate. The judicial power of the Senate arises from its constitutional authority to sit as a Court of Impeachment when Federal officers are tried for "high crimes and misdemeanors."

Without the advice and consent of a majority of the Senate no Federal officer can be clothed with the authority to act as such. Without the affirmative approval of a two-thirds majority of the Senate no treaty negotiated by the President can become effective. On the other hand, a law may be enacted without the approval of the President by passing it over his veto. The House possesses no power to influence the Senate or the President in matters of political appointment or treaty relations, and a treaty may be made effective without the slightest consideration for the attitude of the House, and once ratified it becomes equal in authority with a law of Congress. The House may decide to impeach the President, but it remains for the Senate to sit in judgment, the only limitation upon this power of judgment being that the Chief Justice of the Supreme Court shall sit as its Presiding Officer.

Not only does the Senate possess powers wider in range than those of either the President or the House of Representatives, but these powers tend to give it a dignity and soberness of mind not in evidence in the House. One needs attend only a day's session of the two branches of Congress to see the difference between the House and the Senate. In the House there is more or less noise. In the Senate everything is conservative, staid, and dignified. The House will permit itself to be photographed on special occasions. The Senate in all history has never succumbed to the importunities of the press photographer. Upon such occasions as an all-night session or adjournment day, the House will sing itself hoarse while in recess. The Senate would be shocked from center to circumference if anyone presumed to raise his voice in song within its walls.

A few years ago Senator Tillman, of South Carolina, was addressing the Senate, when Senator Warren, of Wyoming, sitting on the opposite side of the middle aisle spied a bottle in the pocket of the South Carolinian. He drew the bottle from its resting place, took out the cork, smelled of it, much to the amusement of the galleries, and then replaced it. The Senate was shocked by this proceeding and such a frigid atmosphere was created that the Senator from Wyoming has never given vent to his playful impulses from that day to this. Upon another occasion Senator Tillman made a speech in which he likened himself to the interlocutor in a minstrel show, declaring that certain other Senators were the burntcork artists known as endmen, and that "Gum Shoe" Bill Stone could give an exhibition of walking on eggs without cracking the shells. The Senate did not relish this speech, although individual Members of that body were much amused by it; Senator

Tillman heard from various sources that the Senate did not enjoy such a characterization and as a result he declared openly that in the future he would not attempt to make a humorous speech. Such events in the House are regarded as "happy hits" and are of frequent occurrence.

In the House a Member desiring to make a speech often has to beg for a single minute in which to make it. In the Senate there is no limit to the time a Senator may talk, except that imposed by his own powers of endurance. In the House a Member may ask leave to extend his remarks in the Congressional Record and then may print there a speech not a word of which was delivered on the floor. He may even go so far as to place in his printed but undelivered speech interpolations such as "Applause," "Prolonged applause," and "Loud and continued applause," and other little phrases wherever he thinks they ought to go. It is true that only a few deluded Members carry the matter thus far. But in the Senate the practice of extending remarks in the Record is never resorted to, and the cheap practice of inserting such interpolations as those above is unheard of.

The Senate differs from the House as widely in its rules and in the way in which it is constituted as it does in the character of its proceedings. The Senate never dies; one-third of the Senators go out of office and a like number come in every two years, so that two-thirds of the Senate membership is always in office. The House dies every two years and must be entirely reorganized at the beginning of each Congress. There is a sort of rivalry between the two bodies, each asserting itself to be the more powerful and each occasionally pointing the finger of ridicule at the other on account of the difference in procedure.

The rules of both the Senate and the House positively prohibit any Member of either body to speak disrespectfully of the other body, and yet Senators frequently point out that the rule in the House is little more than mob rule, while Members of the House as often declare that senatorial courtesy is carried to such lengths that one man may thwart the will of more than ninety.

Yet each body is proud of its distinguishing features. The House could not be induced to give up its right to cut off debate whenever it desires to do so, and the Senate has never found provocation strong enough to induce it to curtail the right of unlimited debate. Legislation in the Senate is enacted largely on the principle of unanimous consent. In practice the Senate never agrees to set a date for a vote in the future except by unanimous consent.

The principle that every Senator is entitled to speak as long as he desires, and that no motion can take away from him the right to the floor until he is ready to yield it, has produced the unique senatorial filibuster. A Senator in the minority at the end of his speech may yield the floor, and as long as another of the opposition succeeds in following him they are able to protract the debate and prevent a vote. Senators engaged in a filibuster have long odds over those attempting to put it down. Three or four strong-lunged Senators on guard in the interest of a filibuster can usually maintain debate so long that it wears out the efforts of the majority to maintain a quorum, and to bring the issue to a vote, or to a compromise.

According to tradition in the Senate there shall not be any hindrance on free and full debate. This freedom of debate has been used by individual Senators for the purpose of blocking legislation to which they were opposed, especially toward the end of a Congress which expires biennially by limitation on March 4. Thus former Senator Carter, of Montana, once defeated a river and harbor bill by talking it to death, the late Senator Clay, of Georgia, made a lengthy and successful filibuster on a statehood bill, the Democrats of the Senate successfully filibustered against the famous "Force Bill," and Senator Tillman, of South Carolina, successfully insisted upon an appropriation for a claim in favor of his State which had been repeatedly disallowed.

In 1908 Senator La Follette, of Wisconsin, and several other opponents of the Aldrich currency bill started a filibuster against the passage of the conference report on that measure. Every technicality was utilized for the purpose of consuming time. The question of "no quorum" was repeatedly raised and the session which began at noon on May 29 sat for some 30 hours. This brought about the resurrection of an ancient rule whereby Members could be compelled to vote or to give a good reason therefor. Under this rule the Vice President counted a quorum in spite of the fact that a majority of the Members of the Senate had not voted. The Senate also determined upon that occasion that the question of "no quorum" could not be raised when a previous roll call had disclosed the presence of a quorum, if no business had intervened, and it was held that the debate did not constitute intervening business. A long dormant rule which prohibited any Senator from addressing the Senate upon any question more than twice in any one legislative day was resurrected as a means of putting down the filibuster. One-man filibusters usually take place at the very close of a session of Congress, and upon these occasions some champion long-distance speeches are delivered.

Perhaps the greatest filibuster ever conducted, and one which gripped the attention of the entire country, was the one against the "Force Bill" in Harrison's administration. The House of Representatives had passed the bill, and the Republicans were very anxious that it become a law. When it came to the Senate, the Democrats started in to fight it tooth and nail. The Republicans knew that if they could force the bill to a vote they had the necessary majority to pass it. The Democrats realized that the only way they could prevent the passage of the measure and its approval by the President would be to keep it from coming to a vote. The Republicans decided that they would insist upon fixing a time for a vote, and to do so they were willing to break the precedents of a century and vote a cloture, and they attempted thus to cut off the right of unlimited debate. They found that some of their own members, while extremely anxious to pass the "Force Bill," were not willing to do so at the price of breaking this time-honored precedent.

The late Senator Quay, of Pennsylvania, heartily disliked President Harrison, and his support of the Democratic filibuster turned the tide and defeated the bill. There have been many times when the Senate majority, impatient with a filibustering minority, has advocated the curtailment of the right of unlimited debate, but as soon as the members of that majority found themselves in the minority they in turn have been the firmest supporters of that right. It is probable that the Senate never will recede from its ancient position of never fixing a future date for voting upon any issue without unanimous consent.

The Presiding Officer of the Senate is the Vice President of the United States. He is elected by the people and has no powers in the Senate save to preside over its deliberations, and to cast the deciding vote in case of a tie. Since the Senate has no choice in the selection of its regular Presiding Officer, it is careful to hedge about his position with rules which do not permit him to dominate its deliberations. He is required by the rules of the Senate to recognize the first speaker who addresses the chair.

When a new Congress meets every second year, the newly elected Members of the Senate are escorted to the Vice President's desk, where he administers to them the oath of office. They have received their credentials from the legislatures of the States they represent, and these are filed among the records of the Senate. Only one Senator from each State comes in at one time, except under extraordinary circumstances, and his colleague is expected to escort him to the desk of the Vice President for the administration of the oath. As a rule Senators extend this courtesy to their incoming colleagues, even though there have been strenuous political differences between them. Occasionally, however, the incoming Senator and the continuing Senator are bitter enemies, personal as well as political, and refuse to extend this courtesy. When Senator Clarke, of Arkansas, took the oath of office, Senator Berry refused to escort him.

The Senate is a great stickler for its traditions. Back in the earlier days of the Republic snuff taking was popular, and for a while the snuffbox was kept on the desk of the Presiding Officer. Henry Clay was a great snuff taker, and would frequently pause in his speeches to inhale a bit of the tobacco dust. To this day snuffboxes are maintained in the Senate, and, remarkable as it may seem, they are frequently replenished with a fresh supply of snuff. Senators sometimes carry personal peculiarities into the Senate Chamber. Sam Houston, of Texas, was a confirmed whittler, and every morning he had a little bundle of pine sticks brought into the Senate Chamber. If matters in which he was deeply interested were pending, his whittling would take the form of simply making shavings; if the matters in which he had no interest were pending he would carve out little boats, animals, and other designs and present them to his friends. Senator Charles Sumner had a habit of pulling the pages' ears. Upon one occasion he, in a moment of abstraction, caught a page by the ear and proceeded to march him up and down the Senate aisle. The Senator was called and the boy, who is to-day a business man in New York, declares that he still has a vivid recollection of the acute suffering he underwent before he succeeded in bringing Mr. Sumner to a realization of what he was doing. Alabama once sent a man to the United States Senate who was so large that an extrasized chair and desk had to be provided for him, although those in common use will seat comfortably a man of more than 200 pounds. The peculiarities of Senators of bygone days find little counterpart in the Senate of more recent years.

The Senate has frequent secret sessions, usually for the consideration of executive business, during which the public is rigidly excluded and a great effort is made to maintain absolute secrecy as to the proceedings. However, the newspaper men who constitute the corps of Washington correspondents always have intimate friends among the Senators, and it is next to impossible for the Senate to keep the secrets of its secret sessions. It goes into executive session for the purpose of considering nominations sent in by the President, and also for the consideration of treaties. Of course it would be impossible for the Senate to fully and freely discuss grave international matters in the open, without giving rise to complications with other Governments.

It is popularly supposed that younger men are being elected to the Senate to-day than formerly. The Constitution requires that a Senator be at least 30 years of age, 9 years a citizen of the United States, and an inhabitant of the State from which he is elected. It is very seldom that the constitutional age limit is even approached, the average Senator being upward of 40 years of age at the time he is chosen. There have been cases, however, when Senators have come into office at an age barely qualifying them for service in the Senate. Henry Clay was one of these, and Luke Lea, of Tennessee, is another. The length of service of Senators is greater to-day than it was before the Civil War. When Thomas H. Benton, of

GRAND STAIRWAY IN LIBRARY OF CONGRESS.

Missouri, had served 30 years in the Senate it gave him the longest term in Congress that had been enjoyed by any Member of either House. Since the Civil War many Members of both the Senate and the House have served longer than Benton, some of them having 40 years of service to their credit.

Being so much smaller in membership than the House, it is natural that the Senate can afford its Members more comforts and conveniences than are enjoyed by the Members of the House. While each Member of the House has one room in the House Office Building, each Member of the Senate has two and sometimes three large rooms. Nearly every Senator has the chairmanship of some committee, and this entitles him to the services of two or three assistants.

The Senate and House have placed splendid facilities at the disposal of the press. The galleries back of the chairs of the presiding officers of the two Houses are reserved exclusively for the 200 representatives of the big newspapers of the country who belong to the corps of Washington correspondents. Back of each of these galleries are several large rooms which are for the exclusive use of the members of the press. One of these is a telegraph room where the press matter of the day's doings is sent out. Another is the writing room, in addition to which there are lounging and retiring rooms. Only newspaper men whose credentials have been passed upon by a standing committee of correspondents are eligible to press gallery membership. Each gallery is presided over by a superintendent and several assistants, who do all they can to aid the correspondents in getting the news of Congress to the 90,000,000 people it represents. The superintendent of the Senate Press Gallery is James D. Preston and of the House Gallery Charles H. Mann.

CHAPTER XXIII.

THE LIBRARY OF CONGRESS.

Housed in the finest building of its kind in the world, possessing the third largest collection of books and pamphlets ever assembled, containing the world's greatest collection of maps, and centering its activities along lines which will make it in the future a great national institution, uniting all of the great libraries in the country into one huge system of book depositories in which the treasures of all will be available to the student at any one of them, the Library of Congress is one of the most important monuments to literature in the world.

The Library Building is the creation of American architects, sculptors, and painters exclusively. Not only is it a beautiful structure outside and inside, but it is the best-designed building in the world for library purposes such as it is intended to serve. One may get an idea of how accessible are the books on its shelves from the statement that it requires only 15 minutes to procure any desired book in the Congressional Library. Situated in the center of a 10-acre plat of ground, and covering more than 4 acres of this, the Library is one of the best-lighted buildings in the world. It is built in the shape of a large square, inclosing a great central court, which is cut up into sections by bookstacks radiating from a rotunda in the center of the square. It has more than 2,000 windows, is three stories high, and the central rotunda is surmounted by a magnificent gold-covered dome. No other building in America and few in the entire world are so elaborately decorated with sculptures and mural paintings, and these possess a merit that commands praise from every critic.

The main reading room of the Library is 100 feet in diameter and 125 feet from the floor to the dome. It is furnished in mahogany, and has a seating capacity of 290.

When a reader comes into the reading room he fills out an application card, giving the name of the book he desires, and, if he is familiar with the use of the Library Catalogue, the Library number of the book and the name of the author. He signs his name to the card and writes on it the number of the desk he intends to use. He then gives the card to an attendant at the central desk. This attendant knows exactly on what deck, or floor, of what bookstack, the desired book is kept. A pneumatic-tube system connects the reading room with the various decks of the bookstacks, just as the cashier's office in a big department store is connected with the various counters of the store. The attendant at the central desk

THE LIBRARY OF CONGRESS 289

puts the card into a little sole-leather case and that in turn into the tube.

By pulling a lever the card is started on its journey to the attendant on the deck where the desired book is kept. A bell is also rung, and this calls the deck attendant to the tube station. He takes out the card, and the number on it tells him exactly where the book is located. Usually he is familiar enough with the majority of books called for to find them without even the number. If there is no number on the card and he can not locate it without the number, he consults a card catalogue of the books on his desk, and is thus able to find the book.

When he gets the book he places it on a rack and pulls a lever. A specially designed book carrier consists of 18 brass book baskets, mounted on an endless double chain. This book carrier starts in the reading room and goes down vertically to a point below the level of the basement. Here it passes around a wheel and travels through a tunnel in a horizontal direction to the center of the bookstack. Here it passes around another wheel and travels upward again to the top of the stack, where it passes around a third wheel and returns by the same route. The carrier travels at a speed of a hundred feet a minute. When the stack attendant has placed the book on the rack and pulled the lever, the next carrier basket which comes along, automatically lifts the book out of the rack and carries it down beneath the ground and then up again into the reading room, where it is automatically discharged into a cushioned box at the central desk.

When the attendant in the reading room wishes to return the book to the stack, the carrier is so arranged that it can be sent to the proper desk simply by pulling a certain lever. The basket containing the book will pass every other deck and will never deposit its burden except at the right place. This carrier seems almost to possess human intelligence, refusing to carry books in any way that might injure them in transit. In practice, nearly all of the books are sent from the stacks to the central reading room by this carrier, but as a rule they are sent back by a messenger, on a large book truck.

Each of the bookstacks consists of from 9 to 10 stories, with a series of cast-iron frames supporting tiers and shelves. The largest stacks are 65 feet high. The shelves are of cold-rolled steel, and are finished as smooth as glass. The stacks are lighted by large windows of plate glass, which are attached directly to the window frame in such a way as to make them dust and damp tight. There are no sashes in these windows, and they are never opened. As bright sunshine is harmful to books, it is necessary to have an arrangement which will at all times admit light and yet keep out the direct sunlight. Of course it would be a difficult task to open and shut 200 window shades every time the sun seeks to enter, so it has been arranged that they can all be shut or opened simultaneously by a hydraulic apparatus operated by pressing a button.

At the outset there were three stacks possessing a total of 44 miles of book shelves, with a capacity of approximately 2,000,000 volumes. Since that time another stack has been built, which adds another million volumes to the capacity of the Library. It is arranged so that still other stacks may be added, and the ultimate capacity will be more than 4,000,000 volumes, counting 9 volumes to the foot. This would make a single row of books more than a hundred miles long. The new stack, which was built a few years ago, is equipped with some facilities not possessed by the others. One of these is a unique provision for economy in the use of electricity for lighting purposes. At every other shelf there is a push button, by which the attendant may turn on the light for one passageway. This continues to burn for about six minutes, and then the lights are automatically cut out. If the attendant wishes to stay longer he must press the button again. There is an underground book railway leading directly from the Library to a station in the Capitol. This runs through a brick tunnel, a quarter of a mile long. There is an endless chain to which book trays are attached, and they make the trip from the Library to the Capitol in from two to three minutes. Members of the House and Senate and of the Supreme

Court, and the officials of these bodies, have the privilege of drawing books from the Library, and of having them sent to their offices, to the Capitol, or to their homes.

It is one of the cherished ideas of the present Librarian of Congress that the Library shall be made a great national institution, which will unlock all of the treasures of the literary world to the serious students of the United States. Although the greatest library in the Western Hemisphere, there are still many works lacking from the collections of the Library of Congress. The same is true of every other library in America. Not one of them has a complete collection. But what one of them lacks another possesses, and by a properly organized system of cooperation, they may make available for all of them every book possessed by any one of them. Such a system of cooperation will give to the United States a library service superior to that of any other country in the world. The Federal Government has other libraries than the Library of Congress, and they make Uncle Sam the owner of more than 3,000,000 volumes. Each of the principal departments and bureaus of the Government maintains a special library dealing with the subjects with which it is principally concerned. For instance, the Bureau of Education has the world's best library on educational matters; the Bureau of Fisheries has the finest library in existence on aquatic life; the Bureau of Standards possesses a magnificent library on scientific subjects; and the library of the office of the Surgeon General of the United States Army is regarded as the greatest medical library in the world. Already such a system of cooperation has been established between these various libraries that they are practically one so far as research work is concerned.

The first step necessary to a full realization of the high purpose to coordinate the library work of the country will be the making of a complete card index of each publication to be found in the libraries of the country. This will cover many million cards, as each book requires an average of five cards to properly index it, with the appropriate cross references. This index will show in what libraries the rarer works may be had, and application to any library by a serious student will make it available, even though it has come from the most distant corner of the country. When this movement for the nationalization of the Library of Congress is realized, America will be ahead of any other nation in library matters. Already Mr. Herbert Putnam, the Librarian of Congress, has placed his ideas into partial operation and with the most signal success.

The Library of Congress lends freely to other libraries, and even deposits with them, for long periods, such material as they may require in their work, they paying the transportation charges. It also invites other libraries to use its bibliographic service, and is ready at all times to furnish reference lists and aids to specific research. The bibliographers, who prepare lists of all works bearing on a given subject, render an important service. Whenever any subject becomes of general interest to the public, a bibliography is prepared and made available for general use.

Without losing sight of the fact that the Library was founded for Congress by Congress, and that the lawmakers have the first claim upon its attention, the Librarian is seeking in every way to extend the scope and usefulness of its work. The card-index system which has been established, and the plan of printing duplicate cards for gratuitous distribution to the various other governmental libraries, and at cost to other libraries, have proved the emancipation of the library worker. It costs from 25 to 50 cents per volume to catalogue library books and from 15 to 30 cents to print the cards. It requires no more time or expense to catalogue a book for all of the libraries of the country than for one, and duplicate cards, after the work of the cataloging has been completed, are very inexpensive. It is exactly as in the case of a book. The cost of authorship and composition is as much for an edition of a hundred as for an edition of a hundred thousand. More than a thousand libraries are now using the cataloging service of the Library of Congress and the number of subscribers is increasing at the rate of about 16 per cent a year. There are several grades of cards and the lowest grade full set brought down to date may be had for about $200.

As the low-grade manila cards take up so much less space, requiring only about three-fifths as much as the best cards, they are often preferred to the others. Some idea of the magnitude of the indexing and classification work of the Library of Congress may be had from the statement that if a book index of the material on its shelves were to be printed, it would require 15 years to complete the job, at a cost of nearly a half million dollars. Some time in the future this may be undertaken, but the ever-growing list of material received makes such a publication almost, if not entirely, impracticable. The collections of the Library are growing at the rate of nearly 100,000 books a year, and are approaching the 2,000,000 mark. Only the National Library of France and that of the British Museum have larger collections.

There are a number of divisions in the Library. One of the most interesting of these is that of Music. It has more than half a million pieces of music in sheet form, together with thousands of volumes of bound scores, as well as general musical literature. The development of the collection under expert advice during the past decade has made it one of the most famous collections in the world. It includes, for instance, nearly 2,000 scores of modern operas, and more than 12,000 opera texts. The aim of the Music Division has been to encourage and aid serious research, and it has sought, therefore, the full orchestral scores of any orchestral composition rather than a piano or other merely popular arrangement.

Another interesting division is the Map and Chart Division, whose official head declares it to possess the greatest and most satisfactorily indexed collection of maps and charts in the world. The British Museum has a larger collection, but the maps in it are by no means as accessible as those of the Library of Congress. It has more than a hundred thousand maps in sheet form, as well as an extraordinary collection of atlases.

The collection of prints **is also a large one,** and many of these are of **rare historical value.** There is an especially excellent collection of prints and portraits of the public men of the United States, particularly the Presidents. In these collections one may see rare pictures of the Father of His Country at Mount Vernon, and others of Roosevelt pitching hay at Oyster Bay and Taft playing golf at Chevy Chase.

Another interesting division of the Library is that of Manuscripts. Here one may see the papers of the Continental Congress, and of Washington, Jefferson, Madison, and others, transferred from the State Department, together with various collections, the results of gifts as well as of purchases, which are now indispensable to students of American history in search of original material. The total number of pieces in the collection can not be stated with precision, but one single small group contains a hundred thousand pieces.

The Library of Congress is a library of record as well as of research, and it has aimed to make its collections bear testimony on any question concerning which the Government or the people may need information. Its usefulness in this direction may be illustrated in a thousand ways. For instance, in the sixties, 25 head of cattle were driven from a Texas ranch. Eye-witnesses swore that they were driven 50 miles to the left of Twin Mountain. Twin Mountain was not located on any map available to the Court of Claims. If the cattle were driven to one side of Twin Mountain, they were driven by friendly Apaches, and the Government would have to pay for them. If they were driven to the other side, they were driven by hostile Comanches and the Government was under no obligations to reimburse the owner. An atlas of 1867 on file in the Library of Congress was resurrected and it laid the offense at the door of the Comanches.

The venerable and lamented Ainsworth R. Spofford, under whose administration the Library was built, and to whose memory it always will be a monument, once said that there should never be a censor in the republic of books. He asserted that no man could tell what portion of the trash of to-day would be the treasure of tomorrow. A file of the Charleston Courier, bought for a considerable sum, has been widely used to determine the question of loyalty in the case of those who make claims for reimbursement for property destroyed by Federal troops during the Civil War. In a hundred ways the Library as a library of record is invaluable to the Government and the people.

The Copyright Office is now a part of the Library of Congress. Here every book, pamphlet, and other literary production protected by the copyright laws of the United States is registered, and two copies are filed for the use of the Library. Of course, not everything that is published is copyrighted, and consequently the Library misses some very important publications which are needed to make its collections complete, but for the acquisition of which there is no provision, except by purchase.

CHAPTER XXIV.

THE GOVERNMENT PRINTING OFFICE.

THE United States has the largest and finest printing office in the world. It represents an expenditure of more than $16,000,000 for construction and equipment, and an annual expenditure of more than $6,000,000 for maintenance and operation. A thousand different important books and pamphlets are published by it every year, to say nothing of the large number and variety of circulars, bills, and other small jobs which go to make up the year's work of the Government Printing Office. It issues daily and weekly journals, monthly periodicals, and a large number of yearly publications. These range in frequency and importance, from the daily Congressional Record to the annual reports of small bureau officials, and in subject-matter from an abstract report of the Bureau of Standards upon the standardization of pyrometers to a horse book by the Department of Agriculture or a Jefferson's Bible by the authority of Congress.

The aggregate work of the Government Printing Office during a single year is vast in its proportions. In 1910 it set up more than a million pages of type, and printed nearly 3,000,000,000 pages of matter, to say nothing of nearly 700,000,000 blanks, schedules, cards, etc., 72,000,000 letterheads and envelopes, and other things in proportion. Nearly a million and a half copies of various publications were bound. The composition costs were nearly $2,000,000.

In spite of the fact that every known practicable labor-saving device is used at the Government Printing Office, more than $4,000,000 a year is paid out in wages, and it requires more than $300,000 a year to pay for the extra help required when the regular force goes on its vacation. It requires more than a million dollars' worth of paper and upward of $600,000 worth of other material for a year's operation at the big printing office. In a single month it was able to turn out 156,000,000 postal cards. One begins to appreciate the immensity of the plant when he considers how great are the little things on its bill of expenses. The annual soap supply costs $2,000, while $23 of screw drivers, $82 worth of pens, $500 of lead pencils, $2,000 worth of machine oil, 24 tons of printer's ink, and other things in proportion are used. Waste paper is reduced to a minimum, every possible piece being utilized in the operations of the big print shop, and yet $30,000 worth of it is sold annually. Simply by changing the style of the Congressional Record Index, a saving of $30,000 was effected. By changing from egg coal to pea coal, a saving of $10,000 was effected. The printing of the Sunday eulogy editions of the Congressional Record on Monday morning represents an outlay nearly $8,000 greater than would be required if this edition of the Record could be released on Tuesday.

When one goes through the big print shop he finds many wonderful things. One room contains about 80 linotype machines, the largest number to be found in a single room anywhere in the world. In another room are melting pots with a capacity of 15 tons of molten metal. In another room is a series of presses, whose combined output is more than a million impressions every hour. Although there are 87 presses in this room, there is not a pulley or a belt in sight, each machine being driven by its individual electric motor. Printer's ink is applied to 40 tons of paper every eight hours. There are card presses which turn out a million cards each day. The job section is one of the most remarkable in existence. It turns out more work in a single day than the average job office of the commercial world could turn out in a full week. The most perfect equipment that money can buy is to be found throughout the entire plant.

The Public Printer is able to give a good account of himself with this superb equipment when heavy demands are made upon him. When the Naval Court of Inquiry into the destruction of the *Maine* made its report, President McKinley transmitted the document to Congress one afternoon. The next morning it was printed and in the hands of every member of the Senate and House, and of the various members of the press. It contained 24 full-page illustrations, 1 lithograph in colors, and nearly 300 pages of printed matter.

When a congressional committee was making an investigation into the matter of hazing at West Point, the Government Printing Office was able, in 36 hours, to print and deliver to Congress the 2,000-page report of that inquiry. Congress makes heavier demands upon the Government Printing Office than any of the other branches of the Government. Its annual printing bill amounts to more than $2,000,000. The Congressional Record and the printing of hearings, committee reports, and bills cover the major portion of this amount. During a single year the Government Printing Office printed for Congress more than a million copies of octavo publications, 27,000 copies of the Congressional Record every day, some 500 copies each of more than 30,000 bills and resolutions, and numerous other things in proportion.

The next most liberal patron of the Government Printing Office is the Patent Office. The very large expense attached to the issuance of the Patent Office Gazette is responsible for this. This publication is issued weekly, each issue containing the drawings and specifications

GOVERNMENT PRINTING OFFICE

of all patents issued during the preceding week, and also containing a list of trade-marks granted. The Department of Agriculture ranks third. Its most important publication is the annual Yearbook, of which half a million copies are published. Each book weighs about 3 pounds and the total edition would require more than 25 freight cars to transport it.

Nothing is too exacting for the Government Printing Office to undertake. The War of the Rebellion Records, published in 128 volumes, and requiring a 1,200-page index, perhaps for generations will remain the world's greatest undertaking in the printing line. These records contain more than a hundred thousand pages of printed matter and required in their publication 80,000 reams of white paper and more than 3,000,000,000 ems of type. The whole edition comprises about a million and a half volumes. Not only large tasks are undertaken, but exacting ones as well. When Congress wanted to publish a history of the Capitol, it demanded that the completed volume should be one of the finest examples of the printer's art anywhere to be found. The resulting volume is a splendid example of fine printing. When Congress offers to sell a publication, it never counts in the cost of the manuscript, the cost of composition, or anything else except the cost of the paper and other materials entering into the publication and the labor involved in printing and binding. Yet with the history of the

Capitol being sold on this basis, the price of the work was fixed at $10.

Under the administration of Public Printer Samuel B. Donnelly the cost of performing a given piece of work has been materially reduced. During one fiscal year he was able to cut down the scale of charges 5 per cent, and to accomplish more work with 97 less employees. During the next year he reduced this still lower by 3 per cent, the principal decrease being 5 cents per thousand ems in the item of plain composition. The accounts of the office show the cost of operating each division and section, making it possible for the Public Printer to ascertain the cost of the various operations and to determine the comparative efficiency of the different people in the office. Under the present plan of accounting, the Public Printer is able to know at the close of each day exactly how much the operations of that day have cost and what funds remain available for the remainder of the fiscal year.

It is a prevalent opinion that the overhead expenses of the Government Printing Office are not as great as those of commercial establishments. However, these overhead items include power, heat, light, repair to buildings and plant, maintenance of a delivery service, stock rooms, sanitary forces, and payments to employees injured in the service. They also include $50,000 for watchmen, $170,000 for holidays, $358,000 for leaves of absence, and $190,000 for salaries. The overhead charges include all the items entering into the expense of operating a commercial shop with the exception of rent and the insurance. These items are more than offset by the half million dollars required for holidays and leaves of absence. With the amount of money the Government spends for holidays and leaves of absence at the Government Printing Office the Public Printer could pay the rent and insurance upon a building with twice the floor space of the Government Printing Office, and located either in New York or Chicago.

That there is an expenditure of unnecessary money in connection with the distribution of public documents is the belief of the Public Printer. At the present time the product of the Government Printing Office is hauled to the different departments and bureaus, where it is wrapped and addressed and then again hauled to the Post Office and from the Post Office again to the railway-mail cars. It is proposed by the Public Printer that a mailing station shall be established in the Government Printing Office itself, and all mail of this nature hauled to the mail cars direct from the workrooms and storage rooms in the Government Printing Office.

There is an arrangement whereby Senators and Representatives may have their speeches printed for them at the actual cost of the paper and the work of printing and assembling them. The Government Printing Office first sets up the speeches in type for the purpose of putting them into the Congressional Record. When a Senator or Representative delivers a speech which he expects to have reprinted and distributed among his constituents, he orders it held for revision until he has time to arrange it as he would like to have it appear. It is then printed in the Record separate from the regular proceedings, and it is contained in the appendix of the bound sets of the Congressional Record. He then asks the Government Printing Office to estimate how much per thousand the printed speeches will cost delivered at his offices.

In order that every citizen may have full and free opportunity to possess himself of any information contained in any part of the publications of the Federal Government, even though he may not be able to get them through his Member of Congress or through any bureau officials of the Government, the office of the Superintendent of Documents has been created, and this office conducts a regular bookstore with only Government documents on its shelves. After the demands of Congress and the departments are supplied, a sufficient number of additional copies of each publication are run off to supply the needs of the general public.

Many valuable publications are issued under the guise of a public document. And the superintendent of public documents is expected to use such means of advertising them as will bring them to the attention of the general public. These publications are sold at the bare cost of the production after the plates have been made. All other expenses are met by the Federal Treasury. Yet with opportunities like this to buy publications from Uncle Sam's bookstore at a cost even smaller than the actual expense of production, the sales are much more limited than would naturally be expected. The reason for this lies in the fact that people object to paying for a thing at one place which may be had free at another. Nearly every publication which the superintendent of documents has for sale may be obtained from a Senator or a Representative without any cost whatever. The majority of people are aware of this fact, and write directly to their Senators and Representatives for such publications as they desire. However, the total cash sales of documents in 1910 aggregated more than $76,000. That the public is growing more appreciative of the value of public documents is revealed by the fact that the cash sales have increased to this point from $12,000 in only six years. This has been due largely to the use of printer's ink in advertising the fact that the Government has such documents for sale. The superintendent sends out lists of important publications on all the leading subjects in which the mass of the people are interested, and these are posted conspicuously in the small post offices throughout the United States.

The Government also sends out to all of the important libraries of the country which are designated by the Senators and Representatives from the States in which they are located, a full list of Government publications. While many of the libraries seem to appreciate the privilege accorded to them in supplying public documents, others do not care for it. The Government requires the libraries acting as depositaries of public documents to accept the whole list or none. Many libraries are not able to give shelf room and to index the entire list. The Government Printing Office officials believe that every library should be permitted to select only such documents as it finds essential to its particular work.

A few years ago it was determined to eliminate a vast accumulation of worthless public documents from the storage rooms of the Government Printing Office. They were documents which had been returned from libraries and other sources, and were piled together without any reference to their usefulness, the million and a quarter documents comprising the accumulation having been thrown together as they came in. It took more than 400 typewritten pages to list them.

One of the most interesting publications issued at the Government Printing Office is what is known as the Style Book. With hundreds of printers engaged in setting up the type, and with thousands of authors contributing manuscripts, it would inevitably result that there could be no continuity of style with reference to spelling, typography, capitalizing, etc., if some fixed rules were not laid down. There are hundreds of words which may be spelled in two ways, both correct, and either acceptable. But in printing a book or pamphlet one or the other of these spellings must be taken and adhered to. For instance, it would not do to speak of "favor" on one page and "favour" on the next page. In all such cases the Printing Office rules follow Webster's Dictionary, not because Webster's is necessarily better than any other standard dictionary, but because there must be some standard to go by. Another matter which is considered in the Style Book is that of capitalization. It will be observed in reading newspapers that some of them spell Congress with a small "c," and others will "Cap" the word. In thousands of cases capitalization is merely a matter of taste. Yet it must be made uniform in a given office. Therefore, the Style Book deals extensively with the question of capitalization. The practice which the Government follows is to capitalize the names of Government bodies, as, for instance, Congress, the Bureau of Chemistry, and the Office of the Indian Affairs. All State bodies are written, unless accompanied by the name of the State, with small letters, as the board of health, and the bureau of mines. All great natural objects are capitalized in both the singular and the plural, as, Ohio River, Massachusetts and Cape Cod Bays, and the Golden Gate.

In punctuation and abbreviation rigid rules are followed. When three or more adjectives follow one another, the Government style is to put a comma after all but the last, as, for instance, "He was kind, considerate, and gentle." Again, it is right to speak of an "ill-natured man," and proper to write "a man who is ill natured," using the hyphen in the one case and omitting it in the other. It is proper to write Boston and Boone Island Lights, and likewise Massachusetts Bay lights; Grant's Tomb and the tomb of Napoleon.

The existing Style Book of the Government Printing Office was compiled by a committee appointed by the Public Printer, consisting of the leading experts on style in the Government Printing Office. After they had completed their work, they sent it to all of the various officials of the Government who were interested for suggestions as to additions and changes. After these officials had gone over the work carefully and submitted their views, such changes were made as would bring the work in consonance with these ideas, and the Style Book was then formally adopted and is the standard to-day by which all the Government printing is done. It probably represents the world's most authoritative work on printing style.

Not only does the Government spend more than $6,000,000 for printing in Washington, but an additional $2,000,000 may be added for work done outside of Washington. No one ever has undertaken to make an accurate estimate of the expense incurred by Uncle Sam in the preparation of the manuscripts which are printed by the Government. They are practically the product of an expenditure of nearly a billion dollars a year by the Federal establishments; but if one were to consider only such activities as are made primarily for the purpose of publishing information, it is probable that the gathering of material which goes to the Printing Office represents an expenditure of $15,000,000. It has been suggested that if Uncle Sam possessed a proper system of editing, the national printing bill might be cut in two. In a recent investigation into the cost of printing it was stated by an authority that two out of every three of the public documents issued by the Government could be boiled down to half their present size without the omission of any material fact.

CHAPTER XXV.

THE CIVIL SERVICE.

APPROXIMATELY 400,000 persons find employment in the executive civil service of the United States. Add to these those who do work for the Government by contract, such as star-route mail carriers, and those who are connected with the legislative and judicial branches of the Government, and it will appear that there are approximately half a million people working for Uncle Sam.

About half of these are under what is known as the classified service; that is, they are men and women who have been appointed after competitive examination, or who occupied positions when they became subject to examination. The United States annually expends several hundred million dollars for salaries and wages. These salaries range from the $75,000 paid to the President of the United States, down to the $5 a year received by a backwoods postmaster, determined by the cancellation of the postage stamps on mail originating at his office.

Government employees get their positions in different ways. The President directly appoints nearly 10,000 of them. These are the higher officials of the Government, such as Cabinet officers and their chief assistants, judges of the courts, postmasters above the fourth class, United States marshals, district attorneys, heads of important bureaus, and members of various commissions and other organizations. About a quarter of a million employees secure their positions through competitive examinations taken under the auspices of the Civil Service Commission, a body which has in charge the enforcement of the provisions of the Federal civil-service law. Nearly 200,000 receive their appointments without competitive examinations, and are said to be in the unclassified service. Many of these are in positions where mental qualifications are not as essential as physical strength, most of them being merely manual laborers.

The maintenance of a competent force for the operation of the machinery of the Federal Government always has involved many serious problems. During the greater part of the first century of national existence positions in the Federal service were distributed under what was known as the "spoils system." When a new political party came into power it considered that one of its first duties was to turn out the entire force which had administered affairs under the former administration, and to put its own adherents into their places. The evils of the "spoils system" continued to grow more marked until 1883, when the civil-service act was passed, and the present merit system had its beginning.

That this system of appointing Government employees and keeping them in office has been a vast improvement over the old patronage system is agreed by all. But even with this plan of maintaining an efficient force certain objections have arisen. One of these is that employees continue in the service long after the period of their efficiency is passed, and when they are no longer able to render satisfactory return for their salaries. It is agreed that the Government should not turn them out of the service, and yet it is realized that they have passed their term of usefulness. To keep them in their positions after they have become unable to do their work is to adopt, without any law therefor, a sort of old-age pension system.

There are clerks in the Government service who have to be wheeled to their desks in roller chairs, and others have been known to continue on the Federal pay roll long after they have passed the age of 80 years. Although the law strictly requires efficiency in the public service to be maintained, the average departmental chief feels that it would be inhuman to turn the old clerks out, and so they continue in the service. It is estimated that 1 out of every 14 Government employees in the city of Washington is over 65 years old.

As long as there is no law requiring compulsory

retirement after a certain age limit there is no hope of eliminating these people from the service. Of course, Congress will not set an age limit for compulsory retirement without making some sort of provision for the clerks after they are retired. A straight out civil pension is held by many to be out of the question, since it would involve the payment by the Government of perhaps $25,000,000 a year to people who were no longer rendering any return therefor. Another proposal has been brought up which probably will eventually be enacted into law. This proposal is that a certain amount shall be deducted each month from the salaries of Government employees and placed in a retirement fund which the Government will administer for the clerks, paying them 4 per cent interest thereon. Every clerk will be compelled to retire at the age of 70, and will be paid a certain amount, in monthly installments, during the remainder of his life. This amount will be determined by the length of his active service.

The basis proposed is that of 1½ per cent of the full salary drawn by the clerk from the time he enters the service until his retirement. In other words, a clerk who remained in the service for 50 years, receiving an average of $1,200 a year during that time, would have received in the aggregate $60,000. With the retirement pay of 1½ per cent, his annual retirement salary would be $900, or three-fourths of his regular salary.

The average pay of the Government employee

in the United States is $948. The employee in Washington draws an average of $1,079, while the one outside of the District of Columbia gets $928. The advocates of this system insist that the clerks are unable to save anything out of these salaries when managing their own finances, but believe that if the Government made their savings compulsory, they could rise to the occasion and find their old age provided for.

It is to be noted, however, that if the United States finally decides to adopt a system of retiring the superannuated, the Federal Treasury will have to meet the outlays thereunder until such time as the funds collected from the clerks are sufficient to meet the annual demands upon the retirement funds. According to the figures prepared the deductions from the salaries of the clerks would not be sufficient to meet the annuities until after 1975. Prior to that time the Federal Treasury would have to make an annual contribution beginning with about three-quarters of a million dollars for the year the law became effective, increasing year by year until it reached one and three-quarter millions, and then declining again to nothing in a little less than 70 years. The total help the clerks would get in this way would amount to $65,000,000, besides the several million dollars it would cost to administer the fund.

Despite the fact that those who are in the Government service feel that they are underpaid,

THE CIVIL SERVICE

and that their battle with the high cost of living is an unequal one, a feeling that is certainly justified in the case of the man in the service who has to support a family in Washington, there are always a plentiful number of others who would be glad to take their places. There are two eligibles for every appointment made. During a recent year the Civil Service Commission examined 123,657 applicants for civil service appointments. Senators and Representatives are being constantly besieged by constituents who would like to get into the Government service, so much so that it is not improbable that the day will come when Congress will enact a law forbidding any of its Members to intercede in behalf of anyone for appointment to the classified Federal service.

The Civil Service Commission is now pursuing the policy of holding only such examinations as are required for the needs of the service. Formerly examinations were held more frequently, and the result was that there were nearly 50,000 more examination papers a year to be gone over by the commission than necessary for the maintenance of a sufficient list of eligibles. This results in those who succeed being advised of their ratings much earlier, and fewer of those who are eligible decline appointments than when there is a delay in announcing the result of the examination.

The character of examinations is gradually broadening. Many new lines of activity on the part of the Federal Government have resulted in a demand for expert employees of many kinds. Among these may be mentioned apicultural assistants, banking economists, forest engineers, grazing fee collectors, oil inspectors, wireless engineers, tobacco experts, landscape gardeners, scientific assistants in basket willow culture, and engineers of tests. The Civil Service Commission must plan examinations which will serve to test in a thorough and practical manner the special qualifications of the applicants for the proper performance of the duties of the positions they seek to fill. The wide range of the activities of the Federal Government may be inferred from the statement that approximately 500 different kinds of examinations are held annually by the Civil Service Commission, of which 300 are filled by educational tests.

The method by which the Civil Service Commission maintains its lists of eligibles is to hold certain annual examinations for the general public service in various parts of the country. In addition to these, examinations are conducted by local boards of examiners to fill local positions. These examinations are always announced in the newspapers. After the papers have been examined and the ratings of the candidates determined, they are notified, and those who have been successful in passing the examinations are placed on the list of eligibles. Only about one-eighth of the positions embraced in the competitive service are located in Washington. In administering the service outside of Washington, the commission is aided by about 1,700 local boards of examiners having in all more than 5,000 members. None of these local boards is composed solely of the adherents of one political party, except in cases where there are no persons of the opposite party available and competent to serve.

When there is a vacancy in the Government service, the official in charge of the bureau or department in which the vacancy occurs requests the Civil Service Commission to send him a list of eligibles for the position. The commission certifies to him the names of three eligibles for appointment, always giving preference to the three available eligibles having the highest ratings upon their examination papers, except that eligibles who were honorably discharged from the military or naval service by reason of disability incurred in line of duty are placed at the head of all others. Positions in the executive departments at Washington are apportioned among the States and Territories on the basis of population, and when such positions are to be filled, eligibles from the first State in order are certified. Under the present rules no appointing official is permitted to reject a single certified eligible in order to reach a name further down in the list, unless he can show to the satisfaction of the commission that the eligible is mentally, morally, or physically unfit for the position to be filled.

Men have a much better chance in the Government service than women. The list of employees discloses the fact that only one-twelfth of the vast army of workers in the employ of Uncle Sam are women. The law gives the heads of the departments the privilege of calling for male eligibles if they so desire, and this privilege is frequently exercised. Especially is this true in the case of positions requiring confidential service.

Some positions are more easily secured than others. This is true in the case of young men for stenographers. The supply of these has never exceeded the demand, and the same condition prevails in the Railway Mail Service in the far West and Southwest, where nearly all of those who succeed in passing the examination sooner or later are offered positions in the service. In the more important positions the supply of eligibles is far smaller than in the less important ones. There may be a thousand eligibles for appointment to a clerkship, where there is only one eligible to a position as draftsman. The reason for this is that in the ordinary positions Government salaries are considerably higher than commercial salaries, while in technical and administrative positions, the salaries paid by Uncle Sam are often much lower than those paid in the commercial world.

There are exceptions to the rule that all positions in the classified service are filled under competitive examinations. Positions which require highly confidential service are filled without examination. National-bank examiners, receivers in the Office of the Comptroller of the Currency, the cable electricians of the War Department, special agents of the General Land Office appointed to investigate fraudulent entries and other criminal matters, scouts, buffalo keepers, park rangers, and the employees at the leprosy investigation station in Hawaii are instances of the exceptions.

The Civil Service Commission was able to demonstrate its efficiency in mobilizing a capable corps of clerks on a large scale in its work of providing the office force of the Thirteenth Census. It held two extensively advertised examinations in more than 275 cities in which nearly 9,000 persons were examined, of whom 4,800 passed. Of these nearly 4,000 were appointed. The 70,000 census enumerators and a large number of special agents were selected through practical examinations held under the local examining boards of the Civil Service Commission. In all civil-service appointments an effort is made to apportion the positions among the States as equitably as possible. It so happens that in some of the States remote from the National Capital nearly every person who passes a Civil Service examination gets a position, while in the nearby States very few succeed in doing so. That is because the quotas of the nearby States have long since been filled.

A few years ago President Roosevelt issued an

Executive order placing the fourth-class postmasters in 14 States under the classified service, and requiring all new appointees to undergo a competitive examination. The results have not been entirely satisfactory, according to the statements of the Civil Service Commission, because the rate of compensation is too low to attract applicants and the fact that the postmaster must furnish the quarters in which to keep a post office. This not infrequently narrows competition down to the vanishing point, and in the entire territory covered by the order the average number of applicants for each appointment as fourth-class postmaster has been less than two. An arrangement has been made whereby postmasters whose annual compensation is less than $500 may be appointed upon the recommendation of the Post Office inspector in that territory, instead of after competitive examination.

The rules of the Government against political activity on the part of the civil-service employees are growing more rigid and exacting every year. No clerk is allowed to serve on a political committee, as a delegate to a political convention, as an officer of a political club, as chairman of a political meeting, as precinct worker on election day, as editor of a newspaper or writer on subjects discussing political matters, or as a speaker before political meetings. The clerks are forbidden to circulate petitions having a political object, to accept nominations for political offices, to be active in local-option campaigns, or to serve as any sort of election officer.

One of the problems now confronting the Government in its efforts to promote the efficiency of the civil-service employees is that of finding a system of promotion which will give the best possible results. There are four methods of making promotions in the Government service. The first of these is that of free selection by the promoting officer. Formerly this gave poor results, but it is making a better showing to-day. Another method is that of promotion by seniority, which has slight relation to the efficiency of the people promoted. The third method is by competitive examination. The fourth method is by efficiency records maintained in the offices where the clerks are at work. The President's efficiency commission will probably recommend some system of promotions to be made uniform throughout the Government service.

A graphic illustration of the growth of the civil service of the United States is afforded by a contrast of the Government Blue Books published in 1816 and 1905. The one published in 1816 is not much larger than a child's "reader," and had but 176 pages. The one for 1905 had 4,219 pages. The one for 1816 weighed less than a pound, while the one for 1905 tipped the beam at more than 25 pounds. The publication of the one for 1816 cost less than $2,000; the publication of the one for 1905 cost $70,000. The one published in 1911 was so reduced in size by the elimination of useless material that it cost only about $30,000.

The Government service has many attractive features to the person on the outside. The Government clerk is entitled to an annual vacation of a full month. He can utilize another month in sick leave if he needs it. He has frequent holidays, half-holidays every Saturday during the heated term, and goes to work at 9 o'clock in the morning and gets off at 4.30 in the afternoon. To the young man on the farm and in the country town this seems to be an ideal career. Yet few there are who take it up and remain satisfied with their lot. However, it usually takes so much of the self-reliance and independence out of those who make it their lifetime work, that there is perhaps some grounds for the statement of a Senator who observed the operations of the service through 20 years when he told a young fellow who had come to see him that he would rather see his boy a good blacksmith than a Government clerk.

CHAPTER XXVI.

THE SUPREME COURT.

As the head of the American judicial system, possessed of powers which enable it to pass on the constitutionality of the acts of the President, Congress, and the States, and invested with a permanency which makes it independent of changing public opinion, the Supreme Court is in many respects the most powerful factor in the American political system and the greatest judicial organization in the world. Receiving appointment from the President, upon confirmation by the Senate, the justices of the Supreme Court pass beyond the power of either, except under a process of impeachment, in which the House must act as Grand Jury and the Senate as the Court of Trial. The judiciary of England is regarded as the best example of the supremacy of justice in Europe, but the highest English occupant of the bench must be removed by the King, upon the request of Parliament. A justice of the Supreme Court of the United States can be removed for no other cause than "high crimes and misdemeanors," which have never been charged against any justice except Samuel Chase, who was impeached in

1804, but who was acquitted by the Senate. His impeachment grew out of political opinions held and expressed by him, and did not involve the integrity of the man.

An example of how a justice of the Supreme Court may continue in power, even after the whole country has turned its back upon him, is afforded by the experience of Chief Justice Roger B. Taney, who handed down the Dred Scott decision, which in effect nationalized slavery. Taney continued to act as Chief Justice even through the administration of President Lincoln, although he was disliked by the Northern people as only a man can be when he holds opinions against which a people are fighting a bitter war. As long as Charles Sumner continued in the Senate of the United States a bust of Taney was refused its appropriate place in the Supreme Court room.

Although the people have frequently complained of decisions made by the Supreme Court, and have called into question its judgment, its wisdom, and its partisan bias, and although matters of such moment that their ultimate importance could never be measured in dollars and cents have been decided by a margin of one vote, no one ever yet has called into question the integrity of the men who constitute the Supreme Court. Members of the court in discussing the lack of unanimity which sometimes characterizes its decisions assert that it can not be expected that where popular and professional opinion is so

THE SUPREME COURT 327

nearly divided upon the questions involved, the justices, selected from different parties and from remote sections of the Union, and sharing all of the infirmities and prejudices common to their fellow citizens, should be unanimous in their views upon constitutional questions.

The Supreme Court holds its annual sessions from October to June, with recesses at Christmas and at Easter, and at such other times as the consideration of cases which have been heard requires it. When the court is in session its members go to the Capitol every day in the week except Sunday. Five days are devoted to the handing down of opinions and the hearings of cases, Saturday being set aside as a consultation day. Opinions are handed down on Mondays. The court convenes at 12 o'clock noon. Its quarters are in the Capitol Building, the court room being across the hall from the robing and consultation rooms, and is the room which was formerly the Senate Chamber of the United States. Promptly upon the stroke of 12 a passageway across the corridor which leads from the House to the Senate is roped off with silken cords, and the court, headed by the Chief Justice, and followed by the others in the order of their appointment, marches out of the robing rooms, across the corridor, and into the court room. Here everybody arises while the marshal announces the court and the clerk calls out his familiar "Oyez! Oyez!" and announces that the court is now in session and all persons having business before it will draw near and give attention. The justices sit at a high desk, the Chief Justice in the middle, and the others to his right and left in the order of their appointment. Their robes hang in the robing room in the same order that they march in, and they sit around the consultation table in their chambers in the same way.

The justices wear gowns of black silk or like material. When the court was organized, the question arose as to how its members should be dressed. Some thought they should wear the mortar-board cap of a scholar, some the garb of a Roman senator, some the attire of a priest, and others the wig and the gown of the English jurists. When Thomas Jefferson expressed his opinion on the subject he exclaimed: "For Heaven's sake discard the monstrous wig which makes the English judges look like rats peeping through bunches of oakum."

Under the law the justices of the Supreme Court may retire at 70. However, unless overtaken by infirmities which prevent them from rendering efficient service any longer, they prefer to work on. For instance, Justice Harlan was eligible to retire the 1st of June, 1903. But he has preferred to work on, and although the duties of a Supreme Court justice are arduous and trying, he was still in harness in 1911, and had 34 years of honorable service on the bench of the Supreme Court behind him. He has taken part

THE SUPREME COURT

in some of the most important decisions of the court in its entire history. His 34 years of service is more than double the average service of a member of the court. There have been few occasions when the membership of the Supreme Court has changed so rapidly as at the present time. To-day there are only three members of the bench who were there ten years ago. This has come about largely through the numerous deaths that have occurred. Justice Shiras and Justice Brown retired on account of age or ill health, but Justices Brewer and Peckham and Chief Justice Fuller died in the harness. Justice Moody became such a chronic sufferer from rheumatism that although he was far below the age limit, he was retired by an act of Congress passed especially for his benefit, and which carried with it full pay during the remainder of his life.

Until a few years ago the Supreme Court met at 12 and adjourned at 4 o'clock. The justices would withdraw one at a time to eat their lunch behind the scenes, and the attorney addressing the court could often attune his speech to the rattle of the dishes, while perhaps the very justice to whom he was most anxious to address his argument was regaling himself with a dozen fried oysters. This practice probably would have continued indefinitely had not a new member come along and insisted that they adopt the plan of adjourning for lunch and carrying the session further into the evening.

The procedure of the Supreme Court in the determination of the questions involved is an interesting one. To begin with it hears the oral arguments of the attorneys in the case. An attorney who can deliver an effective speech before this court is an artist in his line. Usually the members apparently take little interest in what an attorney is saying, and to the spectator it would seem that the attorney might just as well omit his oral argument and trust to the briefs he has previously submitted. But if anyone thinks that the court is not paying attention, let him watch an attorney stray away from the points his argument is expected to cover or misquote a former decision of the court; he will at once discover that the court is taking mental note and is ready to remind the attorney of his error. Sometimes the court will hear the argument of a plaintiff in error and is persuaded that he had no case upon his own showing. Under such conditions it will advise the opposing attorney that he needs to make no argument. A humorous incident of this kind occurred years ago when the famous Matt Carpenter was the attorney for the plaintiff in error in a certain case. When the opposing attorney began to answer his speech the court declared that it was unnecessary for him to speak further. The attorney was hard of hearing and did not understand the remark, when Matt Carpenter spoke up and said: "The court would rather give you the case than hear you talk."

The justices are not without their sense of humor, even when on the bench. Some years ago a case involving a patent collar button was pending. While the attorney was engaged in arguing it, one of the justices asked him if he understood him to say that "if the button fell out of a man's shirt as he was dressing and rolled under the bed, the owner could recover it without swearing." The attorney replied that no such button was possible of invention.

After a case is argued in the Supreme Court, its members take the printed briefs to their homes and read them. There are a large number of these briefs to be read, and often a single case involves a stupendous amount of study if the members of the court are to become perfectly familiar with it. Saturdays being set apart for conference days, the members of the court meet in the conference room and discuss the cases fully and freely. A friend of one of the justices once asked him what they did in the conference room. He replied that they fought like cats and dogs. Of course, this was overdrawing the picture, but the average justice is a man of great strength of mind and force of character, and, therefore, tenacious of his views; and it is not to be wondered that these discussions sometimes become heated and prolonged. After every justice has expressed his opinion as fully as he cares to, the Chief Justice calls the roll of the court, and each member votes upon the question of an adverse or a favorable decision. After this the Chief Justice assigns to the members of the court the cases upon which they are to write their opinions. Later these opinions are brought in by the members writing them and laid before the whole court. Here again they argue the case, criticize the opinion, and often amend it so much that it has little semblance to its original form.

The court again by a roll call votes upon the question of whether it shall be read as the opinion of the court or not. If there is a dissenting vote on any case, those who dissent arrange among themselves as to who shall write the dissenting opinion. Sometimes the grounds upon which different justices dissent vary, so that there may be one or more dissenting opinions handed down.

The days when opinions are handed down are trying ones on the newspaper correspondents who have to report them. There are a few justices who deliver their opinions in a clear and distinct tone of voice so that they are easily followed and their opinions easily reported. On the other hand, there are others who speak so low and so much like a boy in a hurry to get through with a lesson that it is next to impossible to hear them. The Supreme Court makes little provision for newspaper men, a practice entirely at variance with that of the other branches of the Government. It is true that there are tables for the representatives of the press associations, but the other members of the corps of Washington correspondents must take their chances on two little benches which are filled up with tourists if the correspondents are not there on time.

When a lawyer is admitted to practice before the Supreme Court he signs his name in the official register of the court. Lawyers applying for admission are introduced to the court by some member of the bar, and immediately after the formalities have been complied with they are able to begin their work before the court.

There is perhaps no other body in the world which conducts its business in a more impressive way than the Supreme Court. With the exception of its gown, there is nothing to distinguish the court from any other body of American officials, but silence is so rigidly maintained that the atmosphere is one of dignity and solemnity. Visitors are admitted at all times, so long as there is room on the few benches outside the bar.

There are very often little touches of interest in the course of a day's sitting. When Chief Justice Fuller was still on the bench, he and Associate Justice Harlan were quite chummy. Upon one occasion Justice Harlan leaned over and whispered something to the Chief Justice, and they both began to laugh for all the world like two small boys in school having a hard battle to keep from laughing aloud. Chief Justice Fuller was very fond of his grandchildren, and upon one occasion had a little granddaughter sit on his lap while he was presiding in the Supreme Court.

The Supreme Court has original jurisdiction in comparatively few cases. Principal among these are those cases where ambassadors and consuls are affected and those to which a State is a party. In all other cases the Supreme Court has appellate jurisdiction; that is, the cases are first tried in other courts and if the litigants are not satisfied, may afterwards be carried to the Supreme Court by the party desiring to make an appeal. When the court was first organized it had to wait a full year before a single case was brought to its attention. Original cases have always been very few. Prior to the Civil War there were never more than 350 cases on its docket, while to-day the number is nearly a thousand.

The employees of the Supreme Court seldom change. They are men who have proved their value, and the court cares nothing whatever for patronage. The pages are an interesting lot of young fellows. They must wear knickerbockers as long as they continue to serve as such, and this often brings about the somewhat ludicrous situation of a full-fledged lawyer going around in boy's clothes. They come in when they are small boys and begin to read law immediately thereafter. By the time they are grown they are well advanced in law, and when they reach their majority they are ready to be admitted to practice.

The Supreme Court has a higher standing in the public estimation to-day than it had at the beginning of its career. Chief Justice Jay retired

THE SUPREME COURT 335

from the high position to accept a political office. A governorship was then regarded as more honorable than a seat on the Supreme Bench. Justice Cushing once declined the Chief Justiceship on the ground that he preferred his position as Associate Justice to that of Chief Justice. Many interesting stories are told concerning members of the court. In the early days there was a famous boarding house in Washington where many members of the court lived. Upon one occasion they agreed that they would drink no wine at their meals except when it was raining. Chief Justice Marshall sent Associate Justice Story to the window one day to see if it were raining. Story reported that there was not a cloud to be seen. Marshall immediately assumed a judicial frame of mind and declared that so long as it was raining within the jurisdiction of the court they were entitled to their wine, and that no hour ever passed that it did not rain somewhere in the United States. "Therefore," said he, "let us have our Madeira." When Justice Field was on the bench, the justices who sat on one side of the Chief Justice, were Field, Gray, Brown, and White; those on the other side were Harlan, Brewer, Shiras and Peckham. Those on the one side had no children while those on the other side had both children and grandchildren.

Justices of the Supreme Court sometimes change their minds. When the Pollock case, involving the constitutionality of the income-tax law, was first heard the court refused to declare it unconstitutional. On the rehearing the vote stood five to four against the constitutionality of the law. It is known that between the two hearings some justice changed his mind, as the personnel of the court was the same. Who that justice was, and what his motives were, no outsider is able to say with authority. Upon another occasion, when the Hayes-Tilden presidential election was in dispute and it was decided to create an Electoral Commission to settle it, Justice Clifford ordered his secretary to write a letter announcing that under no circumstances would he accept a place on the commission. The next day he asked his secretary if he had sent the letter and received a negative reply, whereupon he ordered the letter destroyed and accepted a place on the commission. Justice Brewer, afterwards a member of the court, once declared that no one ever knew why Clifford changed his mind.

The present Supreme Court is for the most part made up of young men. Hughes, Van Devanter, and Lamar are all on the sunny side of 55, Lamar, the eldest of the trio, having been born in 1857, and Hughes, the youngest, in 1862. The Chief Justice, Edward D. White, is a Democrat and an ex-Confederate soldier, and was appointed Chief Justice by President Taft, a Republican. Harlan and Lurton admit that they once shot at one another. They were on opposite sides in a small battle in Kentucky during the Civil War.

CHAPTER XXVII.

OTHER FEDERAL COURTS.

THE judiciary of the United States consists of one Supreme Court, nine circuit courts of appeal, and seventy-odd district courts. In addition thereto there is the Court of Claims, in which all claims against the Government are passed upon, the Commerce Court, before which are brought all matters relating to the interstate commerce laws of the country, and the Court of Customs Appeals, where the statutes relating to the customs laws of the United States are interpreted. These latter courts have jurisdiction in special matters provided for by acts of Congress. The Supreme Court, the circuit courts of appeal, and the district courts have jurisdiction over general subjects—in short, over everything not specifically delegated to the special courts.

The judicial system of the Federal Government was entirely revamped in 1911 under an act to codify, revise, and amend the laws relating to the judiciary. The statutes under which the courts acted prior to that time cover over 9,000 sections in the statute books of the country. It was a great undertaking to get all of these together, to eliminate their inconsistencies, and to boil them down into a clear and concise statute and at the same time to change certain features of the judicial establishment.

As the judiciary was formerly composed there was a Supreme Court, with a Chief Justice and 8 Associate Justices; 9 circuit courts of appeal, with 3 judges each; 77 circuit courts, one in each judicial district, which courts were required by law to hold sessions in 276 different places; and 77 district courts, which were required by law to hold sessions in the same places. There were 29 circuit judges and 90 district judges on the bench. Under the old system the aggregate number of days in which the circuit courts of the country were in session was 18,000. The pressure of work had grown so great that the district judges had to preside over the circuit courts for 16,000 days, leaving only 2,000 days in which circuit judges presided. The result produced a sort of judicial anomaly. A district judge would be sitting as such, and during the day the calendar would be completed. No other cases being ready for trial, the district court would adjourn. The judge, without leaving the bench, would call another clerk, who would bring in another docket, and, in many cases, another crier would proceed to open the circuit court, and the district judge, without changing his seat, would proceed to dispose of the circuit-court docket, clothed with the powers of a circuit judge.

OTHER FEDERAL COURTS

Under the new law the circuit court was eliminated from the system. There are now three steps in litigation from its inception to the final decision from which there is no appeal. With the exception of a very few isolated cases, all litigation in the Federal courts begins in the district courts. Appeals may be taken from these courts to the circuit court of appeals. If the litigants are not satisfied with the outcome of their cases there, they may, within certain limitations, carry them up to the Supreme Court. The less important cases are not, as a rule, permitted to be carried up to the higher courts. The law seeks to prevent the crowding of the dockets of the higher courts by providing that final jurisdiction in unimportant litigation may rest in the lower courts.

Each court has its own seal, its own records, and its own officials. There is a United States district attorney, a United States marshal, and such clerks of the court as its business demands in every judicial district. Each district court must hold sessions at a number of different places in the district. The law provides where these meeting places are to be, and the towns designated are usually those which have a Federal building. A large number of cases are not tried by juries, but each term of each district court requires the services of jurors. These jurors, both grand and petit, are publicly drawn from a box containing, at the time of each drawing, the names of not less than 300 persons possessing the necessary qualifications, and whose names are placed therein by the clerk of the court and a commissioner appointed by the judge. The commissioner is a citizen of good standing residing in the district in which the court is held, and he is a well-known member of the principal political party opposing that to which the clerk of the court belongs. The clerk and the commissioner then proceed to place the names in the box, each of them putting in a name alternately without reference to party affiliations.

The district court boundaries of jurisdiction are laid out by law. In nearly half of the States a judicial district is coextensive with the State lines. In other States there are two judicial districts, while in New York there are four. The district judge is not permitted to live outside of the limits of his district, and may be impeached if he does so. His salary is fixed at $6,000 a year. Whenever it appears that the judge of any district court is any way concerned in any suit pending before him in such a way as might render him unfit to preside at the trial of the case, he is required by law to make a record of the fact upon request of counsel. If either party to any proceeding in a court makes an affidavit that the judge who is to preside over the court during the hearing of the suit has a personal bias or prejudice in the case, he must step aside and allow the senior circuit judge of the circuit of which the district court forms a part to appoint some other judge to sit in his stead.

Any suit of a civil nature, arising under the Constitution or laws of the United States or under treaties, may be removed by the defendant from the State courts to the United States district courts. Any suit wholly between citizens of different States may be carried to the United States district court. The law requires that all offenses punishable with death under the Federal laws shall be tried in the county where the offense was committed, providing it can be done without great inconvenience. When a murder is committed on the high seas, the case is tried in the judicial district where the person charged with the murder is apprehended.

There are nine judicial circuits in the United States, in each of which is a circuit court of appeals, consisting of a number of judges. In three of these circuits there are four judges, and in one of them two. In the other five there are three. Each circuit is presided over by one of the justices of the Supreme Court. They seldom sit in cases coming up in the circuit courts of appeals, but more usually look after the work of supervising the administration of affairs in the circuits.

The judges of the Federal courts must take a rigid oath on becoming members of the judiciary. They do solemnly swear that they will administer justice without respect to persons and to do equal right to the poor and to the rich and faithfully and impartially discharge the duties incumbent upon them according to the best of their abilities and understanding, agreeable to the Constitution and the laws of the United States. No judge of a Federal court is permitted to practice law, and may be impeached if he attempts to do so. Any judge who has served 10 years continuously and has attained the age of 70 may retire from the bench by resignation and continue to draw his full salary during the remainder of his life, a privilege few fail to exercise.

The newest court in the Federal judicial system is the Commerce Court. It was created by an act of Congress approved by President Taft on June 18, 1910. It was given jurisdiction formerly possessed by the circuit courts over all cases for the enforcement, otherwise than by adjudication and collection of a forfeiture or penalty, or by infliction of criminal punishment, of any order of the Interstate Commerce Commission other than for the payment of money. It also has jurisdiction in cases brought to set aside any order of the Interstate Commerce Commission, likewise in cases arising under the act to regulate commerce with foreign nations, and among the States, such as formerly were brought in the circuit courts of the United States. The jurisdiction over these matters and over mandamus proceedings of certain kinds is made exclusive, practically giving to the Commerce Court

OTHER FEDERAL COURTS

full control of all of the laws for the regulation of interstate commerce.

The court is composed of five judges. When it was organized these judges were appointed by the President as circuit judges and designated to serve as members of the bench of the Commerce Court. The term of one member of the court expires each year, after which he takes his place as a regular circuit judge and the Chief Justice of the United States designates some other circuit judge to succeed the retiring member.

The member of the court holding the earliest appointment becomes the presiding judge upon the retirement of the next one above him. After a judge of the Commerce Court has served for five years and has retired therefrom to act as circuit judge, he serves on the circuit court of appeals for any circuit requiring his services, upon the designation of the Chief Justice of the Supreme Court. It will probably be the custom when a justice retires from the Commerce Court that he will be assigned to the vacancy caused by the selection of another circuit judge to take his place on the Commerce Court. Each judge of the Commerce Court receives an additional allowance of $1,500 a year, above his regular salary as a circuit judge, for expenses while serving on the Commerce Court in Washington.

The Commerce Court is always open to the transaction of business. Its regular sessions are held in Washington, but the powers of the court and of its officials may be exercised anywhere in the United States. The court may, when it desires to do so in the avoidance of undue expense or inconvenience to suitors, meet in other cities in any part of the country, but its headquarters always will be in Washington.

The machinery for filing suits in the Commerce Court is simple in its operation. The person who desires to have it sit in judgment files in the office of its clerk a written petition, setting forth briefly and succinctly the facts constituting the petitioner's cause for action and specifying the relief sought. A final judgment, interlocutory order, or decree of the Commerce Court may be reviewed by the Supreme Court of the United States, such appeals being taken in like manner as appeals from the circuit courts. No judgment of the Commerce Court shall be superseded or stayed by an appeal to the Supreme Court, unless a member of that body shall so direct. All suits against the findings of the Interstate Commerce Commission can be brought in this court, but the pendency of such suit shall not of itself suspend the order of the Commission. Provision is made; however, for the temporary suspension of such order, in the discretion of the Commerce Court, where irreparable damage would otherwise ensue. The presiding judge of the Commerce Court is Martin A. Knapp, of New York, who served on the Interstate Commerce Commission from 1891 to 1911. The other judges are Robert

W. Archbald, of Pennsylvania; William H. Hunt, of Montana; John E. Carland, of South Dakota; and Julian W. Mack, of Illinois.

The Court of Claims was established in 1855. It consists of a chief justice and four judges, and holds annual sessions in Washington, beginning on the same day that Congress begins and continuing as long as there is business on its docket. On the first day of the regular session the court is required to transmit to that body a full report of all judgments rendered by it during the previous year, the amounts thereof, and in whose favor rendered, together with a brief synopsis of each claim. No Member of Congress is allowed to practice before this court, and if one does so during his service in that body, he is subject to a fine of $10,000 and imprisonment for two years; moreover, he shall thereafter be incapable of holding any office of honor, trust, or profit under the Government of the United States.

The Court of Claims has jurisdiction over all claims, except pensions, founded upon the Constitution or the laws of Congress, or upon any regulation of an executive department, or upon any contract expressed or implied with the Government of the United States. This does not include claims growing out of the late Civil War and commonly known as war claims. The court also acts as a guide for Congress in determining the propriety of the Government paying any claim which can be satisfied only by congressional action. The branch of Congress having a case pending of this nature may, by vote, refer it to the court, and the court then hears all of the testimony, makes the necessary investigations, and reports the facts in the case to Congress and advises that body what amount, if any, is legally or equitably due the claimant from the United States.

If, in its investigation of a case, the court finds that the claimant has a claim of such nature as to come under the jurisdiction of the court, it may proceed to render a verdict therein. The claimant in all such cases is required to set forth fully what action has been taken, and if there is any fraud in the presentation of claims, such claims are thereby forfeited and the claimants are prevented from ever recovering anything from the Government on them.

Another special court created by Congress is known as the United States Court of Customs Appeals, composed of a presiding judge and four associate judges. This court is required always to be open for the transaction of business, and sessions may be held wherever the court may designate. All cases growing out of the decisions of the customs officials of the Federal Government with reference to the construction of the law and the facts respecting classifications of merchandise and the rates of duty imposed thereon come up to it from the Board of General Appraisers. The judgments and decrees of the

OTHER FEDERAL COURTS

Court of Customs Appeals are final in all such cases. If any party interested, whether it be a Government official or an importer, owner, consignee, or agent of any imported merchandise, is dissatisfied with the decision of the Board of General Appraisers he has 60 days in which to carry his complaint to the Customs Court.

The business transacted in the circuit and district courts of the United States is large. During the fiscal year of 1910, 3,464 Government cases were terminated. They resulted in 1,866 judgments for the United States and 254 judgments against the United States. The remainder were either dismissed or discontinued. The criminal prosecutions in these courts are numerous, a total of more than 15,000 cases having been terminated in 1910. Of these 4,355 grew out of violations of the internal-revenue laws, 1,775 represented violations of the postal laws, and 401 violations of the pure food and drug laws. These 15,371 cases resulted in 9,451 convictions and 1,459 acquittals, the remaining cases having been thrown out of court upon one ground or another. There were nearly 10,000 criminal prosecutions pending at the end of the year. The courts dispose of approximately 10,000 suits a year to which the United States is not a party, and have about 45,000 cases on their dockets upon any one day.

When a man or a corporation goes into bankruptcy, the proceedings take place in the Federal courts. During an average year about 14,000 voluntary petitions in bankruptcy are filed and a like number are disposed of. There are always on the dockets of the Federal courts about 30,000 unsettled voluntary bankruptcy cases. The aggregate liabilities of the voluntary bankruptcy cases closed out in an average year is approximately $100,000,000. Wage-earners resort to the bankruptcy courts more frequently than any other class of people. In 1910, 842 petitioners in voluntary cases were farmers, 4,366 wage-earners, 3,667 merchants, 386 manufacturers, and 333 professional men.

When an insolvent fails to make a voluntary bankruptcy petition, outsiders may file petitions to have him adjudged a bankrupt. About 4,000 such petitions are filed a year. Nearly half of those against whom these petitions are filed are merchants.

CHAPTER XXVIII.

THE DEPARTMENT OF JUSTICE.

AFTER the Department of State, the Department of Justice is the smallest of the nine principal branches of the Federal executive service. Yet it is one of the most important of them all. Here the general laws of the country find means for their enforcement and the laws under which the other departments act are construed. Laws do not enforce themselves and the courts are powerless to act unless there is some one to play the rôle of prosecuting attorney. The office of the Attorney General was created for the legal advisor of the President under the judiciary act of 1789. In the early history of the country the chief duty of that official was to guide the Chief Magistrate along legal lines and to represent the United States in the Supreme Court. Since that time his duties have expanded until to-day he is charged with the duties of prosecuting attorney for the Government, the direction of the administration of the Federal court system, and the supervision of Federal prisons.

When the Attorney Generalship was first created it carried with it a salary of only $1,500 a year, and the Attorney General was supposed to pay his secretary out of that. He was not required to reside in Washington and was permitted to continue his law practice while serving as the Attorney General of the United States. In 1814 the duties of the Attorney General were increased, but it was not until 1870 that the office was transformed into a full-fledged department of the Government. Prior to that time the Attorney General held the unique position of being a member of the Cabinet and yet not the head of a department.

When Congress passes an act of legislation, it is usually the workmanship of many hands. The original bill is amended and amended again until it often bears but few marks of its original authorship. The result is that the average law on the statute books is a sort of patchwork of ideas, not especially noted for its plainness of expression. It is often difficult to understand exactly what Congress meant to say, and sometimes one must read carefully the voluminous debates of the House and the Senate before he can interpret correctly the meaning of its legislation. This gives rise to differences of opinion as to the true meaning of many legislative acts and to many controversies before the departments and in the courts. An instance of this is afforded by the great difficulty in the construction of the pure-food law. That law left much doubt as to exactly what constitutes a violation of it. It was this doubt that led to the propounding of the famous query,

"What is Whisky?" That question was thrashed out in the Department of Agriculture, then carried up to the Solicitor General for report, and then to the President who decided it finally.

Probably more public interest is felt in the prosecutions under the Sherman antitrust law than in any other branch of the work of the Department of Justice. Many great trusts have been haled into court by the department's machinery and verdicts secured which have resulted in the breaking up of such large combines as the Standard Oil Co., the American Tobacco Co., and the Powder Trust. Such large combinations of capital as the Paper Board Association, the Window Glass Trust, the Turpentine Trust, and the Wire Pool Associations have been indicted and prosecuted, and, in many instances, verdicts against them secured. The Attorney General also has charge of all litigation for the enforcement of the interstate-commerce laws. When the constitutionality of such a measure as the corporation-tax law is attacked it becomes the duty of the Attorney General to defend the right of the Government to enact and enforce such laws. When the other departments detect violations of the laws in their respective fields of activity it becomes the duty of the Attorney General to prosecute those guilty of such violations. In the investigations into the frauds upon the Government by the underweighing of sugars imported into the United States, the department was able to collect nearly $3,000,000 from the Sugar Trust on account of penalties and duties fraudulently withheld from the Treasury. Other sugar manufacturers were also found to be implicated and more than $1,000,000 has been collected from them.

The Department of Justice is now in possession of a full-fledged secret service of its own. It gives its especial attention to the investigation of violations of the national-banking laws and antitrust laws, peonage laws, the bucket-shop laws, the laws relating to fraudulent bankruptcies, the impersonations of Government officials with the intent to defraud, thefts, murders, and other offenses committed on Government reservations or with respect to Government property. A large number of other matters are investigated by this secret service, including Chinese smuggling, customs frauds, internal-revenue frauds, post-office frauds, violations of neutrality laws, land frauds, etc.

Suits may not be brought against the United States by individuals except in certain classes of cases which may be carried to the Court of Claims and to the circuit courts. In other cases it becomes the duty of the Attorney General to sit in judgment and make recommendations to the President as to the proper course to pursue where individuals seek redress. His opinion in these cases practically amounts to a final verdict from which there is no appeal. The Attorney General also gives opinions upon all questions submitted to him by the Cabinet officers and the President. During a single year 111 formal opinions were rendered by the Attorney General, 19 upon the request of the President and 92 upon the request of executive departments. Opinions were also rendered in 406 cases as to real-estate titles, involving property worth more than $5,000,000. No Government money may be expended for lands or buildings by any of the executive departments until the matter of the title has been settled.

In the rôle of prosecuting attorney for the Government, the Department of Justice looks after all actions at law or suits in equity in which the United States has an interest. If a moonshiner violates the revenue laws, he is placed in the custody of a United States marshal and is prosecuted by the district attorney under the general direction of the Department of Justice. If a man is accused of robbing the mails, he is arrested by the inspectors of the Post Office Department and turned over to the legal officers of the Department of Justice for prosecution. There are more violations of the internal-revenue laws than any other class of Federal statutes. Postal laws, customs laws, and pension laws rank in the order named with respect to the frequency of their violation.

The Department of Justice has no control over the Federal courts so far as the judges are concerned, but the district attorneys, United States marshals, and the clerks of the courts act under its guidance. They are appointed by the President, with the advice and consent of the Senate, but the Attorney General is nearly always consulted before the appointments are made, and in the discharge of their official duties they are expected to be guided by the advice and recommendations of the Department of Justice.

The Attorney General seldom appears in court in person, except in cases of great gravity, involving the construction of the Constitution. He may appear in any court of the Federal judiciary if he desires to do so. His chief assistant is the Solicitor General, who, in the absence or disability of the Attorney General, performs the duties of the head of the department. Under the direction of the Attorney General he has supervision of all cases before the Supreme Court in which the Government is interested. He also assists his chief in the preparation of opinions for the guidance of the President and the members of his Cabinet and in the direction of the law officers of the Government throughout the country.

Next in rank to the Solicitor General is a lawyer known as the Assistant to the Attorney General. He is usually a man who has had a great deal of experience in corporation work, and is popularly known as "the chief trust buster" of the Government. He has charge of all suits growing out of the Sherman antitrust law and other related legislation.

There are a number of Assistant Attorneys

THE DEPARTMENT OF JUSTICE 355

General in the department. Three of these have their offices with the department and act under the directions of the Attorney General. Another is in charge of all suits brought against the Government in the Court of Claims. Another looks after claims growing out of depredations committed by Indians who are still under the control of the Government. Another has charge of all the cases arising out of the administration of the customs laws. In addition to these officials, there is an Assistant Attorney General for the Interior Department who interprets all laws relating to Indian affairs and public lands. The Solicitor for the State Department is an authority upon questions of municipal and international law. When a citizen of the United States has a claim against a foreign Government growing out of such things as deprivation of property brought about by failure to recognize his rights as an American citizen, his case is studied by the Solicitor, and the Secretary of State acts in accordance with the opinions of that official. When a foreign citizen thinks he is mistreated in America and appeals to his home Government, his case is looked into by the Solicitor and the attitude of the United States with reference to it is based upon his findings. The Solicitor also has charge of the examination of extradition papers. He is an official of the Department of Justice. The Solicitor of the Treasury is also an official of the Department of Justice, and is charged with the supervision of much of the litigation of the Government. It is his duty to give necessary instructions to United States attorneys, marshals, and clerks of the courts in matters and proceedings appertaining to the suits under his superintendence. He examines all official bonds, such as are filed in the Treasury Department, and issues distress warrants against delinquent collectors and other custodians of public money. There is also a Solicitor for the Internal Revenue Bureau, one for the Department of Commerce and Labor, and one for the Department of Agriculture.

The Department of Justice also has charge of all pardon cases excepting those in the Army and Navy. When a petition is filed with the President asking him to pardon any person convicted of crime against the Federal Government, he refers the matter to the Department of Justice. Here it is assigned to a special attorney known as the Attorney in Charge of Pardons. He goes over the case carefully and briefs all of the evidence and correspondence relating to it, then turns it over to the Attorney General. He in turn makes his recommendations, and then sends the papers to the President.

A new duty recently was assigned to the Department of Justice—the administration of the law for the parole of Federal prisoners. Under the act of June, 1910, all Federal prisoners sentenced to a term of upward of one year are qualified, after the expiration of one-third of their term, to apply for a parole; that is, to be liberated for the remainder of their term under such rules and regulations as the Attorney General may approve. The board of parole is composed of the Superintendent of Prisons, an official of the Department of Justice, and the warden and physician of the respective penitentiaries. Applications for parole are heard by that board in the first instance. If they recommend the parole, the case goes to the Attorney General for approval or disapproval. It is a condition precedent to the approval of a parole that some responsible person undertakes to look after the prisoner and to provide him with employment. The prisoner is subject also to general supervision by a probation officer. In case he violates the conditions of his parole, he may be returned to prison. A very large number of prisoners have been paroled during the past year. Up to the present time, no prisoner has violated his parole.

It is said by the officials of the department that letters constantly reaching them indicate that there is a somewhat general misconception on the part of the public of the department's relation to the administration of justice. It does not in any way or sense control or direct the action of the Federal courts, nor is it responsible for the final decision of any court, civil or criminal; its responsibility ending with the proper presentation to a court of the facts and constructions of the law germane to the contention of the Government in any particular case. The motto which appears on the seal of the department is: "Qui pro domina justitia sequi ur." Poetically translated, this means: "Who sues for the lady justice?" In other words, the department is charged with the responsibility solely of presenting to the appropriate court the considerations which go to make up a Government case in the event of an alleged infraction of a Federal statute or of any civil cause.

In its work of rendering opinions for the President and the heads of the executive departments on business relating to their affairs, the Department of Justice has uniformly held that the Attorney General is debarred from giving opinions on matters of law to others than the officials named. It was feared in the early days of the Republic that a Department of Justice, unless strictly limited in this respect, might develop into a bureau which would be a source of free advice on legal matters to citizens of the United States in general. In order to avoid such embarrassment, the Attorneys General have held strictly to the law, even declining to comply with the request of a committee of Congress for an opinion on a legal matter.

It costs approximately $10,000,000 a year to maintain the judicial branch of the United States Government. Of this $1,000,000 is expended for the maintenance of the Department of Justice in Washington, another million for the maintenance of prisoners who violate the laws of the Federal Government, and $7,000,000 for the operations of the United States courts. An average of more than 2,500 prisoners are maintained at the expense of the Federal Government all the time, exclusive of those kept in county jails pending trial and under sentence for minor offenses. About 1,500 are sentenced to prison each year, and a like number are discharged in that time. Of these approximately 1,200 are discharged by the expiration of their sentences. Approximately 600 applications for pardon come up each year. The President considers about two-thirds of these cases. He unconditionally pardons a few and commutes the sentences of over a hundred. It costs the United States Government about $200 a year to maintain each of its prisoners. The Department of Justice operates a criminal identification bureau and has upward of 26,000 Bertillion records and 20,000 finger-print records of criminals, great and petty, in the United States. In a single year it was able to identify some 800 criminals by these records.

In connection with the Federal prisoners in Alaska an interesting question has long been pending. It is the custom there that when a person without means is found badly wounded or with frozen limbs to charge him with vagrancy in order that he may, as a United States prisoner, receive the necessary medical and surgical attention at the expense of the Government, the appropriation for support of prisoners being charged with the expense. The Department of Justice feels that the Federal Government ought not to be burdened with the care of these people, hospital bills frequently running as high as $1,000 per person. The Alaska judges declare that these victims are vagrants and that it would be inhuman not to give them necessary treatment.

One of the principal duties of the Department of Justice is that of defending suits brought against the Government in the Court of Claims and in the district and circuit courts of the United States. Nearly 6,000 cases were disposed of during the year 1910 under the general jurisdiction of the courts. The amount claimed in these cases was over $3,600,000; the amount awarded by the courts was slightly over $500,000. The claims referred to the Court of Claims by Congress amounted to $11,730,000; the court awarded the claimants $903,000.

The large growth in volume of new legislation with relation to the regulation of corporations under the interstate-commerce clause of the Federal Constitution has greatly multiplied and expanded the activities of the Department of Justice. The number of suits which it is called upon to prosecute and to defend have been increasing from year to year, and the officials of the department forecast that the volume of business will continue to grow in increasing ratio.

While the department is usually able to command the services of efficient lawyers in the prosecution of its suits against great corporations, it is frequently found that these corporations are ready to employ the department's best men at largely increased salaries. Some of these special attorneys do accept positions with the corporations and leave the Government service. Others, however, stick to the department in spite of the allurements of large salary offers, and sometimes find a rich reward for doing so. Only a few months ago Judge W. S. Kenyon was the "chief trust buster" of the department and stayed with his work in spite of large salaries offered him in the commercial world. His reward came in the shape of an election to the United States Senate by the Legislature of Iowa. It is only in recent years that the Department has been supplied with funds sufficient to command the services of able lawyers in the prosecution of individual suits. Under a more liberal policy on the part of Congress in this direction a number of epoch-making decisions on the interstate-commerce laws of the country have been rendered.

CHAPTER XXIX.

THE PAN AMERICAN UNION.

An eloquent testimonial of the deep interest which the United States feels in the welfare of the 20 other Republics of the western world, the Pan American Union, with headquarters in Washington, is a unique international institution. Organized for the purpose of promoting commercial intercourse between the 21 American Republics, each of which contributes to its maintenance in proportion to its population, its work has expanded and its activities have widened until to-day it is one of the leading factors in promoting trade and increasing the bonds of friendship which tend to unite all of the countries from the Canadian border to Cape Horn.

This interest of the United States Government in her sister Republics began when America was young. When James Monroe was President he boldly announced that the safety and welfare of the United States made it necessary that no country of the Old World should acquire another foot of territory in the New World, whether by purchase, conquest, or otherwise; and that attempts to do so would be regarded as acts of unwar-

THE PAN AMERICAN UNION 363

ranted aggression. The nations of Europe were astonished at the boldness of the new Republic of the west in thus serving notice upon them that they must keep hands off of American territory, but they decided that it would be best for them to acquiesce in this attitude of the United States, and so the Monroe doctrine has become one of the principles of international law tacitly recognized by all nations. To this doctrine the majority of the Latin American Republics owe their political existence. Under it the United States stands as sponsor for practically the entire western world south of the Canadian boundary.

Bound together by so many ties it is but natural that the 21 American Republics should feel a deep interest in the political and commercial welfare of the whole American continent. This interest will be enhanced by the building of the Panama Canal, which will vastly benefit them all and make even more essential close bonds of friendship between them. This growing interest finds concrete expression in the increasing influence of the Pan American Union. The union has its existence by common consent and cooperation, and its administration and duties are fixed by the periodic Pan American conferences held in the capitals of the various countries, to which all of the countries interested send delegates.

The affairs of the Pan American Union are controlled by a governing board composed of the diplomatic representatives in Washington of the other American nations and the Secretary of State of the United States. The affairs of the union are administered by a Director General, an assistant director, and a corps of specially trained assistants. The union is devoted to the development and conservation of commerce and friendly intercourse and good understanding among the American Republics. It was originally organized some 20 years ago as a result of the action of the first Pan American conference held in Washington during the autumn and winter of 1889-90. This famous gathering was presided over by James G. Blaine, then Secretary of State, who long had advocated such close union between the 21 Republics as to make them one great and happy family of people. One of his dreams was of a Pan American railway, to unite the capitals of all of the American Republics and to stimulate commercial and social intercourse so that an era of understanding between the various peoples would inevitably follow.

This first Pan American conference was attended by eminent delegates from all of the countries, and passed a resolution providing for a "Commercial Bureau of the American Republics" which should collect and distribute commercial and general information among them in such a way as not only to foster the exchange of trade, but to remove the great ignorance of each other which existed among their respective peoples. At each of the succeeding Pan American conferences

COURT IN PAN-AMERICAN BUILDING.

the activities and consequent opportunities for usefulness of the Pan American Union have been enlarged. Some idea of the growth of the work of the union may be gathered from the fact that in four years the number of letters written per month increased from 700 to 7,000. In the same length of time the number of printed publications distributed increased from 60,000 to 600,000. No one has been able adequately to measure in money values the great growth of trade that has been brought about by the work of the union. But a careful compilation of easily traced direct results shows that the work of this institution has resulted in a $50,000,000 a year increase in trade between the various countries supporting it. The indirect returns have certainly represented a far greater success even than this. Yet all of this work has been done upon an annual expenditure which has never before amounted to as much as to-day, and which is now approximately $125,000.

Perhaps the most interesting activity of the union, and certainly one which has been a great factor in awakening the people of Latin America to the possibilities of their countries and to the advantages to be reaped from closer union with the United States, has been the monthly magazine of the Pan American Union. This publication carries 200 pages of matter a month, which, in quality, value of material, character of paper and type, number of illustrations, and size, compares favorably with the best of the popular magazines of to-day. Instead of being a dry-as-dust public document, it is a live, twentieth-century magazine, dealing with the progress and development of the 21 American Republics.

Its travel and descriptive articles are second to none published in the current literature of the day. There are a thousand and one things about Latin America which are not known by the average reader, and which are of surpassing interest. Likewise this magazine carries to Latin America messages from the United States, evidence of our interest in them which serves well the purposes for which it was founded. The Pan American magazine is a unique publication in that it carries no advertisements; it is even more unique in that it is a public document and yet partakes of none of the characteristics of such a document except that of accuracy. It also has the original characteristic of being printed in four language editions; in English for circulation in the United States, in Spanish for the 19 Spanish-speaking Republics, in Portuguese for Brazil, and in French for Haiti and general European circulation. Fifteen thousand copies are issued monthly, and although a regular subscription price is charged for it, the demand is larger than the supply.

Perhaps the best library on Latin American subjects anywhere to be found is that possessed by the Pan American Union and known as the Columbus Memorial Library. This library now contains approximately 20,000 volumes, composed mainly of books relating to the American Republics. There is a large reading room where all of the leading publications of Latin America are kept, and where the newspapers of those countries are constantly filed, and prove a great boon to the homesick Latin American whose business brings him to Washington and the United States with increasing frequency.

The 20 Latin American Republics, which, with the United States, support the Pan American Union, occupy about 9,000,000 square miles of territory, or three times the area of the United States. They have already, in the beginning of their industrial development, 70,000,000 people. They conduct now an annual foreign commerce valued at more than $2,000,000,000. One-half of this business has grown up in a single decade. The tremendous "boost" which the completion of the Panama Canal promises to give to Latin America will probably quadruple this great volume of business in less than a single generation. The immensity of the country represented by the Pan American Union is emphasized by the fact that if a merchant vessel steamed out of New Orleans Harbor and sailed around Pan America to San Diego, Cal., its log would show 15,000 miles, or nearly five times the distance across the Atlantic. If, on the other hand, a man inspired by the wanderlust wished to make the unusual journey across the widest portion of South America from Pernambuco, Brazil, by way of the northern coast of Brazil, the Amazon River, and over the Andes to Guayaquil, Ecuador, he would be obliged to travel approximately 3,500 miles. As he entered and sailed up the Amazon, he would discover that the river empties into the Atlantic with a flood four times greater than that of the Mississippi River, so that steamships as large as the *Lusitania* can navigate it a thousand miles, while the largest vessel which loads and unloads at the docks at New Orleans may ascend still another thousand miles farther to the city of Iquitos, Peru.

The possibilities of Latin America in the future are beyond forecast. The little mountainous Republic of Salvador has a population in proportion to area eight times as great as that of the United States. But assuming that Latin America may only become as populous as the United States is to-day, the total population of the 20 Republics would then aggregate 270,000,000 people, or nearly four times as many as they possess to-day. The Latin America of the future promises to be one of the world's greatest food-producing regions, and to possess a wealth which will make even that of the United States to-day look small in comparison.

The Pan American Union is housed in one of the most beautiful of the many beautiful buildings in the city of Washington. In its architecture it differs widely from that of any other building in the National Capital. Since 20 of the 21 American Republics are of Latin origin, the general style of the building fittingly suggests Latin American treatment, while at the same time it harmonizes with the general tone of architecture that is symbolical of the new Washington and which has found its latest verification in the Corcoran Gallery of Art, the Municipal Building, and the Union Station. The building is a monument to the munificence of Andrew Carnegie, who contributed three-fourths of the $1,000,000 required to build it, and to the energy of Director General John Barrett, who developed it. The remaining quarter of a million dollars was contributed by the 21 Republics forming the Union. The United States Government purchased the land for $250,000 and donated it. The construction of this permanent home of the Pan American Union has made Washington an international Capital of the 21 American nations. The building was designed to be the home of the American Republics in the highest sense of the word. Every one of these Republics has its private home in the residence of its ambassador or minister, but the Pan American Union was designed to be the home of all of them, where their representatives may meet as children in the house of their fathers to discuss all questions which may arise, to celebrate public events, or to commemorate glorious days. It was, therefore, determined to make the building nearer the type of a residence than the impersonal public building, although it should still possess that dignity which the subject demands. It was the hope of the Director General that when the representatives of the various countries passed the threshold they should have the impression of entering their own homes; that when the vestibule or staircase and the large assembly hall should shine with thousands of electric lights as a brilliant gathering thronged the rooms to honor a distinguished visitor, the representatives of the 21 Republics might have the impression of receiving guests in their own residences and not in a commonplace meeting room.

Latin American influence in the architecture of this remarkable and beautiful building finds its most typical expression in the patio, over 50 feet square, in the central part of the front section of the building. In this the visitor seems translated to some strange foreign scene, quaint and remote. Here the effect of tropical summer is maintained throughout the year. This large patio is covered with a glass roof, built in two sections, which are operated noiselessly by electricity and constructed so as to slide back over the adjacent flat roof of the staircase when it is desired to have the patio open. In the colder months the glass roof is kept closed, and the steam heat gives to the patio the warmth of tropical sunshine, while in the summer months this roof is kept open and permits the air above to descend unobstructed. In the patio one encounters a large garden of everblooming tropical flowers. The fronds of great palms form the graceful culmination of a diversity of exotic foliage and southern bloom. The unique fountain in the center flows all the year. It suggests the Alhambra and remote Moorish days in Spain.

Well-lighted offices for the Director General and his staff open off of the patio, and at one end is the great assembly chamber, which is called "the Hall of the Republics American," the only room of its kind ever built especially for international conventions and social events. Committee rooms are set aside for important conferences, and in every particular the place is designed to meet the needs for which it was built.

It is the intention of the authorities of the Pan American Union to use funds donated for the purpose by Andrew Carnegie to convert the 5 acres of ground surrounding the Pan American building into an international garden full of significant ideas and suggestions, so as to poetize the site and make it a place apart, inspiring and beautiful. The grounds will be inclosed, but a spacious formal court in front is to be given an inviting air of freedom and openness, so that not until one penetrates to the rear will he fall under the spell of absolute detachment. Once there, however, the isolation will be complete. The garden house at the extreme rear will shut out for all time a distracting view of the few factories that have already crept into this favored neighborhood. It will become an out-of-door apartment, with its walls as richly foliated as the giant hedges of the famous Borda Gardens at Cuernavaca, Mexico, and its floor will have a fine green carpet divided by a long transparent pool, at the end of which a beautiful coral reef of translucent marble will define itself and make all beholders feel something of the lure and charm of tropic seas. Phosphorescent marvels will appear and disappear and make it a scene of entrancing beauty. It is probable that when the work on the grounds of the Pan American Building is completed they will be the most beautiful in the entire National Capital.

One of the great schemes in which the Pan American Union is interested is in the building of the Pan American Railway. It is the hope of every high official of Latin America that the day will come when Buenos Aires and Washington will be connected by rail. Link by link this hope is being realized. One is now practically able to go from Washington to Guatemala City by rail, and construction work is now being carried forward which will enable the traveler to journey from Guatemala City to La Union, Salvador. A railroad is being constructed from Panama to the westernmost part of the Republic of Panama, and a large part of the distance from that point to La Union is now covered by links of railways, the gaps between which will some time be filled in. Of course, few people who have traveled once from the Guatemalan frontier to

Washington by rail will desire to make the same journey a second time, since the water trip is cheaper, almost as quick, and certainly a more pleasant one. But the effect of such connection between Panama and Washington will be such as probably will hasten the construction of the connecting links between Panama and Buenos Aires. It is not probable that at an early date it will be possible to make the journey from Washington to Buenos Aires without break, but when Latin America reaches that state of development to which the United States already has attained, it is certain that one may travel where he will between the capital of the northernmost country of North America to that of the southernmost country of South America by rail.

The officers of the Pan American Union, all of whom have been in intimate touch with the affairs of Latin America during the past decade or more, believe that the opening of the Panama Canal is destined to be followed by an era of development and prosperity that will affect even the remotest of the nations of the New World. They also believe that it will result in the United States assuming a commanding position in their trade relations and in enabling the Pan American Union to scatter broadcast the seed of opportunity, from which the American manufacturer will reap a rich harvest.

CHAPTER XXX.

THE NATIONAL CAPITAL.

The District of Columbia, permanent seat of the Government of the United States of America, is the smallest political division of the country. The city of Washington is merely the name of a geographical section of the District of Columbia, although residents of the entire District are in the habit of regarding themselves as residents of Washington. The city proper embraces about one-seventh of the total area of the District.

It is absolutely unique among the cities of the United States. It is the most American because its population is made up of people from all the States, and yet it is not American at all, for the reason that its residents can not vote. It is the most cosmopolitan because representatives of all other nations dwell in it, yet it has no foreign quarter. Washington's greatest industry is government, and its greatest product is politics, but the issues are all national. It is the only American city where there is no local party politics; in fact, it is the only city of the civilized world which can not choose any of its local officers by vote. The President appoints the executive and judicial officers, and Congress, sitting as a City Council, "exercises exclusive legislation." Despite the anomalous spectacle presented by the Capital city of a democratic country being governed in theory by an autocracy, the people are content, public opinion rules, and the city itself is a masterful argument for the continuation of the present plan.

As it is now constituted, the executive government of the District is intrusted to three commissioners, one of whom must be an officer of at least the rank of major in the Engineer Corps of the Army, or a captain who has served at least 15 years in the Army. The commissioners administer the details of government, prepare the budget, transmit it to the Secretary of the Treasury, who, with such changes as he deems advisable, forwards it to Congress, and the commissioners advocate it and other District legislation before the District of Columbia committees. Because of the fact that the commissioners and Congress are not directly responsible to the people of the District, a system of expressing public opinion has been developed in Washington which is absolutely unique. Under its operation the government is in practice, though not in theory, sensitively responsive to public opinion, being unafraid of elections and independent of party bosses.

Washington is the most beautiful city in the United States, and is claimed by many authorities to have no peer in the world. Paris has more magnificent vistas, but there are quarters of the French capital with never a claim to beauty. There are more shade trees in Washington than in any other city in the world. It has 92,000 trees, while Paris, the next in the list, has only 85,000. It must be remembered in this connection that Paris has nearly 3,000,000 population, while Washington has but 330,000.

The city has 275 little parks less than 1 acre in extent, and 26 others that are more than an acre in size. There are also 10 large parks in the central portion of the city, the largest being the Mall, reaching from the Botanic Garden, at the foot of Capitol Hill, to the Washington Monument, a distance of three-fourths of a mile. The crowning glory of Washington's park system are Rock Creek Park and the Zoological Park, which are practically one. These have a combined area of 1,776 acres. Rock Creek Park is not excelled in beauty by any driving park in the world.

Washington has a greater number of institutions of learning than any other city. Universities, training schools, finishing schools, professional schools, and preparatory schools are supplemented by the excellent public-school system which was started in 1805. The wealthier citizens subscribed funds from their private purses, but opened the schools to all comers. Thomas Jefferson was then President of the United States. He was elected to the board of education and became its first president. The Smithsonian Institution, the Carnegie Institution, the scientific bureaus of the Government, and the great libraries in Washington attract scientists from all over the world, and there are more men actually engaged in scientific research there than in any other city on the globe. The telegraph and telephone are among the thousands of inventions that have come from the workshops of Washington scientists.

More negroes live in Washington than in any other city, approximately 100,000 of the total population of 330,000 being of African descent. Many Washington negroes are among the most advanced of their race, and Washington is the only city where there is a distinct Afro-American society which applies the standards of American morals and manners to its own conduct. The negroes are represented on the school board, hold places of honor and profit under the District government, and enjoy equality before the law.

Much has been written about social usages in Washington, and if one who had never visited the city formed his notions of it from reading such articles, he would imagine a city noisy with the rush of carriages from dinner to dinner, and whose streets were cushioned with a débris of visiting cards from morning calls. As a matter of fact, there are some few people in Washington who do observe with punctilious care all the demands of official etiquette. There are others who observe such of these rules as they choose, and still others whose social activity is sporadic. And then there are some 300,000 who live wholly without the pale of what is called "society."

The conundrum, "When is a lion not a lion?" finds its answer in Washington. Men who have attained prominence and fame are so common that no one turns on the streets to see a great Cabinet minister or a Senator. Celebrities who fill columns of the newspapers when they visit other American cities go in and out among the Washingtonians day after day without attracting notice. The President alone is enough of a hero to command the attention of the people in the street.

The Washington hotels and boarding houses are characteristic. They are parceled out, in a fashion, among the States. A man from Maine will go to the Hotel Hamilton, for there he will find other men from Maine. While the Ebbitt House is officially sacred to the Army and Navy, Tennesseeans also have made it their headquarters for years. So in the boarding houses. A landlady who affects corn bread and hot biscuits will have a Southern clientele, and the fame of a boarding house where brown bread and beans may be had, flanked with the sacred cod, will attract the Bostonian. In some boarding houses there are State tables, all the boarders from Georgia being grouped about one table, those from Illinois at another. This is the last surviving reminder of the congressional "messes" of the early days of the Republic.

There is in Washington a colony of wealthy Americans who have no connection whatever with the business of government or of politics. Millionaires choose Washington for their winter residence, and erect magnificent mansions, which are occupied for only a few months of the year. Some of these have cost more than a million dollars, and a few which approach the million mark are now in course of construction. A rental of $50,000 a year was offered for one of the Washington palaces not long since, and refused. For some the glamour of the American court is the attraction, for others the knowledge that the gates swing inward for the stranger more readily here than in other cities, and for still others the advantage of beautiful surroundings which Washington so richly affords.

The clubs in Washington are of really great importance. At the Metropolitan Club, the men who mold the affairs of the Nation are wont to talk things over in man-to-man fashion. The Cosmos Club is the largest scientific club in the world. Its membership includes the greatest inventors and investigators of the scientific world, and its fine old house, once owned and occupied by Dolly Madison, is the social clearing house of the Smithsonian Institution and the Carnegie Institution. Chevy Chase Country Club is most brilliant socially and the Army and Navy Club is a great organization. The National Press Club is the representative newspaper club of the world. Its membership is the most cosmopolitan and its influence the most extensive of any similar organization in existence.

Washington has not always been the beautiful Capital, political center, and the scene of social activities that it is to-day. In the beginning little attention was paid to the needs of the District. Congress refused to appropriate money to erect public buildings, and the commissioners were forced to borrow from the States, Virginia loaning $120,000 and Maryland $72,000. Congress again refusing to vote money, Maryland let the new National Capital have another $100,000, but only on the personal security of the commissioners. In those days the public credit was poor indeed. The Union was only an experiment, and the Constitution was an untried and sorely mistrusted instrument. Few men thought that the States would stick together. When Mr. Jefferson was President he offered to give a fine building square on Sixteenth Street, which extends north from the front of the White House, to any European nation that would erect a legation building. Not one of the countries of the world thought that the United States would amount to enough to justify the building of a legation at Washington, and no one accepted the offer. Recently Germany paid $125,000 for a site for an embassy building on the same street. Had

THE NATIONAL CAPITAL

Jefferson's offer been accepted by the nations, Sixteenth Street, the handsomest of boulevards, would have been to-day the Avenue of the Ambassadors. Now it is proposed to change the name to the Avenue of the Presidents, because every President since Adams has looked out from his windows on its beautiful sweep to Boundary Hill.

The rivalry between the North and the South was marked in those early days, and the question of the location of the Federal District was debated with heat and earnestness. The Northern States in Congress, led by Alexander Hamilton, favored the assumption of the Revolutionary War debts of the States by the Federal Government. The Southern States opposed the assumption.

Thomas Jefferson met Alexander Hamilton on the street. Hamilton appealed to Jefferson to aid him in passing the assumption bill. Jefferson gave a dinner. At the dinner table it was agreed that a sufficient number of Southern Congressmen would vote to assume the State debts, if a sufficient number of Hamilton's followers would agree to the location of the Federal District in the South. The compromise was put through, and Congress directed that a seat of government be selected on the banks of the Potomac. The State of Maryland ceded 70 square miles and Virginia gave 30 square miles. In 1846 the portion taken from Virginia, including the town of Alexandria, was retroceded to the State, and the District of Columbia was reduced to its present area.

Alexander R. Shepherd, a plumber by trade, first a member of the board of public works and then governor, was the moving spirit in the new government under the reorganization acts of 1871. If Washington was the founder, Shepherd was the builder of the Capital City. He found it a straggling town without a comprehensive system of public improvements, and left it well on its way toward being the most beautiful city of the world.

Disregarding the protests of citizens, he tore away an unsightly market house and made a park of the space. He filled up the miasmatic open sewer that had been the canal of earlier days, and turned the water of Tiber Creek into a great sewer. In less than two years he paved 40 miles of street with wood and 50 miles with gravel. He laid 13 miles of sewers and 14 miles of water mains. The wooden pavements were a failure and soon had to be replaced with asphalt, but once there was a pavement the people would not consent to return to the mud lanes which had disgraced the Capital so many years.

The oldest residence in the city of Washington, the one whose walls have housed the men who have given America its storied past, and which are still bound up in our dreams of a glorious future, is the White House. When it was provided for in the original design of the city it was known as The Palace. When it was first built it was "The President's House." After it was burned by the British it was painted white, and in popular parlance was soon called by its now familiar name, although officially it was known as "The Executive Mansion" until Mr. Roosevelt became its occupant. The White House it is now, and ever shall be, for there is so much of history and legend in the old name that it will always be retained.

In the third year of General Washington's administration as President, a prize of $500 was offered for the best design for a house for the President. James Hoban, a native of Ireland, but then a resident of South Carolina, was the successful competitor. His plans closely copied the design of the house of the Duke of Leinster in Dublin. Originally he planned a three-story structure, susceptible of being extended by means of wings and colonnades. General Washington liked the idea, but the public was aghast at such magnificence. The republican sentiment prevailed, the plans were simplified, and the well-known, two-story building of few rooms was the result. The corner stone was laid by Washington in 1792 and the house was completed in 1799. It was first occupied by John Adams in 1800, and his good wife Abigail hung out the family washing in the East Room. Every President since Adams has lived there and had his office there, until President Roosevelt had an office building constructed to the west of it. Under its roof have been administered the policies which have resulted in the growth of the loose federation of 13 poverty-stricken Colonies into the mightiest Nation of the world.

Burned in 1814 by the British troops, the White House was rebuilt without alteration, except that the scorched sandstone was painted. During General Jackson's administration, the northern portico, the one oftenest seen in pictures, was added. No other important alterations were made until President Roosevelt's time, when a half million dollars was spent in improvements. When Mrs. Cleveland came to the White House as a bride she had visions of entertaining many of her girl friends, knowing what an event in their lives it would be, but it could not be done, for there are not enough sleeping rooms at the White House to permit of entertaining more than one or two persons at a time. Despite the fact that the Nation has outgrown the house, as Hoban and Washington foresaw, it is still beautiful and in its simple grace typifies the democratic spirit of the greatest of Republics.

When George Washington selected the site of the Capital City, he had no difficulty in persuading 18 of the landowners to turn over half their property to the Government in consideration of the enhancement of the value of the half retained. But with Davy Burns, a canny Scot, who owned a farm where the White House and Monument are now situated, it was different. Washington argued with Davy long and earnestly. At length he said: "Had not the Federal City been laid out here you would have died a poor tobacco planter." Whereat the son of Caledonia retorted: "Ay mon, an' hed ye no married the Widder Custis, wi' a' her nagurs, ye'd hae been a land surveyor the noo, an' a mighty poor ane at that." When Davy wouldn't, Washington told him he must, and he consented with characteristic Scotch thrift by extracting a proviso that the site of his own cottage could not be taken and that no lots should be sold for private building in that vicinity.

Just before the Civil War a writer in the Atlantic Monthly said: "Washington is the Elysium of oddities, the Limbo of absurdities, an imbroglio of ludicrous anomalies. Planned on a scale of surpassing grandeur, its architectural execution is almost contemptible. It has a Monument that will never be finished, a Capitol that lacks a dome, and a Scientific Institute which does nothing but report the rise and fall of the thermometer." The prospect must have been discouraging at that time, but what a change we find to-day. The Scientific Institute, whose apparent inactivity was the cause of such sarcastic comment, has given to mankind the science of meteorology. The Monument is completed and it is the most imposing memorial ever raised by man to the memory of a leader of men. The Capitol has been completed, and its Dome, soaring above the clouds, is crowned with the Emblem of Freedom that symbolizes the highest national attainments of the human race. And plans now in process of realization promise to add greatly even to the present glory and beauty of the Nation's Capital, and to make it a seat of government which will be the envy of all nations for all time.